Tombstone Town

Left for dead, marked with a tombstone, a toxic town fights back

~A memoir~
The first sixteen years of the
PINE RIVER SUPERFUND CITIZEN TASK FORCE
St. Louis, Michigan
1998-2013

To Victoria

Jane Keon

Jane Keon

This book is dedicated to the memories of
Dr. Lester E. and Alma Eyer
Dr. George J. and Martha Wallace

Acknowledgements

I am indebted to every member of the CAG, the St. Louis City Council and staff, the professors and students from Alma College, University of Michigan Law School, and Michigan State University, and the people from the governmental agencies and private firms who are assisting in the monumental task of cleaning up the contaminated sites in our community.

Contents

Introduction

On a winter morning, as I went out to the barn to feed the chickens, the smell of a swimming pool rose up from the river that flowed through our small farm. It was no mystery. The chemical factory in town had dumped chlorine the night before, and even six miles downstream where we lived, the river gave off a swimming pool smell.

Every time I smelled it, I thought to myself, if only the chemical plant would shut down and let the river come back to life. At that point, in 1976, I had no idea of the quantities and types of toxic chemicals being piped, poured and dumped into the river. And I certainly had no idea of how intertwined my life would become with the years-long cleanup of our small town.

Finally, in 1978, the State of Michigan closed the chemical plant. The buildings were demolished and buried, and a granite tombstone, engraved with warning words was erected at the gates to the former chemical factory. Nothing was done to clean the river.

Twenty years later, in 1997, the EPA tested sediment samples to see how much DDT remained in the riverbed near the plant site. When they found alarmingly high levels, an Emergency Response was mandated. In October of that year, about 30 members of the community, including myself, signed up to help oversee the sediment cleanup.

This book is a memoir of my years in the Pine River Superfund Citizen Task Force, an EPA-sanctioned Community Advisory Group based in the small town of St. Louis, Michigan. I had the honor of serving as chairperson of our CAG for 12 years, and helped to oversee cleanups in the river, in residential neighborhoods, at a radioactive dump site, and to see the start of the $382 million remediation of the chemical plant site itself.

Despite disliking politics, the law, bureaucracy, and having avoided science as much as possible during my school years, I've learned, out of necessity, some chemistry and biology, some political tactics and bureaucratic tricks, and I've stood in federal bankruptcy court before a judge.

I'm willing, along with many others, to take whatever steps are necessary to restore our land and water, and to reverse our community's reputation as Toxic Town, U.S.A.

Chapter 1
(1997)
A Change of Mind

When I read the announcement in our local newspaper that EPA would meet with the public to discuss the levels of DDT found in the sediment of the Pine River, it seemed pointless to go. The EPA would do whatever it decided to do, no matter what people in the community said. That had been our past experience in dealing with the United States Environmental Protection Agency when Velsicol Chemical Corporation quit production in 1978 and was allowed to leave town without cleaning up the river.

I can see now that I had a touch of the "sickness" that had spread through the St. Louis, Michigan area. The despondency that had settled over people was *like* a sickness. It was contagious, it had symptoms, and it wasn't easy to recover from. Even people who had moved away still suffered from the sickness when St. Louis came to mind. And those who stayed continued to spread the contagion of despondency, one to another.

Over the course of 42 years, Michigan Chemical Corporation (later Velsicol) had used the Pine River as its corporate sewer system, dumping tons of toxic waste into the water to be carried downstream to where the Pine met the Chippewa River and where they both emptied into the Tittabawassee River and onward to Saginaw Bay and out into Lake Huron.

Many claim today that people didn't know better back then. Contrary to this opinion is documented evidence. For instance, in 1935, a few months before the factory opened, the Saginaw City Council passed a resolution objecting to Michigan Chemical's failure to plan for disposal of its waste, except to discharge it into the river. The worry was that the water would no longer be potable for the Saginaw residents, and that it might harm the fish.

Both worries came to fruition and surpassed in devastation anything dreamed of in 1935.

In 1944 the chemical plant began to manufacture the pesticide DDT (dichlorodiphenyltrichloroethane), in addition to other compounds made from the brine deposits that lay deep underground in the mid-Michigan area.

—

In 1971 the manufacturing of the fire retardant polybrominated biphenyl (PBB) began. Tons of waste poured into the Pine River from large outfalls, thickening the water and turning it white or yellow depending on the polluting substance.

Repeated studies by the state Water Resources Commission over the next decades showed increasingly dire results from the chemical plant's discharges into the river. And on land residents dealt with air pollution. Houses located near the chemical plant needed new paint on at least one side yearly because the chemical residue in the air lifted the paint off the houses in flakes and curls. Metal window screens were dissolved by the airborne chemicals and had to be replaced. Clothes had to be hung to dry in the house year round because of the powders and odors they would collect if hung outside on the line. Children were warned to stay out of the river, and when word spread through the neighborhoods that a visiting circus elephant had died after bathing in the water, most of the children heeded the warning.

After the 1970s PBB Disaster, in which the 9 million inhabitants of Michigan were contaminated when the fire retardant entered the food chain, Velsicol Chemical Corporation, which had owned the chemical plant since 1965, feared liability from sick workers, from farmers, and from the State of Michigan, and began to seek ways of avoiding the costs to come. Closing the plant was the most cost-effective option for Velsicol, especially since the corporation was not required to take into account the loss of revenue to the community, the loss of employment for the workers, nor the cost of damage to the river.

Even as the workers and the businessmen in the community worked to develop ways to keep the plant open, Velsicol owners and the government agencies were negotiating behind closed doors to make the chemical factory's leave-taking relatively easy for the company, and disastrous for the community.

When the plant ceased production in September 1978, those of us who viewed the chemical plant as a bad neighbor were glad to see it shut down, yet we sympathized with the workers and others who viewed the closing of the chemical plant as a calamitous end to a long era of prosperity.

It was a trying time for the whole community, and especially for the 400 workers who never received Worker's Compensation payments, and who found that other employers wouldn't hire them for fear the workers had developed long-term health problems from being exposed to chemicals at Velsicol. The unemployment rate was over 10% in our rural county at that time, and predicted to rise to 14% if the workers could not find jobs.

The workers mounted a lawsuit against Velsicol and 13 years later, in 1991, received settlement checks from the company, which were enough to buy from two to four weeks worth of groceries. Some received as much as $500. Some received $300. My mother-in-law received a check for her deceased husband in the amount of $164.79.

Without input from citizens, or from the St. Louis City Council, or from the Gratiot County Board of Commissioners, Velsicol carried on negotiations with attorneys from the U.S. Department of Justice, the State of Michigan, the EPA, and other federal agencies, working to craft a deal. The government agencies purposefully excluded public input during these negotiations to avoid any kind of reactive backlash from citizens. We have a letter in our files demonstrating this intentional exclusion, written to Arnie Bransdorfer, who was serving as a Gratiot County Commissioner at the time the negotiations were underway.

Once the deal was signed, the public objected and raised concerns, but were told by the government officials that this was the best deal anyone could hope for.

The terms of the 1982 Consent Judgment

- Allowed Velsicol to leave the State of Michigan with a waiver from all liability for contamination in the Pine River, both adjacent to the plant site and downstream.
- Stipulated that factory buildings and other off-site buildings contaminated by the chemical operations would be demolished and buried on the 52-acre plant site.
- Stipulated that Velsicol would be responsible for paying for a clay cap overtop the site and a clay slurry wall surrounding the site where it abutted the Pine River.

8

- Stipulated that Velsicol would be responsible for pumping out and disposing of contaminated water that built up within the buried plant site.
- Adding insult to injury, the Consent Judgment stipulated that a granite marker be erected on the site warning people not to enter.

The tombstone placed on the fenced plant site was perceived by our community as a symbol of death. Yes, the chemical plant had died, but did we need a tombstone in the middle of our town proclaiming the death for the next three hundred years? It was unperceptive and unfeeling on the part of the dealmakers to stipulate such a thing.

That is when the despondency set in. Those who were sorry to see the chemical plant end its life in St. Louis and those who were glad to see it go both showed symptoms of the sick feeling of being let down by the government officials whose salaries we paid with our tax dollars.

Soon the downtown area of St. Louis began to suffer. Without the tax base the chemical plant had provided, the city had trouble paying its bills. Road repairs remained undone. Streets weren't swept. The police car wasn't replaced. Stores began to close their doors and were boarded up. Maybe the tombstone was for the town as well as the chemical plant, since the town seemed to be dying.

During this time, those of us who had been disgusted that the chemical plant had used the river as its sewer hesitated to voice our opinions because of the heartache and resentment that flared up when the chemical plant was mentioned. It was almost as if the chemical plant had been a person, and we were not to speak ill of the dead. And the tombstone was there to prove it.

Over the years, real estate agents tried to avoid questions about the tombstone when showing houses in St. Louis. The fenced acreage, when the grass was mown, was mistaken for a park by some newcomers to the town.

That is until they read the signs on the fence warning of toxic chemicals and radiation within, and saw the large, granite tombstone chiseled with six inch letters saying "WARNING."

When the fence began to rust, the churches of the community planted gardens outside it along state highway M-46. Their hope was that travelers' eyes would settle on the flowers and not the fenced site itself.

In 1997 when the meeting notice appeared in the newspaper, I rose above my despondency and my cynicism about EPA, and attended the meeting. Apparently many others did the same thing, because the American Legion hall on Michigan Avenue filled with about 200 people.

I recognized Mayor George Kubin, Ed Lorenz (a history and political science professor at Alma College), Joe Scholtz, (an outspoken person at the city council meetings), several city council members with whom I was acquainted from the years when I covered their meetings as a reporter for the Saginaw News, Melissa Strait (a chemistry professor from Alma College), Kathy Crumbaugh (who with Rex, her husband, owned a large farm), and Jim Vyskocil (a chemistry teacher at St. Louis High School). Over the next months and years, I would get to know several others who attended the meeting that evening, such as Dick Green, Murray Borrello, Gary Smith, Jim Kelly, Jerry and Sally Church, Bill and Carol Layman, Jim Hall, Bernie Bessert, Bill Snowden, and Bill Shrum.

I went to the meeting with the assumption that EPA would recommend excavation of the DDT-laden sediment from the St. Louis mill pond and I was against it. In my opinion, if they dug in that area of the river, it would stir things up and allow the pollution held back by the dam to come downstream to where my family lived. Joe Scholtz and I discussed that possibility before the meeting began. We were both dead set against having EPA disturb the contaminated sediment in the mill pond.

At the meeting, scientists from EPA told us how they had relied upon numbers given to them by Velsicol to determine the amount of DDT left in the river. No one reacted with surprise to hear the EPA scientists say they had found far more DDT in the river than what Velsicol had reported to them prior to the 1982 Consent Judgment. Most everyone knew by now that such a discrepancy was to be expected.

The scientist explained that recently EPA had acquired a new boat and new sampling equipment, and he had been instructed to collect sediment samples from the Pine River near the former Velsicol chemical plant to learn how much DDT remained in the impoundment area behind the dam.

The EPA's impetus for this new testing came from the constantly rising levels of DDT found in fish, birds and mammals downstream from St. Louis. In the late 1970s and early 1980s EPA had theorized that once the chemical plant had closed and was no longer dumping pollutants into the river, then the wildlife downstream would begin to show less DDT uptake in their body fat. Since the opposite had occurred, they determined it was time to find out how much DDT was actually deposited in the impoundment area behind the dam.

As the scientist spoke about levels of DDT, using numbers that I, at least, had nothing to make a comparison with, I raised my hand and asked a question. I wanted to know how much DDT had to be detected in a body of water for EPA to excavate the sediment. As best I can recall, the number was 225 parts per million in sediment samples. And how much were they finding in the impoundment area in St. Louis? That night they said 32,000 ppm. Later they took samples that ranged up to 46,000 ppm.

Those numbers were the deciding factor for me. I changed my mind at that moment, and was in favor of EPA coming to St. Louis to excavate the DDT-laden sediment. I reasoned that with such a vast quantity of DDT deposited in the riverbed, the river could never clean itself, and would continue to slowly poison all the wildlife downstream.

I was fairly well educated about the dangers of DDT in the environment, because I'd grown up in a household in which talk about scientific matters occurred regularly. And even though I disliked science classes in school, scientific facts soaked into me at home as my parents talked about DDT, Strontium 90 fallout, and other ecological worries of the late 1950s and early 1960s.

My parents had met at the University of Michigan Biological Station on Douglas Lake in 1939, married in 1940, and received their masters degrees in biology in 1942. After World War II, my dad used the G.I. Bill to enter graduate school where he earned a PhD in biology, with ornithology (birds) as his area of specialty.

While at Michigan State University, my dad's professor and the chair of his PhD committee was Dr. George Wallace. For those who are familiar with the names of scientists whose research led Rachel Carson to write her masterpiece, *Silent Spring*, the name of Dr. Wallace might be familiar.

It was Dr. Wallace's research on the effects of DDT on robins at the campus of Michigan State University that gave great support to Carson's premise that the widespread dissemination of DDT disrupted animal ecology, from insects to earthworms to birds, and ultimately that it would have deleterious outcomes for humanity. Along with Dr. Wallace, many other pioneering biologists shared their research data with Carson.

Dr. Wallace was only five years older than my dad, and the two of them became life-long friends, as did Martha Wallace with my mother. And I enjoyed the company of the Wallace daughters, especially in playing with the large, elaborate dollhouse that Dr. Wallace had built for them.

I include these homey details to set the stage for how I learned about DDT. Rachel Carson's book hadn't yet been written. My knowledge about DDT came about in the context of being a child and overhearing adult conversations on the topic, and picking up on the concern that the adults expressed.

It was while on bird hikes with the Wallace family, or sharing family dinners, that the adult conversation expressed deep worry about the effects of DDT on songbirds. In 1958 Dr. Wallace gave a presentation on that topic at the National Audubon Society convention, and soon after that Rachel Carson contacted him by mail, asking about the DDT research he had already conducted on the Michigan State University campus.

That same year, when I was 10 years old, I accompanied my dad and a few other adults on an early morning "robin count" on the Alma College campus. Like MSU, Alma College had also sprayed their campus with DDT to kill mosquitoes, and to perhaps preserve elms dying from Dutch elm disease. We found a few dead birds that morning, which we collected, but we were also listening for robins singing their "dawn songs." As I recall, we heard only two singing, instead of the layers of robin songs that we would have heard on most spring mornings.

All of these events were simply part of growing up for me: hearing about the effects of DDT on robins and eco-systems in general; going on early morning robin counts; telling my young neighborhood friends about the benefits of mosquitoes as food for birds; and being called into the house when the DDT sprayer showed up in the neighborhood.

When the spraying truck pulled into a neighbor's yard, set to eradicate their mosquitoes, my mother would call her children in from playing and shut all the windows to keep the spray from coming into the house. When she let us go back outside, we were forbidden to walk on the neighbor's white-sprayed yard, while other neighborhood kids ran around in their bare feet in the DDT residue.

By the time Rachel Carson's *Silent Spring* came out in 1962, its theme was well-known to me. It was a part of the fabric of my life. In fact, when I first became involved in the Pine River Superfund Citizen Task Force and people talked about what a sensation Carson's book had created in 1962, I was puzzled. I knew my parents had known about the dangers of DDT long before 1962, but I didn't understand how they knew, since I didn't yet know about the connection between Dr. Wallace and Rachel Carson.

One evening an elderly gentleman in our group, Gene Kenaga, gave a talk about the uses of DDT during World War II, the civilian uses following the war, and then about the research done by Dr. George Wallace and other scientists that was utilized by Rachel Carson in writing her book *Silent Spring*.

When I heard the name of Dr. Wallace mentioned, it all made sense. Of course the reason I'd known about DDT long before Carson's book came out was due to my parents' friendship with the Wallaces, and their knowledge of Dr. Wallace's research pre-dated any of his publications on the topic, and his acquaintanceship with Rachel Carson.

As I said, I changed my mind that night at the community meeting when I learned about the overwhelming amount of DDT left in the Pine River by Velsicol. And let's make no mistake: it was the U.S. Department of Justice, the State of Michigan, the U.S. Environmental Protection Agency and other federal agencies that had allowed Velsicol to leave town without dredging its waste out of the riverbed.

Under the law in the 1980s, EPA could have cleaned the river, the plant site, and all the other dumping sites and then charged the expenses to Velsicol. Instead EPA and the others let them off the hook.

Near the close of the 1997 community meeting, the citizens were informed about a program that EPA offered which encouraged public participation in a Superfund cleanup. We were told it was unusual for so many people to turn out for a community informational meeting such as the one we were having that night, and the high attendance was a good sign that a Community Advisory Group should form in St. Louis, giving our community a voice in the cleanup process. They asked for a show of hands as to how many might be interested in participating. I raised mine.

An EPA person put out a sign-up sheet, and said he would later convene an informational meeting about how to organize a Community Advisory Group, or CAG.

As the community meeting disbanded, I went to the front of the room to sign my name on the list. Joe Scholtz also came forward. We both had arrived at the same conclusion -- something must be done for our river.

Chapter 2
(1998)
A "Friendship" Rejected

During the first year of our CAG, we took seriously the word "advisory" in "Community Advisory Group." Beth Reiner, the EPA Project Manager, and Stuart Hill, the EPA Community Involvement Coordinator, were visibly caught off guard by our suggestions, our reasoning, and our insistence. Apparently their previous experience with community groups had consisted of meetings at which people sat and listened to EPA's advice without forming independent opinions on how things should be done. To have community members give them advice, or, at times, dissent from the expert advice offered by EPA when the plans seemed detrimental to the river or the community, must have been a new experience for them

Attending the first CAG meetings were people I knew and many not yet known to me, such as Murray Borrello, Ed Lorenz, Gary Smith, Carol Layman and Jim Hall.

Murray was a young geology instructor from Alma College, energetic, idealistic and full of optimism. Being fairly new to the community, he was not aware of the despondency that prevailed in St. Louis and the distrust of government in general and EPA in particular.

Ed Lorenz, a college history and political science professor, had a better idea of the undercurrent of emotion in the community. Although he'd moved here from Maryland in the early 1990s, he had investigated the PBB Disaster and its impact on the community and published his findings in an academic journal.

Joe Scholtz, a native of St. Louis, had gone on record in newspaper articles during the 1970s about the destruction caused by Velsicol to animal life in the Pine River, and how the government had allowed Velsicol to leave town without taking so much as a spoonful of DDT out of the riverbed.

Gary Smith, employed at Total Refinery, also born and raised in St. Louis, wanted to see the buried and fenced Velsicol plant site cleaned up and made useful to the people who called St. Louis home.

While raising her five children, Carol Layman had lived near Kalkaska, Michigan, one location of the state's 1970s mass slaughter and burial of contaminated cows, sheep, pigs and chickens due to the PBB Disaster.

Melissa Strait, a chemistry professor at Alma College, was a transplant from the Pacific Northwest. She had already done some research on the sediments in the river.

Jim Hall was a St. Louis native and worked at Dow Chemical in Midland. Jim had a sense of humor and a love of laughter, but he did not let that keep him from expressing his opinions in a forthright manner.

Phil Ramsey, disgusted with EPA and the plant site during the 1980s, had moved to Texas. He had recently returned.

A contingency from the St. Louis City Council and staff attended, among them Mayor George Kubin who had spoken out against Velsicol's pollution of the river during his high school years in St. Louis; Council Member Jim Kelly, a retired police officer who had been quoted in an early newspaper article about the yellowish-white mass clinging to his kayak when he paddled downstream from the chemical plant; Council Member Peg Boyd, who still mourned the loss of the chemical plant; Council Member Bill Shrum who had retired from working at Dow Chemical in Midland, Michigan; City Clerk Nancy Roehrs, a newcomer to the town; and City Manager Dennis Collison, who had grown up in St. Louis, moved away, and then returned to his hometown.

At our first organizational meeting in January 1998, we approved the idea of forming a CAG, and elected Ed Lorenz as chair, Jim Vyskocil, secretary, Nancy Roehrs, treasurer, and several of us were named chairs of committees charged with overseeing various contaminated sites.

Kathy Crumbaugh was chair of the Injection Well and Breckenridge Radioactive Site committee; Nancy Roehrs and Dennis Collison were co-chairs of the Velsicol Plant Site and Golf Course Site committee; Murray was chair of the Gratiot County Landfill and Smith Farm Site committee; Jim Hall and Barb Shrum were co-chairs of the River Site committee; Dick Green was chair of the Membership committee; and I was made chair of the Public Information committee because of my past experience in writing articles for the Saginaw News.

In choosing our name, we followed our own wisdom and not that of EPA's. Stuart Hill, the EPA Community Involvement Coordinator, suggested we organize ourselves around the remediation of the river and plant site, leaving the other sites for later. He said we would become overwhelmed with more than one site on our docket.

We decided instead to have as our mission the cleanup of all the contaminated sites in the Pine River watershed, both those we knew about and those we might learn about in the future.

This decision later enabled us to intervene in legal actions involving Total Refinery and Oxford Automotive, neither of them Velsicol sites.

Stuart also suggested we name ourselves after Velsicol, such as the Velsicol Superfund Community Advisory Group, but we rejected that idea. Why would we want to name ourselves after the polluter? We chose to name ourselves after our river, instead, and became the "Pine River Superfund Citizen Task Force."

It may be a long and an awkward title, but it describes who we are, where we live, and that we plan to get the job done. A task force, after all, is organized to solve a particular issue and then to dissolve itself when the task is completed.

At the top of our agenda was the Emergency Removal Action proposed for an area in the river near the former Velsicol plant site

As mentioned earlier, the EPA sediment sampling had shown that three to four acres in the riverbed contained 32,000-46,000 parts per million DDT, and we were told that this was possibly the highest concentration in a body of water in the United States of America. EPA scientists told us that the known mass of DDT in the river was about 534,300 pounds. Even though the Montrose facility in California had discharged a greater quantity of DDT into the Pacific, there the poison spread out for miles on the ocean floor, and was not concentrated in a few acres, as it was in our river.

Scientists from EPA and MDEQ (Michigan Department of Environmental Quality) told us that after the 1982-84 remediation of the plant site, they had begun testing the DDT levels in fish living downstream, expecting to see the levels decline. A baseline sample was taken in 1983 and further tests were made in 1985, 1989, 1995 and 1997, and the results showed a constant rise in accumulated DDT in fish tissue.

This meant that the fish constituted a high risk to fish-eating birds, such as the great blue heron. And a human health risk assessment showed that eating the fish from the Pine River could lead to liver cancer, constituting a very high risk for people who ate the fish.

In 1974 a total no-consumption fishing advisory had been placed on the Pine River from St. Louis downstream to the Tittabawassee River. The total ban meant no man, woman or child should eat any fish at any time of any size no matter how rarely from this 36-mile stretch of the Pine River.

One of our CAG's earliest acts took place when we learned that the state was preparing a new Fish Advisory Guide. We wrote a letter asking that the ban on fish consumption start at the dam in Alma, rather than in St. Louis, since the fish could swim freely between the St. Louis and Alma dams, and we knew that any fish that lived above the dam in St. Louis were highly contaminated. Our suggestion was heeded, and the change was made in the new Fish Advisory booklet.

Plenty of fish studies had been conducted in the Pine River from the time the chemical plant began discharging its waste into the river in 1936. To find a type of fish to sample was always difficult, because the fish intolerant of pollution had disappeared, leaving carp as the predominant species.

A study conducted in 1955 by the Michigan Department of Natural Resources Water Resources Commission collected samples of *any* living organism at six locations: two above the chemical plant, one at the plant site, and three downstream from the plant site. Above the Alma dam they found an average of 157 aquatic animals per square foot. At the plant site they sampled both sides of the river and found zero aquatic animal life. In the middle of the river, some pollution-tolerant specimens were found of an aquatic earthworm.

As for plant life, a pollution-tolerant green algae, called Sprongyra, was present but decomposing. Below the St. Louis dam at a one mile test site and at a twelve-mile test site, they found pollution-tolerant species, mostly aquatic earthworms (Tubifididae). At 18 miles below the St. Louis dam, pollution-tolerant species still made up 94 percent of aquatic animal life found.

In 1967 the Water Resources Commission tried to measure the emissions from each of 20 separate wastewater discharge pipes at the chemical plant to determine what was killing the life in the river. They found collecting emissions samples difficult, because the discharges from the outfalls disintegrated the Water Commission's weirs, which were lined with 1/64 inch-thick aluminum flashing. The disintegration occurred within 48 hours of when the weirs were installed.

At one point, Velsicol sought to convince state officials to abandon the health of the river altogether. In 1970, when the state of Michigan requested that Velsicol dredge 15,000 tons of solids from a portion of the river, Velsicol proposed that the river be reclassified "commercial use," which would have exempted them from treating the river any better than they already had been. How they could treat it any worse was the real question.

Our CAG decided to find ways to *promote* the stretch of lifeless river that flowed through the heart of St. Louis. Part of our strategy right from the start was to change the image of the Pine River in the eyes of the people who lived near it, who had learned to avoid it, and who warned their children to stay away from it. We also wanted to convince EPA that our community sincerely wanted the river to come back to life.

Maybe one more description from the Michigan Department of Natural Resources Water Resources Commission to show the river's lifelessness: a memo released in 1970 said the sodium concentrations below the chemical plant had increased significantly from 1967 to 1970, and they found that "all quantitative dredge samples contained large amounts of oil and were *devoid of animal life.*"

In my view, the destruction wrought by one small chemical company on one small river in one small town is an act of barbarism as bad as acts described in the Old Testament when conquering tribes salted the land of their enemies so that nothing could grow or live there for years to come.

Despite this atrocity perpetrated against us, the EPA Project Manager told us she wanted us to befriend Velsicol. She wanted us to "build a new relationship of trust" with Velsicol. She wanted us to "develop a dialogue" with Velsicol. And she wanted a Velsicol representative to join our CAG.

When Beth Reiner espoused these views, most of us didn't know what to say. Some who hadn't lived here through the years of the plant's operation thought her ideas had some merit. Those of us who viewed Velsicol as the enemy struggled with how to react to such a lack of comprehension on her part. Even though she had attended our meetings for six months, and had heard Ed Lorenz speak about the history of Velsicol's corporate shenanigans, including Velsicol's threatening attempt to stop Houghton Mifflin from publishing *Silent Spring*, she wanted us to befriend the corporation.

At a meeting in June, Murray Borrello reported that he had drafted a letter to Velsicol inviting them to attend one of our CAG meetings. After he read the letter out loud, it was followed by a stunned silence. Then Jim Kelly made a motion that such a letter *not* be sent. The motion passed. That wasn't the end of the matter, however.

Our attention was necessarily diverted for awhile. A large technical problem arose, coming between EPA's plans and our wisdom. EPA planned to open the St. Louis dam and draw down the water level in the river to expose the riverbed for excavation.

Our geologist, Murray Borrello, our biologist, Dick Roeper, and our chemist, Melissa Strait all considered the plan unwise as it would potentially allow a release of contaminants into the air when the river sediments dried out, and then to cause scouring of the riverbed when the water was re-introduced, releasing more contaminants into the flowing water that were now trapped in sediment. Our scientists shared data with EPA from a bathymetry survey of the river bottom which supported the CAG's concerns.

When members of our CAG adamantly insisted on finding a different way to tackle the planned excavation process, Beth became angry with us and suggested that EPA didn't have to do anything in the river after all. Dick Roeper asked her if she meant EPA would leave town over this incident, and, with great wordiness, she suggested that as a possible scenario.

This was the CAG's first attempt to offer scientifically-based advice to EPA, and it was not well received.

However, later in the month we learned that EPA had decided to use a barge to float heavy equipment needed to pound in a steel wall for a coffer dam.

Instead of drawing down the entire river, the plan called for sectioning off only one area on one side of the river. The river would flow outside the coffer dam on the other side of the river, while inside the steel walls, the water would be drained and the sediment dredged. When that area was completed, another area would be sectioned off, thereby never stopping the flow of the river. To have the EPA change their plans on the strength of advice from us gave the scientists in our CAG a heady feeling that anything was possible.

Suddenly we learned that we were to be visited by a vice-president of Velsicol Chemical Corporation, a man by the name of Chuck Hanson. The purpose of the meeting was "to develop a dialogue between the community of St. Louis and Velsicol," according to Beth. The only reason I could see for EPA wanting to set up this meeting was in hopes that Velsicol would decide to pay some of the river cleanup costs they had successfully evaded during the 1982 Consent Judgment settlement.

The meeting was closed except to invited participants. The mayor and city manager of St. Louis were there, the representative from the Saginaw Chippewa Tribe, several CAG officers and committee chairpersons, and three people from Velsicol. When Ed had received the phone call from Beth and Stuart about attending a meeting with the Velsicol vice-president, he had been told to bring one or two others from the CAG. Ed insisted, however, that the entire Executive Committee be invited, hoping to evade tactics he perceived being used by Beth and Stuart to divide the leaders of our group one from another.

At the meeting, we were each handed an agenda, a list of invited participants, and a paper labeled "Ground Rules." The first rule said "Be honest, say what you need to say, *but* keep in mind the purpose of the meeting – to establish a *constructive* relationship between the community and Velsicol."

It was beyond the scope of my imagination to envision any kind of constructive relationship with a company which had benefited from the destruction of our community's economy, environment, and reputation.

Ed opened the meeting with his usual warm style, and Chuck Hanson responded in kind.

As I recall, we didn't follow the agenda, because Chuck immediately asked in an expansive way how Velsicol could "make things right with the community."

Jim Hall suggested in a friendly manner that Mr. Hanson first apologize for having contaminated the plant site, the river and other sites in Gratiot County, and if he could do that, it might get us started on the right foot. Chuck diverted the conversation to say he'd heard around town that maybe the community wanted a park, or a recreation center, built on the site. We all listened politely, but didn't give him any encouragement.

Someone asked why Velsicol was denying EPA access to the plant site as a staging area for when excavation began in the river. Beth had repeatedly contacted Chuck with this request, and Chuck would not agree to it. On this day, Chuck answered the question by saying that if EPA wanted to use the site as a *permanent* disposal location for wastes from the river, he would agree to that. Our Executive Committee had already faced this possibility during an earlier meeting and had rejected the idea.

Our collective view was that Velsicol probably hoped EPA would enlarge the plant site with sediment from the river and, when the plant site was found to be leaking, EPA then would be responsible for fixing the leaks, and not Velsicol. At our meeting with Chuck, we politely let him know that we were not interested in having EPA use the plant site as a permanent destination for the contaminated sediment dug from the river.

Someone asked about cleaning up the Smith Farm dump site, and Chuck's warm attitude disappeared. He said Velsicol would *not* clean up Smith Farm. He said Velsicol had spent a million dollars putting up a fence around the property and doing testing. Once they found waste from another industry there, they had quit feeling any responsibility for that site. Chuck had emphasized the word "not" in this statement. That was his first use of the word "not." I spent most of the rest of the meeting counting his "nots."

The next "not" came in a response to someone asking if Velsicol would help clean up the river. Chuck said Velsicol did *not* feel responsible for the DDT in the river, because the DDT was dumped there before Velsicol bought the company. It was Michigan Chemical who had dumped the DDT, not Velsicol.

What about the Gratiot County Landfill? Recently the State Department of Natural Resources had found that the slurry wall around the site was leaking. Chuck said Velsicol would *not* do anything more at the landfill. He said they had been required by the State of Michigan to pay $14 million for clean up back in the 1980s, and they felt no more responsibility for that site.

What about the deep injection well on the Crumbaugh property? Now that a Gratiot County District Court judge had ruled Velsicol couldn't put contaminated water down the well, would they continue to appeal the case? Chuck said they would *not* give up the court battle, because they had documents that said they were allowed to use the well in that capacity.

What about the radioactive waste Velsicol had buried east of St. Louis near Bush Creek – the Breckenridge Site? Would they clean up those wastes? Chuck said they had money budgeted to do so, but their plans had stalled due to a necessity to re-count samples. They had not yet sent the report in to the Nuclear Regulatory Commission and would *not* undertake any cleanup this season.

How about cleaning up the plant site? Would Velsicol be willing to help with that? Since EPA had thought it would cost about $30 million, would he like to help the town with that project? Chuck said they would *not* dig up the mess and truck it away, and they would *not* help if anyone else did it. The legal settlement of 1982 relieved them of any responsibility for cleaning up that site Their only responsibilities were to pump out the contaminated water for disposal, and to mow the grass.

Would Velsicol perhaps be willing to buy a water-tight cover to put over the area where the clay cap had cracked?

At this point Chuck's smile came back, and his attitude softened. He said he had a really good idea for us. How's about, he said in a folksy way, if Velsicol made a gift of the plant site to the city of St. Louis as a place to build a parking garage?

Since the population of St. Louis is about 4,500, and the entire county's population is around 40,000, a parking garage is not something for which we have a great need.

We knew it would solve Chuck's problems, though, in terms of the cracked and leaking clay cap on the plant site.

The parking garage would create a giant roof to keep the rain out, which would mean less pumping for Velsicol.

After Chuck had said what he had to say about his parking garage idea, I spoke up. I'd taken the man's measure, and it seemed to me that he was hoping to hornswoggle us local yokels into receiving the contaminated site as a "gift," which we ourselves would then top with a parking garage. He didn't even offer to pay for the garage to be built.

That's when I spoke up. I said, "Look, Mr. Hanson, we are all busy people. You asked what you could do to make it right with the community. Here's my suggestion: Next time you come, why don't you bring your checkbook, and write us a check for $30 million? That would go a long way towards making things right for the community."

I watched his eyes narrow and his joviality disappear.

I hoped that I hadn't violated the ground rules. 1) Be honest 2) Think before you speak 3) Listen to what the other person has to say 4) Remember the Golden Rule.

Most of the rules were successfully fulfilled, I believe, but I may have done the reverse on #4. I had decided to treat Chuck the way he had been treating us – with some condescension and a little smidge of ridiculousness added in.

The meeting wasn't quite at an end, although I'd tuned out. In response to some remark, Chuck said, "Tell me when we've ever lied to the community," and Jim Hall said, "We don't have all day."

The meeting ended soon after that, and Chuck Hanson didn't come back, with or without his checkbook.

Reasonable people would assume that our meeting with Chuck would have brought to an end the dream of Beth Reiner for a friendship between our CAG and Velsicol, but there was more.

In the above list of Velsicol's Nots, the Crumbaugh's deep injection well was mentioned. The legal battle of Crumbaugh vs. Velsicol had begun about six months prior, and Rex and Kathy Crumbaugh had brought their situation to our attention.

In July 1997, Marcelle Crumbaugh, Rex's mother, had filed for injunctive relief in the Gratiot County 29th District Court to keep Velsicol from injecting contaminated water pumped from the plant site down a deep well located on her property.

—

25

She contended that her deceased husband, Robert, had signed a 99-year lease with Michigan Chemical for disposal of brine waste down the well, and only brine waste. She was not willing to allow Velsicol to dispose of the water pumped from the plant site that was contaminated with unknown chemicals. Velsicol argued that the lease allowed for the disposal of brine "and other waste." The chemical company was in the process of upgrading the well to accept the non-brine waste.

The judge issued a preliminary injunction, barring Velsicol from using the Crumbaugh well, and the case went to trial in March, 1998. I was able to attend one day of the trial, and Gary Smith was able to attend most of it.

During the day I was there, I heard C.W. "Deacon" Dunbar give his testimony on the stand. Deac, a chemical engineer, had served as a loyal employee of Michigan Chemical/Velsicol his entire working life, and he still, as an elderly dapper man in a brown suit, expressed loyalty for the chemical company. It struck me how many men of his generation in America had served their companies loyally and had expected loyalty from the company in return. Instead, Deac and so many others were discarded as easily and as unconscionably as contaminated water.

Deac was loyal to his company, but he would not lie. He testified that he had informed the Crumbaughs that the well would be used only for brine waste.

When Judge Randy Tahvonen ruled in April 1998, he based his decision on reasoning that neither side's attorney had voiced. The judge said since the chemical plant no longer existed, that meant the lease document was null and void. He was quoted in the newspaper as saying, "All evidence shows that the well was to be used in the ongoing operations of the plant. The proposed use of the well cannot be consistent with the lease, because the lease is for an ongoing operation."

The judge gave Velsicol 18 months to remove their equipment from the Crumbugh property, pending an appeal.

As far as we can ascertain, this is the only time Velsicol has met with a cut-and-dried defeat in the courtroom.

That doesn't mean they haven't faced lawsuits before. They've faced many, but were always successful in using delaying tactics, political manipulation, and other tricks to devise settlements that didn't hurt their bottom line very badly.

As an example, consider their 1982 settlement with DOJ, EPA, the State of Michigan and other federal agencies over the plant site, river, county landfill and golf course site: of the $38.5 million assessed in the settlement, only $14 million actually went into the state treasury. Most of the $38.5 million appeared only on paper, such as the "special" clay that supposedly cost $14 million for use in building the slurry walls and caps at two of the sites. How do we know the actual price tag for the clay? We don't. Only Velsicol knows.

Our surprise meeting with Vesicol's vice president Chuck Hanson had taken place on July 16th. Two weeks later Ed was informed by Beth that our CAG would meet at Penny Park near the river prior to our next regular meeting, as she had organized a Chippewa (Ojibwa) blessing of the river. Once again, we were caught off guard by an action planned by Beth.

Back at the October 1997 community meeting at the American Legion hall, Beth had made an offhand comment to the effect that if a Native American tribe was part of our community, we could be more certain of a thorough clean-up. Ed had remembered this comment, and once our group was organized and functioning, he had made contact with people from the Saginaw Chippewa Tribe who lived north of us in Mt. Pleasant. Many members of that tribe had been moved to the reservation from the St. Louis area in the 1800s. In fact, a large Chippewa village had existed on the Pine River downstream from the location of the chemical plant.

Ed became acquainted with Bill Snowden, who was the environmental engineer for the tribe. When Bill learned about a treaty that he thought might help our project, he brought the tribe's lawyer to a CAG meeting to tell us about it.

The tribal lawyer believed a case could be made for the Pine River downstream from the plant site, contending that the treaty had been broken when a total fish-consumption ban had been placed on the river due to the pollution from Velsicol.

On September 24, 1819 the Territory of Michigan and the Chippewa Nation had signed a treaty regarding lands the Indians ceded to Michigan, and lands reserved for Indian habitation. The treaty guaranteed the tribe rights to hunt and fish for food on the rivers that flowed through their new reservation lands and also through the lands they had ceded to Michigan. Even though the tribe wasn't interested in aiding our immediate quest for clean-up of the river impoundment and the plant site, they told us that when we reached the point of addressing the downstream area, they would like to join us.

To start the process, the tribal chief, Kevin Chamberlain, sent a letter to Velsicol's vice president Chuck Hanson, asserting the tribe's treaty right to fish for food in the Pine River. From what we gathered from Beth's comments, Chuck had become upset over this letter, and had directed his anger at EPA, threatening to never let the agency set foot on the plant site, let alone use it for a staging area when they excavated the river. Beth was upset that the chief had written directly to Velsicol, bypassing her. And she was upset that the careful relationship-building that she had attempted with Velsicol had broken down due to both the CAG's obstinacy and the tribe's assertiveness.

We didn't learn about the chief's letter until later, but once we knew about it, we could see the possible reasoning behind Beth's sudden plan for the Chippewa pipe ceremony. It seemed that Beth needed to build a better relationship with the tribe in order to placate Chuck Hanson. And to Beth it may have seemed that a good way to win the tribe's confidence was to invite them to waft tobacco smoke over the river.

We showed up at Penny Park in St. Louis across from the Velsicol Superfund Site, and near the Golf Course Site, to observe the pipe ceremony. Beaver Pelcher of the Saginaw Chippewa Tribe led the ceremony, accompanied by drummers. In the Ojibwa language, Pelcher blessed the sediment removal project that was soon to begin and honored mother earth that had been damaged and needed to be healed.

After the pipe ceremony, Bill Snowden continued to attend the CAG meetings until tribal in-fighting over casino profits turned him into an ex-tribal member.

At that time, the tribal council was reducing its membership roster, thereby increasing the cut of the profits for those left on the rolls. Many people who had been considered tribal members for decades were excommunicated during that purge. We heard that despite the fact that one of Bill's ancestors had signed the 1819 Treaty, he had been expelled from the tribe.

Beth may have finished promoting good will with the tribe, but not with Velsicol.

Gary Smith found out through his connections that Beth had been negotiating with Velsicol about the EPA water treatment plant that was under construction and intended for the processing of contaminated water from the river. Apparently, Vesicol wished to use the water treatment plant for disposal of the highly contaminated water they were still required to pump out of the plant site. Gary told the CAG that he had sent a letter to Beth objecting to her private negotiations without consulting with, or including, the CAG. He made the point that the EPA had encouraged the CAG to form for the purpose of overseeing all aspects of the river clean up, and, therefore, the CAG should have been present when Beth and Chuck Hanson were discussing the possibility of using the EPA water treatment plant for his purposes.

Gary presented a draft resolution voicing the CAG's position on this issue, and the resolution was adopted unanimously.

Beth was not in attendance at this meeting in December 1998, which made it easier to discuss our concerns regarding EPA. The general consensus, after some very sharp comments were voiced, was that the EPA seemed to be drifting away from a commitment to our CAG. The Executive Committee was asked to write a letter to Beth, addressing these concerns.

Even though most of us had held reservations about EPA based on past experience, we were slow to want to admit that EPA's behavior toward us this time around again seemed more like that of an adversary than a friend. We were slow to want to see it, but things seemed to be shaping up that way.

Chapter 3
(1999)
A Community Divided

Our resolution sent to EPA, MDEQ and the City of St. Louis made it clear that when they held meetings, the people affected by the decisions made at those meetings must be included in the decision-making process.

Ironically, the next month's first two items on the agenda were about meetings that had not included CAG members. Stuart Hill, the EPA Community Involvement Coordinator, had met with students from St. Louis High School to tell them what EPA was doing at the river site. This wasn't wrong, but we would have preferred to have a CAG person in on the presentation. As chair of the Public Information committee, I had already informed the schools and organizations around town that I was available to give a 15-20 minute talk on the river cleanup. Just before Christmas, I'd presented a program to the Alma/St. Louis Rotary Club, and the Rotarians donated $50 into our treasury. After Stuart's meeting at the high school, I cornered him to remind him of my willingness to give talks, and he told me quite bluntly that going out into the community to talk to people was his job.

I didn't persist, but I continued to let people know I was available to give talks, and I gave several in those first couple of years. Most of the talks I gave resulted in a donation, while none of Stuart's talks brought money into our treasury.

We had developed a little distrust of Stuart in the early months of our CAG, which may have disposed us to wonder about his motives in everything. He had told us that he would mail out the notices for our monthly meetings at EPA's expense, and at first, he did so. Then one time he forgot, and our meeting attendance was quite low.

We gave him another chance, and he forgot again. After that, we sent out the mailings ourselves at our own expense. When Stuart told me we were wasting our money, since EPA would pay for the postage, I explained that we preferred to do the mailing ourselves, and left it at that.

As for the other secret meeting, we later learned it was called the "EPA/St. Louis Community Consensus meeting," and included people from EPA, MDEQ, the City and Velsicol. Since no one from the CAG had been invited to participate, it was beginning to look as if the people in the CAG were not considered to be the authentic "community," at least in the eyes of EPA.

Maybe the city was beginning to view us in the same way, because the city manager, Dennis Collison, stopped coming to CAG meetings, and city council members came less often. When I asked one of the council members about his lack of attendance, he told me that various people from the city took turns coming so that at least one person was there "to keep an eye on us." Even though he said it in a jocular manner, it indicated a rift.

I've described many of the people who signed up to get the CAG rolling. We seemed an ordinary bunch, in my estimation, except that each of us was willing to give volunteer time to this endeavor. Looking around at our diverse, yet amiable group, I didn't see extremists of any kind. We were average citizens who felt strongly about cleaning up our corner of the world, and were willing to give of our time and talent to see that it got done. Along with the city council people, we were representative of the community at large. From what we learned later, this was part of the problem. In EPA's opinion, because we represented the community at large, our voice was too strong.

In March we received EPA's response to our resolution. The letter said if formal negotiations took place, the CAG would be notified. The skittishness of this reply was not lost on our group. *Formal negotiations? Notified?* Informal negotiations were as important as formal for reaching decisions. And even if formal negotiations took place, we were not assured inclusion, only notification.

One certainty arose from this response. We weren't imagining the distancing of EPA from our CAG.

Some of us began to wonder if we should back out of being an EPA-sanctioned Community Advisory Group and form our own coalition. We had learned the year before about EPA Technical Assistance Grants (TAG) available to groups like ours, which provided a $50,000 grant for the group to hire consultants.

Obviously, to have money like that to work with over and above dues and donations was attractive. Yet the requirements for how the money could be spent were very narrow, and also necessitated the hiring of two people: a Technical Advisor and a Grant Manager.

At a meeting of the Executive Committee, we struggled with these issues, with the majority deciding we should apply for the TAG grant and go forward as a CAG, but continue evaluation of our progress in the constraints of the CAG/TAG programs. In essence, we would see how long we could stand it. Ed encouraged us, saying that he thought we could try to stretch the rules of the TAG grant and maybe make them more lenient for ourselves and for newcomer citizen groups that might form in other places.

Our CAG was beginning to expand with new voices, several of them from people who lived downriver. Some of them expressed the same worries Joe and I had voiced about contaminants flowing over the dam and further polluting the downstream stretch of the river.

Once excavation had begun in the riverbed, the EPA On-Site Coordinator, Sam Borreis, promised to find out how much DDT was going over the dam. A few months later his successor, Callie Bolattino, reported a baseline of 73 grams of DDT passing over the dam daily, and she said that the amount should not increase during excavation, because the coffer dam would contain the area being dug up. The worries were somewhat assuaged.

Two new people, Harry Vitek and Fred Brown, drove over from Midland and Saginaw counties to attend our meetings, as did Professor Dave Swenson and his biology students from Saginaw Valley State University. A few men from Midland County involved in a conservation club also came with regularity in those first few years.

Both the Midland and Saginaw daily papers published articles about our activities fairly often. And our local daily and weekly papers sent reporters to our CAG meetings. As chair of the Public Information committee, I rarely had to write a press release. Instead, the reporters talked to me after the meetings or called me on the telephone.

We saw this widespread coverage in a positive light, but we learned that the city resented the notoriety they believed we were bringing to St. Louis.

Before she had become inactive, Nancy Roehrs, the city clerk and CAG treasurer, had told us it wasn't Velsicol who paid taxes on the land where the chemical plant had been located, but NWI Land Management.

Ed Lorenz researched NWI and learned that when William Farley had sold Velsicol to its five principle owners, including Chuck Hanson, he had spun off the most contaminated sites in Michigan, Illinois, New Jersey and Tennessee and "sold" them to his newly created NWI company, whose sole function was to own those seven sites. That allowed the five principle owners to buy Velsicol with no major liabilities. NWI was simply a name on a paper and legal holder of the property deeds.

During one of our CAG meetings, someone wondered out loud why Velsicol, a well-known and prosperous chemical company, would have desired to purchase Michigan Chemical Company which, in 1978, was old and decrepit, facing lawsuits from the workers following the PBB Disaster and from the State of Michigan for extensive pollution.

Ed assigned some students to this question, and we learned that the purchase of Michigan Chemical by Velsicol did not take place in 1978 after the PBB disaster, but years earlier. Everyone had assumed the sale had taken place in 1978, because that's when the sign in front of the chemical plant had been changed to "Velsicol."

Actually, Michigan Chemical had been acquired by William Farley in 1963 and was merged into Velsicol in 1965. Like all the profitable companies he bought, Farley squeezed the earnings out of Michigan Chemical without putting money into maintenance or upkeep.

It's instructive to compare photographs of the Michigan Chemical plant from the late 1950s and early 1960s with those of the 1970s. The neat and tidy buildings from earlier years had become dirty, piled with junk, and the whole plant took on a run-down, ramshackle appearance.

Soon after Ed shared his history lesson with the CAG, Beth announced to us that from now on EPA would be dealing with NWI and not Velsicol.

Yes, Velsicol was still responsible under the terms of the 1982 Consent Judgment to pump out and dispose of the contaminated water that accumulated in the plant site under the clay cap, but was not the owner of the property. NWI owned it.

Beth began to talk about NWI as if it was a real corporation, telling us that NWI wished to use the city's water treatment plant for disposal of their waste; that NWI would help the city get a grant from EPA to make a re-use plan for the plant site; and that NWI would be sending a representative to our CAG meetings.

Whew! For a company that had no buildings, no people, and no cash flow, they had become quite busy all of a sudden.

Beth's demeanor had changed. She seemed to have made up her mind to get tough with us and tell us how things were going to be. She wasn't going to try to get us to be friends with NWI, as she had with Velsicol. She had decided instead to force the NWI person into our midst.

His name was John Hock and he worked for Memphis Environmental, the in-house contractor for Velsicol/NWI, under the leadership of Chuck Hanson. His job was to sample and characterize contaminated Velsicol/NWI sites, and to compile reports that showed that the sites were contained and that contaminants were not migrating.

John told us that he would be doing tests periodically at the plant site, including the measurement of amounts of contaminated water pumped out of the site for disposal. He also planned to conduct tests at the radioactive site.

As for the plant site, our CAG let John Hock know from day one that we were sure the site was leaking contaminated water into the river, and that he needed to get his company to determine which sections of the slurry wall had broken down.

Gary Smith, who was running the Plant Site Committee now that the city manager and the city clerk had quit coming to meetings, reported on a conversation he'd had with EPA workers at the site. They had said the slurry wall was leaking, but that tests were needed for verification. Gary stressed that we needed to know for sure about the slurry wall leaks before the Plant Site Committee could move forward with plans for brownfield reclamation and other ideas for site usage.

Another attempt at divisiveness was launched by our Community Involvement Coordinator, Stuart Hill. He told us that he would be meeting with the Michigan United Conservation Clubs to help them form a CAG. He said that since they were a major environmental organization in the state, they should have a voice in how the river was cleaned up. This statement caught us off guard. We didn't quite understand how two CAGs were needed. And we already had several people who belonged to MUCC as members of our CAG.

Murray, the youngest member of our Executive Committee, had joined the CAG expecting the best of everyone, especially EPA. This was the night when he lost his idea of utopia. He rose up and said, "I smell a rat," or words to that effect. He demanded to know when and where the meeting with MUCC would take place. He needed to know, he explained, because he had meant to join the MUCC and he had decided that the night of the upcoming meeting was when he was going to pay his dues.

With smiles and heartiness, Fred Brown and Harry Vitek, two of the MUCC members, encouraged Murray. In fact, they said, he could ride to the meeting with them. And by the way, they wanted us to know that whatever happened at the meeting involving EPA, the MUCC would not undermine the efforts of our CAG to clean up the river. Murray followed through, went to the meeting and joined MUCC. He told us that the conservation club members listened to Stuart's spiel on forming a CAG, but voted not to do so.

Later, when I was speaking with Stuart after one of our meetings, he mentioned that we needed more CAGs in the area because our CAG was too strong. I asked what he meant by "strong," and he said we had too many people who were outspoken and opinionated. He added that he had tried to remedy this adverse situation by getting the MUCC people to form a CAG, and they wouldn't do it. He said that Fred Brown had talked them out of it.

Dr. Fred Brown was definitely opinionated and out-spoken, and our CAG benefited from his wealth of knowledge. When he first began to attend our meetings, we had no idea of his extensive background in protecting the rivers of Michigan.

He had been a research chemist at Dow Chemical Corporation in Midland, and had risked his job in 1969 to stand against Dow on the issue of selling the waters of Michigan. As president of MUCC, he had led the conservation clubs in opposing a plan, promoted by Dow, to allow industry to impound the state rivers and sell the surplus water. The battle went to court and the judge found the industry plan unconstitutional.

Fred had led the Michigan Water Resources Commission, and later he was appointed by the governor of Michigan to a permanent seat on the commission

When Fred had seen an article in the Saginaw newspaper about our group's efforts to clean up the pollutants left by Velsicol in the Pine River, he thought he might be able to help us. I, for one, wasn't sure we wanted his help – at least at first.

I confess that I clashed with Fred during one of the CAG meetings. He presented a very logical viewpoint that perhaps EPA was putting the cart before the horse in cleaning up the river before they cleaned the plant site. He offered information from already published reports which indicated the plant site was leaking. But when he suggested that EPA halt its plans to begin excavation in the river and to spend the $30 million "or some portion thereof" on an investigation of the plant site instead, I had to speak up.

We had been waiting for decades for a clean up of the river. Now that we had EPA in town and ready to do the work, we didn't want to call a halt. I talked about the "hotspot" in the river, the 2-3 acre area of sediment with DDT levels as high as 46,000 parts per million. As long as the hotspot was sitting there, the downstream portion of the river would continue to be poisoned. The hot spot needed to be removed now. Even though I agreed that it would have made sense for EPA to clean the plant site first and the river second, now wasn't the time to stop the plan that was in place to clean the hotspot in the river. The community had waited too long to ask them to stop the forward progress of the river cleanup.

In later years, as the evidence mounted showing that the plant site was not only leaking but *pouring* contaminants back into the river, Fred asked me whether I didn't agree that it would have made sense to clean the plant site first, and of course I agreed with him.

Even so, I think it would have been a mistake for EPA to halt the Emergency Removal Action. On the other hand, the subsequent riverbed acreage (almost 36 acres in all) should have awaited excavation until the plant site had been cleaned, because re-pollution of the cleaned river continued non-stop from the leaking plant site.

Of course, to go back even further in time, it was in the 1980s when the plant site and river should have been properly excavated and the contaminants should have been buried far from the moving water of the Pine River, with Velsicol paying the costs rather than the U.S. taxpayers.

By May, sheet piling had been pounded into the bed of the river to form a large cell, and dewatering of the cell had begun. The previous fall the EPA contractor, EQ (Environmental Quality Management) had successfully floated a barge carrying a 30-ton crane with a vibratory hammerhead that did the pounding. Even loaded, the barge drew only 32 inches of water. The whole city shook and resounded as the sheet piling was hammered to a depth of 15 feet into the sediment and the hard, gravelly clay beneath it. We could hear the hammering downstream at our house.

Then a large pump was activated, piping water from within the cell through a hose and back into the flowing part of the river. Once the cell was de-watered, and after several days had passed for the mud to dry enough for heavy equipment to drive down into the cell, excavation began. Truckloads of contaminated sediment were driven out of the cell and up to a concrete pad where the loads were dumped. The water that ran out of the dumped sediment was captured for processing in the on-site water treatment plant. After Beth had successfully persuaded Velsicol to sign a letter of agreement, this whole operation had been set up on the north end of the former Velsicol plant site.

At our May meeting a few families attended who lived on North Street next to the excavation process. Joe Fuentes told Beth that the odor and the dust from the operation were affecting the everyday life of the residents who lived on the shoreline of the river, from dirty cars, to gardens they didn't dare plant for fear of the chemicals drifting in the air from the stirred up dust, and how they had to keep their windows closed.

What would they do when hot weather came? He asked that his family be moved to another house at government expense during the time of the excavation.

Beth, with her new "take charge" attitude told him that moving families who lived in the area "would not be a consideration entertained by EPA." Case closed.

CAG members suggested ways that EPA could change their operation to lessen the effects on close-by residents. How about using water spray to keep the dust down? How about using a spray solidifier to help dry the sediment instead of using lime dust? How about offering car wash certificates to residents? And was there a phone number people could call with complaints?

Because the residents heard our thoughtful suggestions in contrast with Beth's refusal to help, they could see that our CAG wanted the best for the community during this time of upheaval. Moreover, we were pleased when EPA followed through and implemented our suggestions, including publishing the number of the telephone located at the trailer where the On-Site Coordinator and other workers spent time.

Later in the year, when Beth began maternity leave, she gave a parting speech, about the "antagonistic atmosphere" of our meetings and urged us to work at having a "less strained relationship" with EPA. We listened politely, but most of us felt that the strain didn't originate with the CAG, but with EPA.

She also introduced our new interim Project Manager, Stephanie Ball. Stephanie was slight of build, appeared to be about 16 years old, and showed obvious signs of nervousness to be taking on the responsibilities of her job.

As excavation of the hotspot continued throughout the summer, Stephanie took pictures of the work and showed them as power point slides at our meetings. Not only were thick layers of white chemical waste dug through during the excavation, but also black layers of petroleum waste.

Dr. Fred Brown had informed us that petroleum waste, particularly benzene, would react with DDT, making the pesticide move more readily. He said that DDT by itself generally settled into sediments and stayed put, but when benzene and other petroleum distillates came in contact with it, the DDT attached itself to them and moved with the flow of the river.

Our Executive Committee discussed how to address the petroleum waste that had come and was still coming downstream from Total Refinery, which refined crude oil into gasoline, heating oil and jet fuel. As an employee of Total, our treasurer, Gary Smith, was familiar with the refinery's use of Horse Creek as a sewer line that emptied into the Pine River. Recently, Murray Borrello had taken a shovelful of the sludge from the confluence of Horse Creek and the Pine River, let it dry, and then and had set it on fire as a vivid demonstration for his students.

Since Total was a going concern, employing almost 300 people in the community, we were cautious about addressing the problem of their contamination of the river. We didn't want to disrupt a profitable company that provided good-paying jobs to local residents.

Then Gary heard that EPA had fined Total $13.9 million for an air pollution violation.

A little investigation showed that the entire amount of fine money would go into the U.S. Treasury. It seemed a shame that the money couldn't come to our community, which had suffered from the air pollution.

A little more research turned up a policy entitled a Supplemental Environmental Project, which allowed a portion of fines from a polluter to be diverted into an environmental project in a community. The SEP process also benefited the polluter, since the company was exempted from paying taxes on fines diverted into a Supplemental Environmental Project, while it was required to pay taxes on fines paid into the U.S. Treasury.

This looked like the way to go for our CAG. Not only would we benefit the community, but Total Refinery as well. Ed acquired the necessary paperwork to apply for a SEP, and we held an Executive Committee meeting to discuss possible community projects.

We settled on a cleanup of Horse Creek, since there was no question that it had been polluted by the refinery, and because the creek flowed into the Pine River, contributing to the pollution downstream where sediment cleanup was taking place adjacent to the former Velsicol plant. The rules allowed us to apply only for a portion of the fine money, and we asked for $9 million to be set aside from the fine money for a cleanup of Horse Creek.

Ed sent the paperwork to the EPA Region 5 attorney, as directed in the instructions, and the attorney, Nicole Cantello, informed us that we, as an EPA-sanctioned CAG, could not intervene in any area outside the Superfund Site.

We pointed out that the mandate our CAG had adopted from the start was to oversee the cleanup of the entire Pine River Watershed. With Horse Creek being a tributary of the Pine River, it was well within the territory of our mandate. On the strength of our written arguments, EPA Region 5 accepted our application for a SEP for Horse Creek.

We saw this as two victories in one: the first was the SEP itself, and the second was stretching the rules for a CAG.

In the midst of these activities, it was announced in the newspaper that Total Refinery was for sale. Actually, they planned to close down and sell the tanks, piping and equipment to another company, which turned out to be UDS (Ultramar Diamond Shamrock).

Total's decision to leave the community was based on international reasons, not local. They were a French-owned company, and they wanted to drill for oil in the Persian Gulf waters controlled by Iran. At that time, the United States had sanctions against Iran (the Iran-Libya Sanctions Act). If Total, a foreign company with U.S. assets, were to drill in Iranian waters, they would face stiff penalties. Instead Total chose to divest themselves of all their U.S. assets to allow themselves to drill in the Persian Gulf. Some people in the community thought that our "environmental group" was responsible for Total Refinery leaving, but that wasn't the case.

When we heard that Total was closing down, and that EPA was overseeing the closure, we tried to get a seat at the table for the negotiations over a consent judgment. We were determined to be included in decisions regarding the closure of this company and the disposition of its contaminated site.

We had no intention of giving in when EPA, UDS and the DOJ let us know that we were not welcome, declaring that Total was not part of the Velsicol Superfund Site, and therefore none of our business. At the first intimation that we were not to be included, Ed and Murray began to wage a campaign to change that situation.

Murray made a Freedom of Information Act request to EPA, asking for all letters and documents regarding the negotiations. The initial response received pointed out that the parties were involved in an on-going court procedure and EPA could not release the documents. When the 10-day FOIA deadline had come and gone, Murray got on the phone, and was told that EPA could not find the records.

This battle went on through the year, and finally in December Murray called the EPA lawyer and said he was prepared to personally take EPA to federal court. But instead of complying with the FOIA request, EPA began to look for exemptions to the FOIA guidelines to let themselves off the hook.

Another EPA lawyer was assigned to take Murray's frequent phone calls. After his threat of a lawsuit, she told him the files had been found, but that EPA was not required to release them due to a clause that made information received for law enforcement purposes exempt from FOIA.

Murray went to his own lawyer (his brother), who told him EPA was misusing the clause. Murray informed the EPA lawyer of what he had learned from his lawyer, and after using colorful language about Murray's persistence, the lawyer said she would ship the documents to him.

Sure enough, in another week large boxes of materials arrived at his house. He and a few of his students began reading the letters and reports, compiling the information to enable our CAG to better respond to the planned remediation of the Total Refinery site.

Meanwhile, Ed hurriedly organized a meeting to gather information from the public regarding the closing of the refinery and its effects on the workers, on the tax base of the city of Alma, and also about the pollutants in soil and water being left behind. Included in the meeting were ordinary citizens, local officials, and two aides to one of our members of Congress. EPA was not happy to be excluded from the meeting, and a UDS spokesperson also expressed displeasure at being left out.

That encouraged Ed to put pressure on the Department of Justice, EPA, MDEQ and the refinery owners to take part in a formal public hearing. The DOJ was reluctant to commit itself, and it was not until May of 2000 that the public hearing finally took place.

Meanwhile, something noteworthy happened with our new EPA Project Manager, Stephanie Ball, and our new MDEQ Project Manager, Brian vonGunten. As they were winding down the Emergency Removal Action for the hotspot in the river, they were simultaneously wrote a work plan for the cleanup of a much larger area in the bend of the river that surrounded the former Velsicol plant site. During the December meeting they announced that when a draft of the work plan was completed, they would like to share it with us to get our comments and suggestions before finalizing it.

This simple statement struck us with a great sense of relief and encouragement. It looked as if Stephanie and Brian were going to seek our input without us having to insist that they listen to us.

That was the chief bright spot in a year full of struggles with EPA officials and with the gulf widening between the city and the CAG. We suspected that Beth and Stuart had helped encourage the division between ourselves and those who served in city government, but it was not until several more years that we learned the full truth.

Chapter 4
(2000)
A Closed Door

Even in our earliest years, the CAG had a sense of past, present and future. Having a history professor (Ed Lorenz) as our chairman for the first four years helped us to keep the past in focus, which enriched the present-day intentions of our group, and gave us the resolve to not let the outcomes of the past become the outcomes of the future.

We reminded each other often that we needed to pursue every possible angle to achieve the best clean up of our sites for the sake of those who would come after us. Once we were gone, we wanted our children and grandchildren to read the newspaper accounts, or look through our expanding files of letters written, presentations made, and reports compiled, and we wanted them to see that our CAG had persisted in every way possible in the pursuit of pollution cleanup for our community. We were determined to right the wrongs of the past, and to prevent new wrongs from occurring.

The year 2000 tested our determination. We insisted that our voice be heard in regard to the Total/UDS legal settlement, the Fruit of the Loom bankruptcy proceedings, by the state health department, and by EPA concerning their water treatment facility.

Meanwhile, a change in personnel caught us by surprise. Our new MDEQ Project Manager Brian von Gunten was suddenly replaced with another new person, Scott Cornelius. The change upset us. Our relationship with Brian had begun well, with him showing respect for our views and soliciting suggestions from us. We didn't like to lose him.

And the circumstances around this change seemed odd, even to other MDEQ employees. We learned that Brian was going to the Kalamazoo River site, and Scott, who had been at the Kalamazoo site, was being sent to us. That switch in project managers actually had been ordered by the director of MDEQ, Russ Harding, which was highly unusual, we were told, and perhaps the only time such a switch had been ordered by the head of the agency.

In our heightened state of alert, we thought the switch may have had something to do with our CAG being outspoken and opinionated.

In hindsight, I think it had more to do with Scott Cornelius being outspoken and opinionated. Scott told us that one of the corporate PRPs (potentially responsible parties) at the Kalamazoo River site had asked for his removal, and the MDEQ director had met the corporate man's request.

We were angry to lose Brian, angry to see the director of our state agency bow to the wishes of a polluting corporation, and angry to have to bring yet another project manager up to speed. A motion was made to send a letter to Russ Harding expressing our displeasure with his intervention in switching project managers, and we did so.

It was into this angry atmosphere that Scott Cornelius was received. Joe Scholtz predicted Scott would not last six months with us. Joe was wrong. Scott was with us for twelve years.

Excavation continued in the river, with reports of 17,000 tons having been removed, and then 50,000 tons, and then 88,000 tons. The runoff water from the sediments had to be stockpiled, though, while EPA and MDEQ argued about how much DDT could remain in the water after it had passed through the water treatment plant and was returned to the river.

The State of Michigan standard was more stringent than the federal standard, and EPA did not want to spend the extra money it would take to meet the state standard, instead, wanting the state to grant them a variance to allow more DDT to be returned to the river. Our EPA Project Manager, Stephanie, said we should ask the state to provide the variance, because without it, the project would come to a halt and a whole season of work would be lost.

The members of our Technical Committee took a good look at the data, and then wrote a resolution addressing the problem. In it we asked MDEQ to wait on issuing a variance until certain conditions were met by EPA, including the start up of a monitoring program to determine the chemical content of emissions from the water treatment plant, and testing those emissions for other chemicals besides DDT. Once these conditions were met, the MDEQ could consider the variance issue again.

Helping to craft this resolution was an elderly gentleman who had quietly joined our group a few months earlier.

It was after Ed had given a presentation at the Chippewa Nature Center, located at the junction of the Pine River and the Chippewa River in Midland County, that he had met Gene Kenaga and invited him to come to our meetings. Ed had no idea that he'd invited a World War II DDT expert, but that's what Dr. Eugene Kenaga was. He had retired from Dow Chemical where he had worked as a research entomologist.

Gene's knowledge of chemistry was a treasure trove for us. His presence, however, and that of Fred Brown, required us to make a change. Because of the scientifically detailed discussions that Gene and Fred brought to our CAG meetings, which were above the heads, or boring, to many of the CAG members, I suggested that we form a separate Technical Committee, and the others agreed. That way the scientists could delve into detail at the afternoon Technical meeting, and then Murray, chair of that committee, could bring a summation of their discussions to the evening CAG membership meeting.

It was Gene who had suggested a clause in the variance resolution that set the condition to test emissions from the water treatment plant for other chemicals in addition to DDT, explaining that there were chemicals far worse than DDT that could be in the water.

After sending the resolution to both agencies, the Technical Committee initiated a conference call with Stephanie at her office in Chicago. At the end of it, Stephanie and her bosses agreed to upgrade the water treatment plant, and we were once again assured of a full season of excavation. The PVC piping in the water treatment plant was replaced with steel, and diatomaceous earth was used to help clean the water.

45

In addition, our new MDEQ Project Manager, Scott Cornelius, and his bosses had decided that if EPA was able to reduce the DDT discharge levels to a point near the state standard of 0.14 parts per billion, they would then issue a variance for the remaining amount.

As it was, the EPA was able to meet the state standard, and a variance was not needed, which pleased us, because in the long run it was better for the health of the river.

Not only did EPA meet the state standard, but they also met our conditions. We were grateful that the Technical Committee had made it a condition to test the emissions from the water treatment plant, and to test for other chemicals besides DDT, because we were soon facing another problem of toxicity.

When the first report came out showing emissions data, Fred Brown questioned why a certain toxic chemical showed up in the emissions data and not in the contaminated water entering the treatment facility. EPA sent samples to the state lab, and it was found that the rogue chemical had come from the water treatment system itself.

One of the chemicals used for cleaning the water was actually toxic, and it was being introduced into our river from our very efforts to clean the river. That was maddening, yet we were glad that the emissions testing plan had been put in place so that the toxicity was discovered at an early stage.

To shift to another important development, we learned that the State of Michigan planned to begin destroying infant blood spot cards. From the time our group first formed, we had been seeking ways to obtain a comprehensive health study of the people in our area. We had brainstormed about the possibility that the blood spots on the cards, collected since the 1960s, might provide us with baseline data to help us obtain a grant for a health study.

Michigan had led the way in obtaining tiny drops of blood from the heels of newborn babies and storing them on cards in files, in conjunction with the National Newborn Screening Quality Assurance Program. The dried blood spots were used to screen for genetic and metabolic problems in individual newborns.

After Ed Lorenz and Melissa Strait had attended a national meeting of the American Chemical Society, where they learned of a study that was using infant dried blood spots to assess the presence of pesticides and other organochlorine compounds in newborns, our CAG theorized that a health study matching the infant blood spot cards with the now adult subjects could give us a before-and-after look at DDT exposure from the 1960s to the present day.

Now, however, the cards were scheduled to be destroyed.

Since the blood spot cards contained genetic material and private information about the baby and his or her parents, they were considered to be in violation of the new genetic privacy law enacted by the Michigan state legislature. The legislature had directed the Department of Community Health to develop a schedule for the destruction of the cards.

We wrote a letter to the person at the state health department who was in charge of the blood spot cards, presenting our view that the cards should be spared because they could help us with our health study, and perhaps help other communities assess their exposure to environmental pollutants from the 1960s to the present day. The letter was also sent to our state legislators.

Despite our petition, the destruction of the cards began. Cards from the 1960s and into the 1970s were destroyed before a moratorium was called. It seemed like such needless destruction of an important resource.

Even though our community had never been the recipient of a comprehensive health study, we had provided an interesting pool of people for many researchers to study, especially following the PBB Disaster in the 1970s. The community's experience with researchers, however, left it with a low regard for them.

The researchers would come to town from universities and research hospitals, find their subjects, gather their data, leave town and never be heard from again.

Our ill-fortune in having been exposed to PBB and DDT was the good fortune of the researchers. They were enriched by having a ready-made pool of live subjects to write about. They were enriched by having their articles published in journals, which advanced their careers.

Yet they gave nothing back to the people who had agreed to give them blood samples, fat samples, descriptions of their symptoms, and a portion of their dignity to be a subject in a study. No copies of the reports or journal articles were sent to St. Louis residents or to the public library. No thank-you notes arrived.

Despite all the research, the community still didn't know what to expect from its years of exposure.

No one knew whether or not the increased problems with breast cancer, thyroid gland trouble, prostate cancer, early menstruation in girls, and learning difficulties in children were attributable to the chemical exposures through air, water, garden soil and through the animals hunted or fished for food, or to something else.

Our CAG applied for a grant from the National Institute of Environmental Health Sciences (NIEHS) to fund a comprehensive health study in our community, and the roundabout response we received said we didn't have enough data about the health of people in our community to receive a grant to find out about the health of people in our community. The letter, however, encouraged us to gather more data, and to re-apply.

Ed Lorenz received a small grant from the Gerstacker Foundation in Midland and used the money to hire college students to do a preliminary health survey in the community. The local school superintendents and a family physician were willing to share data with us, and the data showed an abnormally high level of "special ed." students in our county, and heightened levels of asthma in children. The physician who headed up our county health department, Dr. Robert Graham, helped the college students gather more data to strengthen our request for a grant. Then we contacted Dr. Wilfried Karmaus, an epidemiologist in the College of Human Medicine at Michigan State University, to write the grant application.

With all of this professional assistance, we felt that our chances were good to receive a 5-year grant, but our proposal was rejected. Undeterred, we made some adjustments in the request and applied again, adding some new data.

We had hired students from Alma College to conduct a short survey of people fishing in the Pine River. The statistics they presented to us were disturbing: Of the 69 people interviewed, 83% of them ate the fish they caught; 96% who ate fish ate them more than once a month; 35% of those who ate fish ate them on a daily basis; 94% of those people who fished had caught fish with visible lesions and tumors; 74% of the women who fished ate their catch at least on a monthly basis, including a 14-year-old pregnant mother with a toddler.

Despite our best efforts, our grant application was again turned down.

Meanwhile, the NWI/Velsicol/Memphis Environmental representative who was assigned to attend our meetings, John Hock, mentioned that Fruit of the Loom had filed for bankruptcy. His announcement didn't seem relevant to most of the people at the meeting. What connection did the underwear company have with Velsicol? Only Ed had a clue as to the significance of John's announcement.

Ed explained to us that in the 1980s the business mogul, William Farley, had renamed the old and profitable Union Underwear company "Fruit of the Loom" and had made it the parent company of his various acquisitions, which included among others Northwest Industries (NWI) and Velsicol Chemical. It was through NWI that the former Velsicol plant site was linked to Fruit of the Loom, since Fruit was the parent company of NWI which now "owned" the plant site. After this explanation, Ed speculated that maybe our CAG should file a claim against Fruit of the Loom in bankruptcy court.

John Hock laughed out loud, thinking it was a joke. We tentatively laughed with him, puzzled as to how we could do such a thing, yet trusting that Ed might be onto something. Ed asked John to keep us posted on the progress of the bankruptcy filing, and John said he would.

In July, we learned that the Fruit of the Loom bankruptcy had moved to the stage at which we could file a claim. I made a motion for the Executive Committee to explore the steps for filing a claim, to determine the amount of the claim, and then go ahead and file. The motion passed.

At the Executive Committee meeting, Murray reported that his brother, the lawyer, said we did not have legal standing to file a claim. After some discussion about our unlikely chances of having the judge recognize our claim, we decided that despite our lack of standing, we should go ahead and file. We had nothing to lose.

That decision was followed by more discussion about the dollar amount we should ask for in our claim. Ed reported that one of his students had gone on-line and learned that Fruit of the Loom had a $100 million pollution insurance policy through an AIG (American International Group) subsidiary.

I suggested that we file a claim for the entire $100 million in the pollution insurance policy. The money would be earmarked for a full remediation of the plant site and also the Breckenridge radioactive site, since both were covered by the insurance policy. The others agreed with me, and we filled out the paperwork and filed the claim.

At the next meeting, when John Hock heard that we'd filed a claim for $100 million, he laughed and shook his head, but I think he kind of enjoyed our audacity.

A more serious matter arose a month later. John reported in a very bland manner that in recent months NWI/Velsicol/Memphis Environmental had not found any water in the plant site to pump out. He blamed it on low rainfall. We said again that the wall around the plant site was leaking, and suggested that John get his employers to patch the holes.

For two years we'd been telling EPA that the site was leaking, and we'd asked repeatedly for them to test to find out where the slurry wall was breached. We pointed out that the same kind of slurry wall built at the Gratiot County Landfill had leaked in 1998. Why would the wall at the chemical plant site last any longer? EPA informed us that they were not going to do tests on the plant site, because their only responsibility was the river remediation.

Meanwhile, upstream, discussions were underway on the Consent Judgment for Total Petroleum. In a scenario eerily similar to the closed door sessions in the 1982 Velsicol settlement, the presence of citizens was being resisted during the settlement negotiations among Total Refinery, EPA, the U.S. Department of Justice, and the State of Michigan. There was one difference, however. Our CAG did not stop hammering on the closed door.

In the previous chapter I described Murray's relentless quest to obtain documents related to the settlement talks, and Ed's resolute calling of one public meeting after another. Murray's reward was the boxes of documents and reports, and Ed's was a commitment on the part of EPA, MDEQ and Total/UDS to be present at a large, public hearing for the community. After one excuse after another, DOJ also finally agreed to attend, and the date was set for May.

To educate the members of the CAG in preparation for the meetings, Murray asked one of his students to give us a presentation about our SEP project, Horse Creek, which flowed into the Pine River. "Flowed" is a relative term, since the creek was clogged with over seven feet of smelly black sludge. The black hydrocarbon sludge was also present in a wide swath at the confluence Horse Creek and the Pine River. In addition, the river sediments contained high levels of lead. If a body of water contained over 200 parts per million lead, it qualified for remediation. The samples from the confluence of Horse Creek and the Pine River measured up to 5,700 ppm.

Even though Horse Creek had been accepted as a SEP (Supplemental Environmental Project), we had our sights set on a cleanup of the riverbed from the refinery site all the way to the chemical plant site. We knew it was a long shot, but nothing ventured, nothing gained.

On May 10, 2000 we congregated in a private room at Alma College for an afternoon CAG meeting with our guests from DOJ, EPA, and MDEQ. Dinner would follow. And then we would move to the large auditorium on campus for the public meeting involving the refinery property owner, UDS/Total, and the wider community.

We have a transcript of the afternoon meeting. Ed spoke first, and contrasted our well-organized, well-supported situation in the year 2000 with that of 1982 when the Velsicol Consent Judgment was being negotiated. He was letting the gathered attorneys know, without saying it directly, that we intended for the outcome of these negotiations over Total to be very different from those in 1982.

Annette Lange, the attorney from the U.S. Department of Justice, said that in crafting the decree with UDS/Total, "we were very conscious of not creating a situation that would leave the community with the same feelings that it had with respect to the Velsicol site." Of course, it wasn't only the *feelings* we were left with, but also a lot of toxic sediment, polluted soil, and contaminated groundwater.

Annette then told us how the process would work, with a comment period following the consent order and prior to the judge signing the decree. She put a good spin on it, saying we would have several weeks to write our comments before the June 8th deadline, as if that were ample time.

Dr. Fred Brown spoke up and said that he would like to ask for a 30-day extension of the comment period. We had been through two EPA comment periods during the river clean up, and we knew that asking for a 30-day extension was usual practice. In light of that knowledge, Annette's reply seemed a little odd. She said, "Thirty days is quite a long time."

Sitting near Fred, I saw his eyes lock onto Annette's face. With an unmistakable emphasis in his pronunciation, he explained that in order for us to write an intelligent comment, we would need time. Annette said she would take his request back to the Department of Justice.

Then she turned to the written questions we had submitted, the first one asking whether or not $9 million was enough to clean up Horse Creek. She told us that no one knew if $9 million was enough, but that the cleanup had to fit the money.

Did that mean the work would stop, with the project unfinished? She didn't answer directly, but said the written consent judgment did not release Total/UDS from all liability.

Murray questioned the truth of that statement, and asked her to point out where those words appeared in the document.

At this point, she grew defensive and sarcastic, saying she was sure we had read the consent decree, but she doubted if any of us had read the complaint, and that it was the complaint that set the legal basis for the decree. Our group, of course, had gone over everything, but we didn't correct her misapprehension.

After much explanation, she said again that the decree did not relieve Total of liability for corrective action under RCRA (Resource Conservation and Recovery Act). Murray asked where in the decree those words could be found. She told us we wouldn't find any words in the decree about Total being released or not released from liability under RCRA.

In response, Murray referred her to page 34, paragraph 55 where there was an explicitly worded sentence about Total being released from liability. He suggested that a re-wording of that sentence might be necessary if the decree did *not* intend to release the company from all liability. She maintained that the sentence referred a reader back to section 6, even though the words of reference were not there.

At one point, CAG member and biologist Dick Roeper asked if EPA and MDEQ had performed sampling in the river upstream from the confluence of the river and Horse Creek. In a highly defensive manner, Annette said a judge would never ask Total to clean up the river. Nicole Cantello, the EPA attorney, said the Clean Water Act could not be applied to dumping that took place prior to 1972, and who could tell where all that "mud" came from in the river?

Murray informed her that forensic chemical analysis performed on river samples revealed that the sludge was partially refined petroleum products. Those results indicated that the "mud" in the river had come from the refinery.

Dick asked if the Clean Water Act applied also to Horse Creek. Would the sludge be excavated only to the 1972 level, and not the 1935 level (when the refinery opened)?

Annette had said repeatedly that the decree did not release Total from corrective action under RCRA, or from Superfund. Our CAG was sure that the Total site could not become a Superfund Site as oil refineries were not included in the Superfund law. Why did she keep hinting that Superfund was a way to get the Total/UDS site cleaned up when she knew Superfund was not even a possibility for the oil refinery?

Years later when we learned that a refinery *could* become a Superfund Site based on lead contamination, we wondered if this explained Annette's broad references to RCRA law and Superfund during our conversation with her. If so, it would have been kind of her, or one of the other attorneys, to educate us on that point.

Mike Vickery had persisted about the Horse Creek situation. What if the creek wasn't cleaned to the standards the community expected when the $9 million ran out? After Annette made it clear that no cleanup standards were stipulated in the decree, Nicole said, "If there is a shortfall, yours will now be the only community that finds themselves in this situation." We didn't quite understand what she meant. Annette explained that in the entire country, there were only six sediment remediation projects ever brought to settlement under the Clean Water Act.

I guess they were telling us that the situation of a shortfall of money had not come up before because there were so few sediment remediation projects underway, and, further, that we should feel privileged that we were getting a sediment remediation project at all.

They meant well in telling us this, but I find it highly discouraging that in our vast country such a small number of sediment remediation projects had taken place from 1972 to 2000 under the Clean Water Act. In hearing the hesitancy expressed by both Annette and Nicole of even trying to bring such cases, I can't help but think that DOJ and EPA might be part of the problem. Why aren't they actively bringing such cases to court?

And, of course, citizens need to take the initiative by writing letters asking for Supplemental Environmental Projects, and insisting that DOJ and EPA follow through in the best way possible.

This is a lesson we have learned and re-learned in our years as a CAG. Citizen groups make the jobs of state and federal agencies easier when we ask for specific actions and insist that things be done right. The people on the ground, such as project managers and on-site coordinators, appreciate working with a group of ordinary people who insist that government agencies help them achieve specific goals. We can ask for actions that aren't "on the list," so to speak, and our insistence aids the project managers in getting the necessary funding to do the job to meet our standards.

Citizens can be squeaky wheels when project managers cannot. And when the project is completed, the citizens are satisfied and the project manager can chalk up a success for his or her career.

If this theory holds true, we helped Annette and Nicole further their careers by asking for the Horse Creek clean up and insisting that it be done right. That meant cleaning not only to 1972 levels (whatever they would have been) but down to the 1935 levels when Total (then Leonard Refinery) first began operating.

At the evening meeting, as Annette made her opening statement, she again said something that seemed intended to make us feel good, yet again struck me as an indication of a slack-off attitude in the Department of Justice.

She told the crowd that this legal action against Total/UDS was "one of the largest non-Superfund single facility settlements DOJ has ever entered into." Really? A fine of only $13.9 million was one of the largest DOJ had ever won? What in the world was DOJ spending its time, talent and our tax dollars on?

One of the questions from the audience was an echo of what the CAG had asked during the afternoon. Was UDS/Total required to expend only $9 million, even if Horse Creek was not cleaned to the community's satisfaction? The UDS/Total spokesman said he didn't know what was meant by "clean," but then eventually agreed that the company was only required to spend $9 million. Both Annette and Nicole agreed that UDS/Total was not required to spend more, and that we were lucky to get the $9 million, and if we held up the proceedings too long by asking for extensions, the money could go instead into the U.S. Treasury. The threat was not lost on us.

It looked as if once more a major polluter of the Pine River would be allowed to leave town without cleaning up its mess. And it looked as if the consent decree would release that major polluter from all future liability.

Murray and his students continued to search through the old reports they had received from EPA through the Freedom of Information Act, and he uncovered operational records from Midwest Refinery, which had been bought out by Leonard Refinery, with both later becoming Total Refinery. Spills from the Midwest Refinery were documented, including one report that confirmed direct contamination of both the Pine River and Horse Creek.

During the meetings with DOJ, Annette had contended that no direct link could be established between the refinery and pollution in the river and creek, and on the grounds that no direct link could be found, the DOJ had rejected our requests to include compensation for cleanup of the river in the consent judgment.

Now that we had documentation that proved the direct link, a letter was written to DOJ with copies of the relevant reports. When Annette received the reports, she asked the judge to put off signing the Consent Decree until December 15 to allow DOJ to review the documents.

Their motion, however, made it clear to the judge that waiting was merely a formality, because she wrote that the information we'd provided them "does not raise any new issues" and "that the United States already considered these issues."

Her statements were true in that DOJ had previously considered *the issue* of spills or dumping into Horse Creek and the river, but they had rejected the issue because of a lack of evidence. Even though she now had the evidence, she didn't want to use it. The settlement hearing went forward without consideration of the pollution left in the Pine River by Total/UDS.

Not yet giving up, Murray and Ed met with officials from the city of Alma, thinking the court might heed the city's voice. The Alma officials agreed to speak at an upcoming hearing in federal court in Bay City in an effort to convince DOJ, UDS/Total, and the judge that language in the document needed to clearly state that the settlement applied only to the specific violations mentioned in the indictment, and was not a complete release of UDS/Total from all liability.

At the court hearing, all of the parties agreed to the language change suggested by the city officials, and the decree was modified and signed in early 2001.

One change in wording may seem a small victory after the long, hard fight, yet we viewed it as more than a consolation prize. We viewed it through the lens of the future. If our grandchildren needed to refer to the 2001 UDS Consent Judgment, they would see that we had kept the door open for them to litigate against UDS/Total or whoever later bought the refinery property.

One last item for the year 2000: when EPA had moved onto the former Velsicol plant site to begin the excavation of 30-plus acres of river bottom, they had to make room for their equipment inside the fence that surrounded the 52-acre plant site.

Something was in the way.

It was the granite tombstone, decreed by a judge in 1982 to forever stand on the site, warning people to stay away, alerting them that this was a dead zone. The tombstone had been unearthed and dumped with a pile of rocks behind the on-site trailer.

When Bill Shrum noticed that the tombstone had been dug up, he suggested to Stephanie that it be donated to the St. Louis Historical Society. Stephanie said the stone needed to stay on the plant site to comply with the 1982 Consent Decree.

From that moment on, we had a new goal – to reach a time when the tombstone could go to the historical museum and become an artifact of our past. It would be a great day when we could ceremoniously move the granite block across town to the museum, and close the door behind us on our years of being Toxic Town U.S.A, marked with a tombstone.

Chapter 5
(2001)
A Question Answered

The separation of the city from the CAG continued. It wasn't a complete cutting off from one another, because on occasion City Manager Dennis Collison would attend one of our meetings to bring us up to date on an issue regarding the river. For instance, when the St. Louis hydroelectric dam needed repair, he came to let us know. And various CAG members maintained one-on-one relationships with people at city hall. The overall atmosphere, however, was thick with suspicion on the part of the city. For reasons we couldn't discern at the time, the city people "kept an eye on us" and also kept their distance.

We didn't have much time to consider this nebulous atmosphere because plenty of concrete activity was underway at the river impoundment site, the plant site, the Breckenridge radioactive site and upstream. Sometimes it seemed burdensome to be overseeing so many sites, yet we still believed we'd been right to shoulder this large responsibility. With all the willing workers in our group, and most with leadership skills, we were the right people for the task.

A few victories along the way kept us encouraged. To cross a site off the list re-energized us, and the first one was the Crumbaugh deep well. The State of Michigan Court of Appeals upheld the decision made by Judge Randy Tahvonen in the Gratiot County 29th Circuit Court, barring Velsicol from using the well for disposal.

When Rex and Kathy Crumbaugh announced this outcome at a meeting late in the year of 2000, we broke into applause. Velsicol had to remove their equipment from the Crumbaugh farm and plug the deep injection well, bringing the dispute to an end.

We asked John Hock where Velsicol was now disposing of the water pumped out of the plant site, and he told us it was trucked to a disposal site near Detroit.

We learned, however, that the amount trucked was minimal. Instead of the 1 to 2 million gallons a year pumped out, they hadn't pumped at all recently.

Then John told us that data he'd reviewed for NWI showed that 11 million gallons of water was missing. When we heard that news, the roomful of people was shocked into silence. Then it erupted into excited talk. This was the smoking gun, we thought. This proved that the plant site was leaking.

Not so fast, Scott Cornelius cautioned us. Our new MDEQ project manager encouraged us to wait for data that he and his contractor would gather from test wells they planned to place inside and outside the slurry wall. First of all, the bentonitic clay wall, built between the plant site and the river, needed to be found. To do that, they would use ground penetrating radar with special probes to find the wall. Then a pair of wells would be dug at every 300 feet, with one well inside and one well outside of the wall. Dye would be used to determine if water was escaping from inside the plant site to the outside. A heat source test would also be employed. In addition, plans called for testing samples from the monitoring wells for about 150 chemical compounds.

Velsicol/NWI/Memphis Environmental/Fruit (their name kept expanding) managed to delay the start of Scott's tests. The protocol required Scott to ask the responsible party at the site if it preferred to do the testing, or if it preferred to have MDEQ perform the tests. Scott had sent a letter to that effect, and received no reply. He sent a second letter that demanded an answer within 15 days, and if an answer was not forthcoming, work at the site would begin within 30 days. Hydrogeologists from EPA and an engineer and a geologist from the state would work to locate the slurry wall, determine if it was leaking, and then devise the action to take.

At our July CAG meeting, John Hock questioned Scott's letter, both in terms of the work to be done and as to who would pay for the work. He said that NWI/Fruit was not interested in paying for tests of the wall. That information didn't surprise us. We knew Velsicol didn't want to know if the wall was leaking, since it was part of their responsibility under the 1982 Consent Decree to maintain a secured facility.

Scott assured John that the DEQ and EPA would pay for the work. We, of course, preferred that NWI/Fruit *not* perform the tests, as we had low confidence in any data they produced. Finally, an agreement was reached, and Scott procured $500,000 in state funds to pay for the test wells.

When the ground penetrating equipment arrived on site, a major difficulty was encountered. They could not find the slurry wall. Even a detailed 1984 map drawn by the original contractor who had built the wall, Conestoga Rovers, proved of little use. Scott planned to try another piece of equipment, a geo-probe unit.

Where was the wall? Why couldn't it be found? Had it ever been there? Had it crumbled and dissolved? These were the questions that reverberated among our members as the months went by and the wall could not be found.

Meanwhile, a firm we had hired, Public Sector Consultants, reviewed reports and examined existing data to answer the question, "Is the plant site leaking?" Scott was endeavoring to answer the question by gathering new data and the consulting firm by looking at previously published studies. In September we had a visit from Bill Rustem of Public Sector Consultants to walk us through the document produced by his company. It was clear. Without a doubt, the plant site was leaking and had been for some time.

If EPA had read their old reports, they would have seen for themselves that our claims about the site leaking were accurate. The evidence had been available long before our CAG had formed. The Public Sector Consultants document we had paid for was expensive, but it was well worth the cost to have this question answered, and to have it neatly packaged in a professional report. We believe that it helped convince the agencies to address the leaking plant site.

The other question we had asked the consulting firm to investigate was how soon we would be able to eat the fish, and the answer to that was unknown. Certainly the fish would remain toxic for consumption until the plant site was no longer leaking.

Meanwhile, Scott and his crew from Weston Solutions had found the wall and were gathering fresh data about its state of repair.

Suddenly, EPA also became interested in the structural integrity of the wall. During excavation of sediment from the edge of the river next to the plant site, the wall of the riverbank began to crumble down. Seeps of dark liquid were visible within the soil, and tests revealed them to be DNAPL (dense non-aqueous phase liquid).

60

Around the same time, in scraping the hard base of the riverbed with a big machine, they broke through, revealing a pool of DNAPL underneath the floor of the river. The presence of DNAPL brought the attention of EPA to the slurry wall itself, or to what was left of the slurry wall. The "containment system" was now an issue they were willing to address.

When tested, the DNAPL measured 44,000 ppm DDT. The seeps also contained other contaminants at unacceptably high levels.

Clothed in protective gear, due to the toxicity of the DNAPL, workers investigated the crumbling riverbank/slurry wall, and a sand trench was found running underneath the slurry wall and into the plant site itself. It was a conduit which had allowed contaminants from within the site to flow into the river. Even if the wall hadn't failed, this sand seam (and many others like it) had allowed the plant site to leak nonstop. Other tests showed that the bottom of the supposedly contained plant site had been breached, allowing contaminants access into the groundwater underneath the city of St. Louis.

Later, when portions of the standing slurry wall were found, they didn't only have cracks in them, but also gaping openings, measuring as wide as eight feet. Tests done in the lab using a mixture of the chemicals from within the site applied to portions of the slurry wall revealed that the chemical mixture ate through the material of the wall, destroying it.

Once we had the answer to our question of whether or not the slurry wall was leaking, and when we knew how bad it was, the CAG then decided that the entire plant site needed to be excavated, demolished buildings and all, and incinerated on site.

We were not in favor of an attempt to fix the wall, or to have EPA install a new wall. Walls made no sense with the discovery that pathways existed for chemicals to travel through the bottom of the site and into the aquifer below. The only thing that made sense was to do what should have been done in the 1980s, and that was to dig the site up and incinerate the remains or bury them in a properly lined landfill far away from the river.

Meanwhile, another victory emerged from our fight with DOJ and EPA over the upstream portion of the river.

Armed with sampling data from upstream and the operating records from the old Midwest Refinery, Murray set up a meeting with MDEQ officials, city of Alma officials, and a few other CAG members at the state attorney general's office in Lansing. He set forth his reasons for a complete cleanup of the Pine River from the old Midwest refinery site down to the Velsicol site in St. Louis. At this meeting, the MDEQ officials expressed a willingness to investigate upstream by taking more sediment samples and doing further research of historical documents. They welcomed input from the CAG, and agreed to report their findings to our Technical Committee.

This outcome was a direct result of the CAG's hard work in gathering data to argue with the Department of Justice that the river sediment near the UDS/Total refinery required a clean up. Even though our data did not convince DOJ, it persuaded MDEQ to continue the investigation.

Additional sampling of the river sediment upstream found hexavalent chromium. Its origins were not Velsicol nor the refinery, but another factory that had existed in Alma since the 1920's. Lobdell-Emery had begun as a factory making wooden bicycle rims, wooden steering wheels for cars, broom handles and dowels, and had transformed into a factory that made parts for cars. It was now owned by Oxford Automotive. Chromium plating had taken place at the factory during the decades of chrome car bumpers, door handles, and knobs.

Two of our CAG members had worked there, and they told stories about contaminated wastes being dumped into Horse Creek and directly into the Pine River. Documents found by Melissa Strait and Murray Borrello confirmed the dumping. We thought we'd found another PRP (potential responsible party) that could help pay for cleanup of the sediments in the upstream portion of the river.

Another rogue chemical was discovered in the sediment near the Velsicol site--chlordane. We knew Velsicol had made chlordane at their facilities in other states, but it had not been manufactured in St. Louis. Where had the chlordane come from? Had it been shipped here as waste from other Velsicol factories and dumped into our river?

If we could prove that Velsicol had done that, it could be grounds for re-opening the 1982 Consent Decree. Throughout our early years, we kept watch to find a way to re-open the decree, hoping to get a better deal for the community. It bothered us that everything was locked up tight until the year 2012 when the judgment would be re-visited.

Another item of interest came out of the UDS/Total battle. Gratiot County Drain Commissioner Brian Denman attended one of our meetings to talk about Horse Creek. Accompanying him was an attorney from a law firm in Lansing.

Brian told us that he had sent letters to Annette Lange and UDS/Total during the DOJ comment period on the consent order, apprising them of certain requirements under the Michigan Drain Code, since Horse Creek was designated a county drain. Brian said the response from Total was "unfavorable," and that Lange had not responded at all.

He explained to us that the Michigan Drain Code gives the local Drain Commissioner power to force a cleanup, but not to incur costs. The costs for the cleanup have to be assessed to the property owner. Should the property owner default, the land could then be sold to recoup the costs of a cleanup. In fact, Brian had already put things in motion to carry out this plan.

This whole scenario seemed interesting to us, especially if UDS/Total spent their $9 million and then quit the job without cleaning up all of Horse Creek. Maybe then the drain commissioner could enforce them to finalize the cleanup. For others in the group, it was appealing to think of the county drain commissioner possibly coming into ownership of the 90 acres of Total refinery property and selling it for the proceeds.

Later, when Horse Creek received a thorough clean up, probably costing more than $9 million, we wondered if Brian's letters about the Michigan Drain Code had helped bring about the complete restoration of the tributary.

In November we learned that Berkshire Hathaway (Warren Buffet's company) had bought the assets of Fruit of the Loom, but not their liabilities. We didn't know how this might change the bankruptcy proceedings, and affect our $100 million claim.

—

To educate ourselves, we contacted a professor at the University of Michigan Law School, Dr. Nina Mendelson, and she assigned three students to investigate our position in light of this sale, and report back to us. Even though we continued to hope that our $100 million claim against Fruit of the Loom would make it through the bankruptcy court, it seemed unrealistic to think it would. We needed to find out what other action we might take so that some of the bankruptcy money would come back to our community to clean up the plant site and the Breckenridge Site, which were both covered under the policy.

The Breckenridge radioactive site was small in size, only 2.2 acres, with the area of disposal less than that. In the 1960s Velsicol had been licensed by the Atomic Energy Commission to bury its radioactive wastes there.

Because they had been licensed, and since they had met the requirements for disposal as set in the 1960s, Velsicol argued they shouldn't have to do anything more at the site.

The radioactive waste had come from Velsicol's uranium extraction process that yielded the rare earth yttrium used as a phosphor in color television picture tubes, and also to produce synthetic diamonds and crystals for use in electronic devices. During the filtration process that took place during extraction, both uranium and thorium remained in the leftover material, called "filter cake." According to Velsicol's documents, the final burial of radioactive wastes at the Breckenridge Site had taken place in 1970.

In recent years, after the Nuclear Regulatory Commission had performed radiological assessments, they informed Velsicol that more needed to be done at the site to close it properly. At the time our CAG had organized, nothing had been done, and we wrote a letter in 1998 after our meeting with Chuck Hanson, asking Velsicol to move forward with cleanup at the site

By 2001, still no activity had begun, and it worried us to hear John Hock say that NWI did not have the money to clean up the Breckenridge Site when we knew they had a $100 million pollution insurance policy to draw upon. It was this statement that prompted Ed to write a letter to NRC, urging them to make a claim against the $100 million Fruit of the Loom pollution insurance policy.

Bruce Jorgensen, Chief of the Decommissioning Branch at the NRC, wrote back to assure Ed that NRC was involved with other federal and state agencies to coordinate efforts in securing funds from the NWI/Velsicol/Fruit property owners to develop permanent solutions for the sites covered under the policy. That was our first clue that something big was in the works regarding the Fruit of the Loom bankruptcy settlement.

Long before we had faced any legal situations, Ed had been curious to know if the EPA Technical Assistance Grant money could be used for consultations with attorneys about legal issues. The TAG guidelines spelled out clearly that the monies could not be used to sue EPA, but as far as consulting lawyers and getting their views on situations, there was no express prohibition, although that was how our local EPA personnel interpreted the rules.

When the Fruit of the Loom situation became a legal concern for our CAG, Ed wrote out his arguments in favor of allowing TAG grants to be used for legal consultation, and sent them to the national office that was charged with overseeing TAGs. Because of our rocky relationship with our then-EPA project manager, Ed had decided to skip over top of her and her bosses at Region 5 and pitch his argument to the national EPA staff.

The National TAG Coordinator agreed with Ed's argument, and stated specifically that the use of TAG funds to pursue legal action against Fruit of the Loom's environmental reserves, and the Velsicol Superfund Site containment failure, were eligible uses and within the scope of the TAG program's statutory authority.

When we received that reply from the National TAG Coordinator, we decided to establish a Legal Committee and consult with an attorney in hopes of gaining the best settlement possible in the Fruit of the Loom bankruptcy. We still had not heard if our claim had been accepted or rejected by the judge, but we thought we should be proactive and prepare for any eventuality.

Meanwhile, work went forward in the river impoundment area behind the St. Louis dam.

In June, dewatering took place in Cell 1,2,3. The cell had originally been planned as three units, but was later combined into one, hence the name.

65

Before dewatering began, the water within the cell was pretreated, and then tested for DDT. When surface waters showed non-detectable levels of DDT, mass dewatering of the uppermost two feet of water in the cell began, with a large, loud pump lifting thousands of gallons up over the steel walls of the cell and into the river. With the clean water removed, the rest of the water in the cell was piped through the water treatment plant for cleansing before being released into the river.

The cofferdam cells were constructed along one shoreline to the middle of the river, allowing half of the river to flow unimpeded. After several years of work on the south side of the bend in the river, the plan called for building cells on the north side and then that sediment, too, would be removed.

The south side of the river was called Phase I, and the north side portion of the project, Phase II. We also had an Operable Unit 1 and an Operable Unit 2, which made for some confusion. OU-1 was the plant site and OU-2 the river. In 2001, OU-2 was in Phase I, to give a glimpse of how confusing the terminology could be to new people joining the CAG.

Sediment core samples taken from 81 locations from outside Cell 1,2,3, and going around the bend and south to the M-46 bridge showed DDT levels ranging from 71 ppm to 2500 ppm. There was plenty more work to be done, since the sediment was to be cleaned to 5 ppm or less.

Later in the summer, when sediment removal began in cell 1,2,3, huge earthmoving machines dug themselves down to a depth of 10 to 15 feet below the riverbank where the sediment used to lie only four feet below the surface of the water. Big, bouncy-wheeled mega-trucks hauled the sediments up specially constructed roads to the surface, where the sediments were unloaded onto a vast concrete pad.

Runoff waters were captured and sent through the water treatment plant, which was housed in a white, fiber-clothed temporary structure on the site, reminiscent of a large, oblong circus tent. Residue from sugar beet manufacturing, called beet lime, was mixed with the partially dried sediments to further dry the mass. Then the sediments were loaded onto semi-trailers owned by local truckers.

Each truck and trailer was washed of residue before it was allowed to drive off the site. At first, about 25 trucks a day hauled load after load from St. Louis to various hazardous waste sites around the state.

Our CAG had made it clear from the outset, and we had repeated our statement, that we were willing to have the sediment buried in Gratiot County, as long as it was buried away from rivers and creeks, and as long as the landfill area was properly lined. EPA, however, preferred to work with already established sites near Flint, Harrison and Pierson, rather than create a new one in our area. Our CAG also had requested on-site incineration, but without ever explaining why, EPA turned us down on that issue as well.

Even though EPA had set up constant water sprays to control the dust from the excavation, the job was still dusty and smelly. It was also busy and loud. I know some of the city fathers were ashamed to have such activity taking place in the middle of their downtown area, although some were pleased that work was underway to clean up the mess which had branded our town as toxic.

Council member and CAG member Bill Shrum voiced the latter view fairly often, remembering how helpless the townspeople had felt when the chemical plant was closing and the decisions for the plant site and river were being handled behind closed doors, with DO NOT ADMIT signs on those closed doors, and, especially, do not admit the people the decisions are going to affect.

Complaints from citizens were voiced at our meetings about the dust, the noise and the smells. Stephanie, who was now our EPA project manager, patiently reminded people about the free car wash certificates, and she saw to it that more spray devices were installed to better control the dust. She made her Chicago office phone number available to residents, in addition to the on-site number. Her whole manner of dealing with the citizens was accommodating and mannerly. It was a refreshing relief.

Chapter 6
(2002 Part 1)
A Reluctant Leader

The undertone of animosity aimed towards the CAG from city staff and city council members became almost an audible hum by the end of 2001.

They were unhappy that people from "out of town" were involved in the CAG (meaning people from the neighboring towns of Alma, Ithaca, and Breckenridge, as well as people who lived downstream on the Pine River in Midland County).

They were unhappy that college students were involved in the CAG, including those from Alma College, Central Michigan University, Michigan State University and Saginaw Valley State University.

They were unhappy that the CAG wanted to clean upstream and downstream in the river instead of just concentrating on the Velsicol site within the city limits of St. Louis.

They were unhappy that the CAG asked questions that led EPA and MDEQ to find more contaminants, because the new discoveries were slowing down redevelopment of the plant site acreage.

Most of all, they were unhappy with the CAG in general, because, in their view, we were to blame for the negative press about St. Louis, meaning the news stories that talked about contaminated land and water and plans to clean them up.

We understood their viewpoint to a certain extent. We knew they wanted the city of St. Louis to break free from its reputation as a toxic town, and that was our long term goal as well. We differed, though, in our levels of realism. While the CAG was willing to uncover the truth and find out how bad things really were to ensure a thorough cleanup, the city wanted to keep the extent of the mess hidden, believing it would somehow go away if it wasn't seen and known. Their viewpoint was clearly unrealistic, yet it was a real sentiment in their hearts.

Most of their anger and blame were aimed at Ed and Murray, since those two had led the charge since 1998 and were most often quoted in the newspaper articles.

The animosity took the form of critical comments made to Gary Smith, Joe Scholtz and Bernie Bessert about Ed or Murray's personalities, or their academic goals, or the fact that they weren't "from around here." (Although Ed grew up in Baltimore, Maryland, Murray was raised in Saginaw.) Lately, though, accusations had been flung at Ed and Murray to their faces. This was shocking to them, as was some behind-the-scenes gossip that got them called on the carpet at the college. Both Ed and Murray felt that the undermining tactics being used against them were jeopardizing their jobs.

Ed began to say that he needed to step down as chairperson and we needed to elect someone who lived in St. Louis. At first it seemed an off-hand comment, but later he became serious about it. Our biennial elections were coming up in January 2002, and I expected Gary, Joe, Bernie or Jim Hall to step up as leader. I was surprised when Ed asked me to think about running for the position. Later Murray sent me an e-mail about some other issue, but ended it by saying "Jane for President!"

The three of us ate lunch together one day, and I explained to them that if I did get elected, I would expect them to still run the show – "The Ed and Murray Show," as we had jokingly come to call it. I would lead the meetings, sign the letters, organize the mailings, but that would be the extent of it.

I knew there was no way I could do what Ed had done as chairperson. The man was brilliant and tireless, with a file cabinet for a memory. He could go to that file cabinet and pull out the exact document needed, and quote from it word for word. Not only that, he could see connections and possibilities that the rest of us were deaf and blind to until he spoke them out loud. Coupled with Murray's scientific knowledge, and Murray's own legal way of looking at things that he'd inherited from his father, a judge, the two were unstoppable. And what made The Ed and Murray Show entertaining was the way Murray, the funny man, and Ed, the straight man, played off each other at the meetings.

I could see the wisdom of having a St. Louis person as the figurehead, and I was willing to perform that role, even though I wasn't really a resident of St. Louis.

I'd grown up in Alma and had lived in St. Louis for only 27 years. And I didn't even live in town, but downstream in an area that the city said it didn't care about seeing cleaned up. Even so, I was closer to being a St. Louis resident than Ed was. And Gary, Joe, Bernie and Jim, all of whom lived in town, were not willing to run for the office of chairperson.

Sure enough, after I was elected, Bill Shrum, who sat on the city council, reported that the city "approved" of me as the new Chair of the CAG. I took it as it was meant – not as flattery of my abilities, but that I was in and Ed was out. Not a single one of us thought this change would solve our differences with the city, though.

Our most pressing business at the beginning of the year was to write a letter. Essentially, Ed and Murray wrote it and I signed it. Our lawyers at the University of Michigan (Dr. Mendelson and her students) had encouraged us to pursue a claim against Fruit of the Loom based on natural resource damages. The claim we had originally filed, a statutory claim, would fall far behind the claims of suppliers, creditors and bondholders of Fruit of the Loom. For this new claim our attorneys said we would need proof of natural resource damages that extended beyond the Pine River to Lake Huron, such as fish migrating from the Great Lake into tributaries like the Pine River, where they would become contaminated, and then swim back to Lake Huron, carrying the contaminants with them.

I remembered having heard my grandfather tell stories about giant sturgeon that swam up into the Pine River from Saginaw Bay. Murray did a search for any studies on the migratory habits of sturgeon and found a recent one that showed sturgeon coming into the Pine River in Midland County.

He also found a similar study about redhorse suckers. It was important to include this fish information in order to tie in with the trusteeships held by Fish and Wildlife and NOAA, the agencies in charge of natural resource damages claims.

We had little time to gather the data and write the letter because on January 25th, Fruit of the Loom would file its bankruptcy plan with the court, and our claim needed to be submitted before then.

Murray and Ed drafted a long, detailed letter filled with historical and scientific proof. In our letter, we named three federal agencies that we said should receive money from the bankruptcy settlement to fund a natural resource damage assessment on the Pine River: the U.S. Fish and Wildlife Service in the Department of the Interior, the National Oceanic and Atmospheric Agency in the Department of Commerce, and the U.S. Department of Justice.

We sent the letter to all three agencies, asking them to seek damages for natural resource injuries in its bankruptcy-related negotiations with Fruit of the Loom and NWI Land Management. We also asked them to consider bringing a CERCLA claim (Comprehensive Environmental Response Compensation and Liability Act) against Velsicol Chemical Corporation if a natural resource damage assessment in the Pine River warranted it.

In February we received word that our own $100 million claim against Fruit of the Loom had been rejected. There was no explanation. The judge had the discretion to throw out claims, and he threw ours out. Now we were awaiting a response about the NRD (natural resource damages) claim that we had asked the federal agencies to file for the Pine River.

Meanwhile, we learned that the city was considering taking ownership of the Smith Farm Site and making it into a park.

The word "farm" in the title was a misnomer. The area had been used for at least two decades as a dumping ground for Velsicol, Alma Products, Alma Iron and Metal, and Lobdell-Emery. A family (named Smith) had lived in the house on the "farm" until the property was condemned.

The site was relatively small, about 14 acres, and the Superfund Division at MDEQ was overseeing surface cleanup there. Since the early 1990s, hundreds of barrels of dumped waste had been pulled from a pond on the property, as well as asbestos clutch facings, hundreds of tires, and piles of other trash found in both the pond and on land.

Reports showed that the soil and pond sediment contained vinyl chloride, mercury, lead, DDT and PBB, among many other substances.

The city's strategy was to own the property to keep an industry from buying it.

The city had spent money and expended a lot of patience in trying to get an automobile junk yard cleaned up that had been located on the other side of State Road from Smith Farm. With State Road serving as an entryway into the city from the south, they preferred to have presentable sights for travelers to see as they drove into town.

We thought the park was a great plan, as long as the site was cleaned up first, but from what we had heard from various sources, it sounded as if a cover-up and not a cleanup was planned for the site.

The MDEQ project manager at the site was Kim Sakowski, who had been our first MDEQ project manager on the river impoundment cleanup. Kim hadn't thought much of our CAG, and Murray was finding her resistant to sharing information about the Smith Farm site.

He had invited her to give a presentation of her data to the Technical Committee, but she didn't respond. Murray was able to get a copy of the work plan for the site and saw that it called for a geo-textile liner overlaid with 2 feet of soil. No excavation was planned, and no remedy was planned for the sides or bottom of the site.

After four months of inviting Kim to attend a meeting, Murray suggested that someone else call Kim, as he believed that she was avoiding his phone calls. Jim Hall volunteered, and we all agreed that Jim's ways were sweeter than Murray's. Apparently they weren't, because Kim still did not come to our meeting.

As leader of our group, I knew it was time to extend a more formal invitation. In a short letter, I requested her presence at our May 15th meeting to answer questions, and I attached a list of questions to help her prepare.

I told her that the CAG would like to see the property converted to a park, but we had concerns about the nature and quantity of contaminants at the site, and about a vinyl chloride plume in the groundwater.

I sent copies of the letter to her bosses, our legislators, the Bethany Township supervisor (since Smith Farm was located in Bethany Township) and the St. Louis city manager. Right away I received an e-mail response from Kim that said, "This note is to confirm my attendance at the May 15th meeting."

Murray worried that her terse response would mean she would communicate very little at the meeting, but as the new leader of our group, I felt a sense of victory that she had responded at all and had agreed to attend.

The next thing we knew an article appeared in the newspaper quoting St. Louis City Manager Dennis Collison, who said that I had written a letter trying to get Kim Sakowski fired from her job. He said the letter was a personal attack against Kim. He told a reporter that he was going to send a "counter-letter" because our letter was "so negative and attacking one person, instead of the department."

This overblown reaction was another indication, in my opinion, of some deeper issue going on within the city.

I called Dennis and told him I would like to sit down and chat with him if he could work me into his schedule. He said, "Just you?" with a note of suspicion in his voice. I said, "Just me," so he agreed to have me come to his office. Interestingly enough, even though he had wanted me to come alone, he had invited another city person to join us, Building Inspector Chad Doyle.

After some blustering, and even hostility, on their part towards the CAG, and an attempt to gang up on me with loud interruptions when I started to speak, we settled into some pretty good conversation, and talked for an hour. Afterwards, I knew that we hadn't reached the heart of the issue, but I had gained some insights.

Frankly, they hated Murray, considering him their enemy, and also an enemy of Kim Sakowski. Dennis and Chad seemed to see it as their duty to protect Kim from Murray. As they talked further, they acknowledged that Kim had been instrumental in helping the city get grants for other city projects, so they also felt they were protecting the best interests of the city when they stood up for her.

Chad talked about how the CAG was making the community look bad, and how it made his job difficult in dealing with real estate agents and people who might want to move here. After listening for awhile, I pointed out the reality of the situation – the contamination was still with us. Someday in the future we might be contamination-free, but that day hadn't yet arrived.

Then Chad said he resented having Alma College students attend our meetings, which turned a community meeting into a classroom. I told him I agreed that the CAG meetings were often learning situations for all of us. I used the example of NAPL (non-aqueous phase liquid), a substance most of us were only now learning about, adults and students alike. Then I went on to share my viewpoint – that when these students graduated from college and went out to live in other communities, they would take with them a picture of how a group of citizens could confront a challenge. Their knowledge could help bring about good things in the communities where they chose to live. Chad said he appreciated hearing my viewpoint, and that he had never thought about it in that way.

That's how the dialogue continued, with one or the other of them saying something pugnacious and with me offering them a different viewpoint. Finally, I asked if they could agree with me that we all wanted the community cleaned up, and they did so. And I asked if they could agree with me that it would be beneficial to find ways to work together. Again, they willingly agreed with me.

I left the meeting feeling calm, but not content. There was more to learn, I felt sure. We had not reached the core of the issue. How could they have arrived at such a state of hostility toward us with us being ignorant as to how we had offended them? I knew we needed to have a meeting of the CAG Executive Committee with the St. Louis City Council members and staff. All of us needed to sit down at a table and talk.

Upset about the city's reaction printed in the newspaper, and knowing how the city manager felt towards him, Murray resigned.

He wrote me a brief letter of resignation, saying, "Unfortunately, this fight for a clean environment has been interpreted by some as a fight to stop the cleanup process, or in some way to cast a negative light on the City of St. Louis…it is clear that my participation with the CAG is posing a serious threat to community unification."

Murray's letter of resignation seemed to assume that unity between the CAG and the city was the highest good. I could only agree with that assumption to a certain point.

Unity would be good only if we could agree on the goals. Unity would not be good, or even possible, if our goals differed sharply from their goals, and it wouldn't be the end of the world to maintain separateness in that case. In fact, it would be the right thing to do. If the city wanted to build a park on a dump site leaking vinyl chloride and the CAG wanted to try to prevent such a thing from happening, then so be it. We would have a war and one side or the other would win.

I asked Murray to delay his resignation until after the upcoming meeting that Kim Sakowski said she would attend. I also asked him to consider how his resignation might reflect on the CAG if the city manager chose to accuse Murray of a "sour grapes" attitude. And I worried that Dennis might choose to think that I'd "fired" Murray after finding out how much the city disliked him. Both of those scenarios would be hard to discount, and would take even more energy and time away from our mission of cleaning up the contaminated sites in the community. Murray agreed to wait and, in his words "let the Kim issue play out."

At the CAG meeting, Chad Doyle and a few other people from the city attended. I thanked Kim for coming and gave her the floor. She said that before she answered any questions, she wanted to begin with a clarification. She wanted to make it clear that Smith Farm was not a Superfund site, but a 201 site, referring to the Michigan Part 201 criteria for cleanups of contaminated sites.

She went on to say that what was being proposed for Smith Farm was not a complete cleanup, but an interim response. This response would not address the groundwater or the pond. She said this was an opportunity for Clean Michigan Initiative money to be used with the object of putting a site into a condition to be redeveloped.

She was asked if further cleanup would take place after the interim response. In other words, what would be the next step? She said there would not be a next step; the only goal was to clean the tax-reverted property to a legal standard that would allow it to be put to use. The plan called for using a geo-textile fabric and 18 inches of soil (not 2 feet as originally planned) to protect people from direct contact with contaminants.

Someone said there seemed to be confusion between the CAG's understanding about the groundwater and the pond, and the city's understanding. The city expected the pond and the groundwater to be cleaned before they received the property. Kim's answer was terse: "There is no remediation planned for the groundwater or the pond."

Fred Brown said that according to the law, no redevelopment could take place on a brownfield site from which contaminants were migrating into the groundwater. Kim said that under state law, she could get a liability exemption for a site such as this one. When pressed, she did say some "hot spots" had been identified in the groundwater, and eventually a study of the groundwater would take place, but not before the site was "capped." Due to money concerns, the groundwater study was on hold, so the attempt to find the extent of migration from the site had stopped.

At an earlier meeting Murray had read to us from an MDEQ report that listed chemicals that the Smith Farm Site contained. The soils contained PCB at twice, PBB at 3 times, and chromium at 14 times the legal limit for direct human contact. The pond contained levels of lead at 58 times, PCB at 78 times and mercury at 153,846 times the amount allowed for surface water. He had sent a copy of the report to the city prior to our meeting with Kim.

We had hoped that with all of this information, the city would decide that it was unsafe to establish a park for their residents on the Smith Farm property without a full excavation of the contaminated soils, a dredging of sediments from the pond, and perhaps a pump and treat system installed to pull back the contaminants moving in the groundwater underneath State Road.

After the meeting with Kim, Murray told me to hang onto his letter of resignation and to put it into effect whenever I saw the need for it. I was relieved that he had changed his mind about quitting the CAG.

Since a theme in Kim's answers had been that a lack of funds restricted the thoroughness of the cleanup, Joe Scholtz decided to get an appointment with the Director of MDEQ to see if he could find supplemental money to complete the project correctly.

In the midst of his appointment with Russ Harding, Joe mentioned how difficult it had been to convince the MDEQ project manager to attend our meeting to answer questions. We don't know if Harding spoke to Kim, but from that point on, she regularly attended our meetings. Over time she lost her hostility toward us and became a friend.

At an Executive Committee meeting soon after our meeting with Kim, we decided to take a definite stand against the proposed interim response at the Smith Farm Site because it did not include a monitoring system for chemicals that might migrate from the uncontained site, nor a plan to address the contaminated groundwater that was known to be migrating from the site. I wrote a letter to the city about the position we had taken, and I also sent one to Kim. We hoped the city would agree with our stance, but if not, so be it.

Meanwhile, the CAG urged EPA to fully excavate the Velsicol plant site as more and more DNAPL (dense non-aqueous phase liquid) seeps were found when thermal infrared imaging was utilized, and as the slurry wall sections were found to contain not cracks, but gaps big enough to drive a truck through, such as the two that measured about 8 feet high and 7 feet wide.

We wondered how Velsicol could have found any water at all to pump from the site, and Scott said their records showed that no water had been pumped since 1997. John Hock had indicated to us that it was a recent development of no water to pump, not something that had been occurring for years.

He hadn't attended our meetings in quite some time, and he wouldn't have liked to hear some of the things that were said that night when we learned that Velsicol, after having complained to us about the expense of pumping the water and disposing of it, had, in truth, quit pumping water even before our CAG had formed.

EPA had designed and was in the process of installing an interceptor trench to capture the DNAPL flowing out of the riverbank by the plant site. The trench was 12 to 15 feet deep, lined with an HDPE liner, and at the bottom of the trench was a 6-inch perforated pipe intended to intercept the flow of DNAPL.

It was emphasized that the collection trench was a temporary measure and not part of the permanent remedy for the site. EPA told us that on-site tests seemed to agree with old photographs of the chemical plant in revealing that the DNAPL was concentrated underneath the former DDT manufacturing facility on the plant site. DNAPL was also found dripping out of an old pipe that ran out from the plant site into the river.

EPA did not know how deep the DNAPL went within the plant site or under the river. They took borings of up to 20 feet deep on the plant site, and no deeper, because they knew they were near the aquifer that the city drew its water from, and they did not want to puncture it.

Borings were also made in the riverbed, 12 to 32 feet below the waterline, to delineate the extent the DNAPL had traveled in a northeasterly direction under the river and away from the plant site, beneath the residential neighborhoods. The furthest edge was not found. By October of 2002, 54 barrels, or almost 3,000 gallons of DNAPL, had been collected, and it kept on coming.

Out of the blue, I received a call at home from Stuart Hill, our EPA Community Involvement Coordinator. None of us had seen or heard from Stuart in quite some time, although we occasionally spotted him around town when he came to meet with City Manager Dennis Collison.

Stuart said he was calling to obtain my home address to give to an attorney for NOAA (National Oceanic and Atmospheric Administration) who had contacted him. He said NOAA wanted to mail me "a response." Stuart had no idea of a response to what, but I knew it must be to do the long letter we had sent asking NOAA, Fish and Wildlife and DOJ to file a Natural Resource Damage claim in the Fruit of the Loom bankruptcy hearings on behalf of the Pine River.

Stuart also said we were "in" the Federal Register. I went on line and found the article in the Federal Register that referred to St. Louis, Michigan. It was a notice of a filing on May 2 of an environmental settlement in reference to Fruit of the Loom, Inc., with a 30-day comment period starting on that date, and here we were still awaiting notification on May 17th.

In fact, if the lawyer from NOAA hadn't contacted us, we might have missed the comment period altogether. After all, how many ordinary citizens glance through the Federal Register on a daily basis? Most of us don't even know bankruptcy filings are published in the Federal Register.

The letter from NOAA attorney Gwendolyn A. Wilkie arrived promptly. In the letter she thanked our CAG for having contacted NOAA earlier that year about our concerns of natural resource damages in the Pine River. I called Ms. Wilkie to thank her, and she said that a thick document was also being shipped to me that would give the details of the proposed Fruit of the Loom settlement.

The document arrived by UPS, and I sat down with it. It was the first legal document other than mortgages that I had ever read. I used three colors of markers, an ink pen and a pencil as I read my way through the pages. I called an Executive Committee meeting and did my best to explain the details of the document to the others. In fact, I had drawn a flow chart to show which money would come from which source and go into which trust account. Each of the seven NWI sites would have its own trust account, and a Trustee would oversee the accounts. The Trustee was actually named in the 89-page document: Jay Steinberg. We said to each other, "Who is Jay Steinberg?"

Ed volunteered to notify a person he knew in Memphis who was working to get the Hollywood Dump Facility cleaned up, and he said he would try to find contact people at the other Velsicol sites to let them know about this proposed settlement. We assumed they, like us, would not know about the notice in the Federal Register.

Two major details from the document referred to our sites:

- Money would come off the top of the settlement funds for the Breckenridge Site, allowing it to be cleaned up early in the whole process of money distribution
- Of the money flowing in to be divided among the seven sites, the St. Louis Facility would always get a 28% share.

Later we learned that the greater percentage earmarked for our site was to reward our CAG for having filed the original $100 million claim, and also following up with the NRD claim.

Ed wrote to the Department of Justice and requested two things: an extension of the public comment period, and a public meeting to be held in St. Louis, Michigan. Both requests were granted, and the DOJ and representatives from all the agencies would come to our little town in the middle of Michigan on June 19th to explain the settlement and answer our questions.

When I agreed to serve as Chair of the CAG, I had hoped for a quiet first year. The year was not halfway through, and already had been loaded with big issues. I knew I could handle a two-year term as Chair of this busy CAG, and then I would gladly hand off the leadership role to someone else. That was my unspoken agenda midway in 2002.

Chapter 7
(2002 Part 2)
Who Is Jay Steinberg?

We decided to spend funds from the CAG savings account to host a nice catered dinner at Alma College prior to the Fruit of the Loom settlement meeting. Guests attended from an alphabet soup of agencies: NRC, NOAA, EPA, MDEQ, and the DOJ. The Fish and Wildlife representative was not able to come.

The public meeting itself was going to be held in the American Legion hall on Michigan Avenue in St. Louis. During the week, when I saw a road resurfacing project underway on Michigan Avenue, I made a phone call to find out their completion date, and it was the day before our meeting. The day of the meeting, I left the dinner at the college a little early and breathed a sigh of relief to see that the paving project had indeed finished.

Inside the hall, I looked around to see if any more preparations were needed. Chairs were set up. Several long tables stood end to end at the front of the room for the panelists. I had called the local public access television crew ahead of time, and they were there, setting up their equipment to capture the meeting on tape. When I greeted Ann Hall, she pointed out the lack of microphones on the long tables for the panelists to speak into, and she was concerned about picking up their voices with only the small microphone on the camera.

Stuart Hill was at the podium, and I decided to check with him about microphones. Stuart had called me a week or so before to tell me that he would come to town to organize the venue for this meeting.

At first I had felt a little conflicted about his take-charge attitude. We hadn't seen or heard from him in many months, perhaps a year, and now, when something momentous was happening, he re-appeared and insisted on being in charge.

And then there was the matter of trust. By his own admission he had tried to form at least one other CAG to compete with us. And I had often wondered if he wasn't a contributor to the city's distrust of the CAG.

I greeted Stuart and asked about microphones for the panelists. He said there weren't going to be any. I'm not sure what he was doing at and under the podium, but he kept on doing it. I waited until his head came up again, and then I said I planned to give a few words of welcome to the guests and the audience before the panel began their talks. He grew very red beneath his tan, and said something very rude to me.

Just then Mayor George Kubin walked in. He heard what Stuart said. I'm sure my eyebrows were still up in surprise when I turned to speak to George, repeating to him that I planned to give a few words of welcome before we started. George said that's what he had planned to do as well. Stuart literally threw up his hands, and said we could do all the welcoming we wanted, and then *he* was going to introduce each representative from each agency and handle the walk-around microphone for questions from the audience. George and I both assented.

For me, the whole little scene remained as an ugly memory, but years later George told me that it was somewhat of a turning point for him to see Stuart's rude behavior toward me.

The panelists were Bruce Jorgenson, the Chief Decommissioning officer from the NRC, who had been keeping us in the loop about the Breckenridge Site by copying us on letters to and from NWI. An NRC attorney, Bruce Person, also attended. Gwendolyn Wilkie came from NOAA. It was great to meet her. From EPA we had our Project Manager Stephanie Ball and EPA attorney, Gaylene Vasaturo. From the State of Michigan our MDEQ Project Manager Scott Cornelius attended, and with him, from the State Attorney General's office, was James Stropkai. Alan Tenenbaum represented the United States Department of Justice.

Throughout the whole evening, Alan seemed to be operating from the mindset that our community might reject the proposed settlement altogether, which I don't think anyone was contemplating. Whenever a question was raised that he didn't want to answer directly, he would ask this rhetorical question: "Are we better off with this agreement or without it?" At first, I thought he didn't understand the questions being asked, but later I saw that he was using his question to divert us, and to avoid answering.

Most of the citizens in attendance asked about certain clauses, paragraphs, and wording in the document, but no one seemed to think we should protest the agreement or reject it altogether. To us it looked like a carefully constructed way to get millions of dollars to flow to the seven NWI sites to help clean them up. Were Fruit of the Loom/NWI and Velsicol benefiting also? Yes, and in looking back, perhaps more so than the community.

Tenenbaum explained that each of the various sources of money listed in the document could produce a lot or a little, and that no one knew for sure. He wouldn't even offer ballpark amounts for most of the sources, although the highest dollar amount was spelled out in the agreement document.

It was at this meeting that we first heard that Velsicol had purchased a pollution insurance policy from the AIG subsidiary AISLIC (American International Specialty Lines Insurance Company), much like the one held by Fruit of the Loom. That news set our CAG on a long quest to procure a copy of that policy.

When Fred Brown raised his hand to ask a question, Stuart made some joke about the TV host Jerry Springer as he carried the microphone to him. Even if Fred had known who Springer was, he would have ignored Stuart's attempts at levity.

Fred asked what role citizens would have in regard to the Trust Accounts. Alan said that there was nothing in the agreement that would preclude citizen involvement in the sites. (Not a direct answer.) Fred replied, "You say there's nothing in this document that *precludes* the participation of citizens. There is also nothing that says we *can* be included. Experience tells me it is very hard to be included if it is not written into the document."

He also raised the point that the document said in one place that it allowed taking money out of a Trust Account for one site and putting it into a Trust Account of another site. Alan was sure it didn't say that, and he read and re-read the sentences, trying to find a way to interpret them differently, but he could not. Fred offered new language, and Alan asked him to send it to him in a written comment.

Murray raised his hand to ask a question, and when Stuart brought the microphone to him, he gave Murray a little lecture about not talking too long, because there were lots of other people who wanted to ask questions, too.

I wondered why Stuart was being disruptive. Here we were with serious questions which took concentration to get our points across, and Stuart was trying to make jokes. He was like the disruptive kid in the classroom who wanted attention.

Several of our CAG members asked in different ways if the public could have access to the Trustee's financial records so that we could see when money flowed into our accounts and from which source. Alan gave wordy non-answers to these questions, or veered into talking about a 5-year review for the Velsicol site. It was reminiscent of the kind of answer Annette Lange had given us during the Total/UDS meetings. DOJ must teach that skill to its attorneys.

City Manager Dennis Collison and Building Inspector Chad Doyle asked several questions about using the settlement money for re-development of the plant site. Alan, Gaylene, Stephanie and Jim Stropkai all tried to explain to them that the money was earmarked for response actions. It was to pay for stopping the leaks at the plant site and for cleaning up the contamination spread by those leaks.

Stuart made a joke at this point in the meeting, too. Dennis wanted money to redevelop, and Stuart tooted his own horn a little and said he was now active in an EPA brownfield-style program. Then he said, "But that doesn't address your main concern – money." He reached into one of his pockets, as if to get out money. "I'm a little short," he said, smiling. It didn't seem to bother him that no one laughed at his jokes.

They did laugh, though, when Norm Keon got up and said, "The question for tonight is, 'Who is Jay Steinberg.' How do you know he exists? How did you choose him for this job?" So many of us during the past few weeks had asked each other, "Who is Jay Steinberg?" that when Norm said it at the meeting, it got a big laugh. I'm sure the agency people had no idea why it was funny to us.

Alan explained that the DOJ had recommended Jay Steinberg; that he worked under the U.S. Trustees program; and that the bankruptcy court had appointed him. Someone in the audience asked if Jay would visit our site. Alan said, hesitantly, "I suspect...it is likely that ...he will...I think."

Gary Smith asked how we could contact Jay, and Alan said, "The thing is he is not being paid yet. It would not be appropriate if people were to contact him now."

So Jay Steinberg remained a mystery man for a while longer.

One of the other seven NWI/Velsicol sites had a representative in attendance at our meeting. Rita Harris, who had traveled up from Memphis, Tennessee, was an Environmental Justice Organizer with Sierra Club for the Hollywood Dump Site and Cypress Creek. She let DOJ know that the only way she had learned about the settlement was through Ed's phone call to her.

Ed addressed this circumstance in his comments written later to the DOJ. He wrote that when a government agency places an announcement in the Federal Register, it assumes it is inviting citizen participation, but citizens are not likely to read the Federal Register, or even to have access to it. Few low-income people had internet access, and, in our community, the only library that had formerly received the Federal Register had been removed from the list of recipients by recent regulatory changes.

The meeting had gone on for more than two hours, and Bruce Jorgenson from NRC hadn't yet spoken. I invited him to talk about the Breckenridge Site. He stood up and said that the Breckenridge Site was not a current hazard, but it did not meet NRC criteria. He said the first money that came in through the Fruit of the Loom/NWI settlement would pay for the excavation of the radioactive materials buried at the site, which would be hauled to Utah where they would be deposited in a landfill licensed by the federal government.

We asked if the $700,000 in the consent agreement was enough money to complete the job, and he assured us that it would be "sufficient" to accomplish cleanup of the site.

How wrong he was.

John Witucki, a man who lived downstream, stood up and reminded the roomful of people that Bay City drew its drinking water from the Saginaw River, which was linked to the Pine River.

He pointed out that the St. Louis Velsicol site was the worst contaminated site in Michigan, and he encouraged us to insist on excavation and removal of the site, and not to allow EPA to persuade us to rely on another "seawall."

His comments received spontaneous applause. He had addressed his comments to Dennis Collison and Chad Doyle, remarking that their desire for re-development of the site should be secondary to its clean-up.

I agreed with John, and I also agreed with Chad's reply. He said redevelopment was critical, "because that graveyard has sat there for 20 years." Yes, the poisonous mess needed to be dug up first, but we all wanted the graveyard gone and the tombstone tucked into the historical museum.

The two men began a heated exchange without the use of the microphone. Murray, who had taken the mike, spoke into it and thanked the panelists. Then Stuart took the microphone from Murray and dismissed the meeting.

Afterwards, we decided two letters were needed when writing our comments on the proposed Fruit settlement.

The first included the historical reasons for desiring written assurances that the settlement would not be used to free the companies or the governmental agencies from operation and maintenance responsibilities at the Velsicol sites. We also requested that the CAG have a role to play in spending decisions as the money came into the St. Louis Trust Account. Finally, we wanted to be assured that the end goal of the plant site was a return to public use, saying, "It is not good land use policy to maintain forever a capped, fenced, factory cemetery filled with a soup of dangerous contaminants."

The second letter made the point that the settlement failed "to reveal sufficient information regarding the appropriateness of the companies' payments," referring to Fruit of the Loom, NWI, Velsicol and True Specialty, all named in the document as sources from which money would flow into the Trust Accounts. Without seeing the companies' budgets, income, cash flow, short term debts, and federal and state income tax information, it was impossible for members of the public to determine whether the settlement was reasonable or not. We requested a confidential proceeding at which a representative of our CAG could view the company's financial records.

In the final settlement agreement, signed by the judge and all the parties, our comments were addressed in detail, as were those of the city and of the Memphis group.

As for our request to view Velsicol's documents, we got a resounding "no," with the further comment that such a practice would have "a chilling effect" on defendants' willingness to enter into "ability to pay" settlements with the United States.

The Memphis group also got a "no" as to DOJ finding another avenue besides the Federal Register for letting a community know about legal actions they were taking against the polluter of an abandoned site.

The response added a section to address our desire to keep informed about the flow of the money by directing the State of Michigan and EPA to place copies of requests for funding made to the Trustee in the St. Louis public library.

Also changed was the wording that Fred had pointed out, and the agreement stated that the United States agreed with the citizen group's request for this clarification.

Even as we held this public meeting and prepared for a meeting with the city officials and council members, work went on deep down in the riverbed. The previous October, a wall had failed in Cell 4, flooding the almost completed cell with new, contaminated river water. Much work had to be repeated, including dewatering the cell, testing the sediment, and then digging and scraping. In Area 3, where the pool of NAPL under the river had been discovered, the majority of the excavation had been completed. Later they would cement over the hole in the till where the excavator shovel had broken through, and much of the thin till layer in that area. Work in Cell 1,2,3 was nearly finished. Confirmation samples in two areas showed high DDT levels. Once those areas were scraped and further confirmation samples were checked, the cell would be finished.

Having a lab on site to test for the chemicals was speeding up the work process. The lab found, though, that samples of the DNAPL were so high in DDT that it masked any other chemicals that might also be contained in the samples. An LNAPL (light non-aqueous phase liquid) source was also discovered which contained principally chlorobenzenes and benzene.

Now, about 40 trucks a day carried loads of partially dried sediment out of the plant site, south on Bankson Street to M-46 and then onward to one of the hazardous waste landfills.

Not only were the contractors washing down the trucks before they left the work site, but they also washed the neighborhood streets to help control the dust. A group of Alma College students offered to wash the houses of people who lived near the excavation activity. Jim Hall went around the neighborhood and got the permission of homeowners for the students to use garden hoses to wash the dust off their houses.

The evening came for our scheduled meeting with the city, and we gathered around a table in the council chambers. Mayor George Kubin raised the first issue that bothered the city, and it was the name of our CAG – Pine River. The name referred to upstream and downstream, as well as within St. Louis. He stated that the Velsicol chemical plant site needed its own group that would focus only on that one site. Since I had heard the exact words come out of Stuart Hill's mouth in the past, I wondered if George had been coached by Stuart.

Peg Boyd brought up her concern that the CAG was overly-aggressive with EPA. It appeared to her that we thought all EPA people were bad. She said the CAG had "an aura of arrogance," and she asked, further, "Why do we even need a CAG? Hasn't the U.S. government done projects like this elsewhere without a CAG?"

I reminded the city council members that when I'd attended their meetings in the 1990s as a reporter for the Saginaw News, the city had expressed hostility towards the EPA and MDEQ. What had caused them to change their thinking?

Jerry Church said it was when Stuart had hired a facilitator to build consensus between EPA and the City. The old view, he said, was that the EPA was bad, but after the staff got to know the EPA people through the facilitation process, they'd changed their thinking.

He went on to say that the CAG had a tendency to mistrust government agencies. Murray said that was true, "and here's why." He gave the example of trying to get the EPA documents about Total and how he had been stonewalled by the agency.

The city responded that they didn't care about upstream or downstream. They only cared about the portion of the river that was located within the city limits of St. Louis.

Peg asked where the idea had come from that the city wanted to put a park on the Smith Farm Site. Her remark caused Dennis and others to erupt in a loud and confrontational outburst, accusing Murray of having made up that story. Murray defended himself, and said that Kim Sakowski from MDEQ had given us the information. The city people didn't want to believe that, and they accused the CAG in general of knowing more than they did, whatever that meant, especially since, later in the meeting, they said just the opposite.

I wasn't willing to let the topic of Smith Farm go. I asked how the city could build a park on it since it was located in Bethany Township. To give some background: the city had a poor relationship with Bethany Township, and the township was not pleased that the city had included a plan for a park at the Smith Farm Site in their 5-year Parks Plan when they didn't even own rights to the property.

In Bethany Township's view, the city had pulled a fast one on them in the 1980s by annexing township land for a prison, and the township had not forgiven the city for that deception. When I asked the city how they could build a park on land owned by the township, Dennis Collison replied that the city could either buy the land or it could be given to them.

As we passed the one hour mark, George said we needed to get together more often instead of fighting things out in the newspaper and through the government agencies. Dennis said he didn't think it was worthwhile to meet together. Then he went on to say that the city knew much more than the CAG knew about the Smith Farm Site through Kim.

He stated that the site would be fixed in the same way the Velsicol site was fixed. Melissa said that the site at Smith Farm was *not* going to be fixed in the same way as the Velsicol Site, since it would not even have a slurry wall around it.

That's how the meeting went. Thoughts and feelings were aired, and some insight was gained into the city's animosity toward us. Some of the reasons for their animosity had names: Beth Reiner, Kim Sakowski and Stuart Hill. Maybe George had the same insight, because he suggested that we meet again in late August and this time he wanted people from the agencies there as well: Scott, Stephanie, Kim and Stuart. We agreed.

As data came in from the borings taken within the plant site to check for the extent of the DNAPL, we began to worry about the aquifer under the city from which St. Louis drew its drinking water. The borings showed that the gravelly clay underlying the plant site was not 70 feet thick, as had been thought, but only 40 feet thick.

Sand stringers were found throughout the supposedly impermeable bottom, allowing movement of groundwater and contaminants. Even though it was said that DNAPL was too heavy to move with groundwater, we already had the experience of it seeping through the riverbank near the river, and somehow it had moved offsite underneath the river to parts unknown. Suspicions were rising that perhaps the DNAPL had penetrated through the bottom of the plant site and into the aquifer.

Two days before our next meeting with the city, an article appeared in the newspaper with the headline "Chemicals in Saint Louis Aquifer." The sub-headline said "Velsicol seepage hasn't mixed in with the city's water," but the headline itself had upset the mayor and other city people.

The information had come from MDEQ as reported at our CAG meeting. Scott had told us that contaminants moving through the bottom of the plant site had reached the top of the aquifer. The contaminants had mingled in the upper area of the aquifer, high above the 150 to 200 foot level from which the city drew its water. DNAPL had not been detected (at that point), but benzenes were present.

Mayor George Kubin led the next joint meeting, and he immediately brought up the newspaper article. He said it was an example of the key problem with the CAG – information from meetings went into the paper before the city knew about the issue.

He turned on Scott and asked if he thought the headline for the article was appropriate. Scott couldn't, or wouldn't, answer that. After all, he hadn't chosen the headline. Scott said he understood George's concerns, but he couldn't withhold information from the public.

I was going to give my usual speech about facing the reality that we were living in a contaminated community, but Gary Smith spoke up and gave the speech instead. I looked forward to the day when the city could recite that speech to themselves and others.

Gary went on to agree that the city should have been notified of this information before either of our meetings took place. The city shouldn't have had to wake up to that headline in the paper.

We commented that people from city government were certainly welcome to attend our meetings. It turned out that Chad Doyle *had* attended our Technical Committee meeting and heard the information first hand when Scott reported it, but he had not shared it with other city officials.

As we talked, it became clear that the article itself did not trouble the city, because it contained factual information, presented in a non-threatening manner, and that the real problem was the headline.

I offered to set up a meeting between the mayor and the newspaper editor to talk about the headline, and also to discuss other activities going on in St. Louis of a positive nature that would interest readers.

Peg Boyd again questioned the necessity for a CAG, and Stuart Hill described how a CAG is formed within the Superfund program, and then becomes an autonomous group. He said EPA had no function other than the administrative startup of a CAG.

He said the fact that we had enlarged our scope to include more than the Velsicol plant site led to the dilemmas faced by Scott and Stephanie, as their limitations were within the Superfund program. He said most other CAGs functioned differently, with fewer in attendance and less interest in technical matters.

George told Stuart he should start attending the meetings of both the CAG and the city council, and serve as a liaison. Soon after that, George adjourned us. No one suggested that we should meet again.

Phil Hansen, the head of the St. Louis Downtown Development Authority, shook hands with me after the meeting and he hung onto mine a little longer and said he wanted me to know where he was coming from.

He said he recognized the "woe is me" attitude of some of the city council members, and he wanted our group to know that he and others fully supported our efforts and were grateful that we were sticking with it.

Our EPA project manager, Stephanie Ball, also spoke with me after the meeting. She told me that two important people had visited the plant site and river site: The EPA Region 5 Director of Superfund and the Director of the Office of the Emergency and Remedial Response. I was glad to know that those people now had a picture in their minds of our site from having seen the on-going work for themselves, and the extent of what was left to do.

I followed up by contacting Rick Mills, editor of the newspaper, and soon afterwards he and George and I had lunch together.

George aired his displeasure with the headline about the aquifer. Rick listened, and then widened the discussion to talk about the balance of stories that could be perceived as good publicity and bad publicity for St. Louis. Rick wrote down ideas that George and I came up with for potentially "good" stories about St. Louis. There were quite a few. George and the city had been active in using grant money to improve the appearance of the downtown area. Also, some of the boarded up stores had new owners who were using Downtown Development Authority grants to re-model buildings and open small businesses downtown.

George raised the issue again about how the articles that came out of our CAG meetings seemed to make St. Louis look bad, meaning contaminated. Once again I tried to explain that the present reality was that St. Louis *was* contaminated, and because the CAG was uncovering the fact of more contamination that had been buried for years, stories about contamination would dominate the news for awhile. In time the stories of completed cleanups would dominate. George wanted to know when the balance would shift. I told him my hope was in two more years. I based that estimate on what Scott and Stephanie had said about finalizing the Feasibility Study for the plant site by the end of 2002, with another year needed for the site's remedy to be designed. I didn't know how overly optimistic I was being.

In the Fruit of the Loom bankruptcy settlement, we had received word that the final document had been signed and that on or about Sept. 21st the initial $1.2 million payment would flow into the St. Louis Trust Account. It would not stay there long, as about a month later, the president of the LePetomane Trust, Jay Steinberg, would ask to borrow the money.

We still did not know who Jay Steinberg was except that he was the mystery man who was willing to hold the deeds to the seven most contaminated NWI/Velsicol sites. In September our MDEQ project manager, Scott Cornelius, e-mailed me to ask if we'd like Jay to visit us and attend our monthly meeting. We all looked forward to making his acquaintance, and we weren't disappointed. Jay looked and talked like the tough, Chicago lawyer that he was, with a little bit of cowboy in him, which, I'm sure, was needed for the non-traditional job he held. He seemed genuinely interested in getting to know us as people, and we enjoyed his sense of humor.

Jay had come for a visit because he wanted to borrow at least $99,000 of the first money deposited into our St. Louis Trust Account. He explained to us that he had no office, no staff and he only used a trial lawyer when needed. The settlement had allowed him some start-up cash for administrative purposes, but he had designs on getting big money out of the Fruit of the Loom pollution insurance policy held by AIG. That would require the services of a lawyer, filing fees and other costs involved with negotiating a settlement. EPA and the State of Michigan had agreed to accept his promissory note for the cash borrowed from the St. Louis Trust Account, and he would like our approval as well. I'm not sure we had a choice, but we were in favor of his efforts to get money out of the Fruit policy for the plant site. After all, that's what our CAG had first tried to do when we filed the $100 million claim in the Fruit of the Loom bankruptcy proceedings.

Jay also made it clear to the CAG that night that he was not the Trustee. His company, LePetomane, was the Trustee, and he was merely its president. Over the years, this got to be a joke with us, because Jay signed the various documents with the words "Jay Steinberg, not individually, but solely as President."

The Total Refinery property, now owned by Valero, was undergoing big changes. The huge towers and tanks were being dismantled and trucked away to other refineries. At one point the giant "cracker" tower was scheduled for implosion, and several of us CAG members stood on the opposite side of East Superior Street to watch the tower come down.

The holding ponds and lagoons were being emptied and excavated, the holes properly lined, and then the excavated sediments piled back in. They mounded up quite high when put back in the holes. Then a geo-textile cover was put over top of the contaminated soils to keep them sealed from wind and rain. It bothered us that another site was being buried, but at least they were doing it in a more secure manner than what had been done in St. Louis and at the Gratiot County Landfill.

As I mentioned earlier, Scott Cornelius originally had told us that by the end of 2002, the Feasibility Study would be completed and a remedy chosen for dealing with the leaking plant site. Of course, that timetable was delayed due to finding the benzene in the aquifer and not knowing the extent of the NAPL contamination. This became a pattern -- the finding of more contamination which further delayed the FS for the plant site.

Another pattern also began in 2002. The first confident bioremediation firm contacted us to say if we were to buy and release their microbes in the plant site soils, the critters would eat up all the pollution and our worries would be over. I know these organisms do successfully consume wastes at some sites, and maybe someday a species will be found that can eat both benzenes and DDT and not die from the 200-plus other chemicals contained in the former Velsicol plant site.

Meanwhile, Scott gave a sample of our soil to the company to take back to their lab for testing. We invited them to return to report their findings to us. We never heard from them again. Throughout the years, it became a predictable pattern, with the companies coming in with a power point presentation and brochures, taking home a soil sample, and never being heard from again.

This was a further indication of the severity of contamination within the plant site. The sooner the site was dug up and hauled away, the better.

Chapter 8
(2003)
Who Are We?

Knowing that the plant site had leaked at least a small amount of benzene into the upper regions of the St. Louis aquifer, and having the suspicion that EPA would advocate for another wall and cap without addressing the bottom of the site, we wrote a letter to Thomas Skinner, Regional Administrator of EPA Region 5, listing our concerns. We advocated excavation of much of the site to capture the source of the NAPL and to make the site usable for redevelopment in the future.

Meanwhile the NAPL trench was collecting the NAPL and contaminated water as it exited the site. Every time the NAPL trench was mentioned, Gary Smith asked to have it reaffirmed that the trench was a temporary measure, and EPA and their contractor, CH2MHILL, continued to say that it was.

We had an uneasy feeling that the unspoken permanent plan for the plant site was a cap, a wall, and the collection trench to capture the runoff out the sides.

We knew we were ignorant about NAPL, and since it seemed certain that the presence of NAPL on the site could be the "driver" for how much of the soil was actually excavated, it seemed prudent to find our own NAPL expert to instruct us. It was time once again to dip into our TAG grant money and hire a consultant.

We began to find names and make phone calls, and we soon discovered that most NAPL experts were employed by chemical corporations, and not interested in assisting a group of citizens.

We finally found one who was willing to share general information with us over the phone, although he would not commit himself to coming to our site to talk with us and the project managers.

He told us that NAPL moved through things that it shouldn't be able to penetrate, and that it didn't always obey the law of gravity, because it had been shown to move uphill. Even controlled laboratory tests had not resulted in definite information on how NAPL behaves, except to say that it is unpredictable.

When we told him that 3000 gallons of NAPL had been collected from the plant site the previous year, and about 100 gallons a month were still being collected, he said in reply: "Although 3,000 gallons may seem like a lot, I suspect it dwarfs what's actually there." He told us it was a misconception to think that NAPL would pool in one location. He said it rarely pooled, but remained dispersed.

When we told him that the NAPL had gone through the "impenetrable" layer of clay under the plant site and may have entered the aquifer from which St. Louis draws its water, his response was this: "I assume there are early warning detection systems in place." When we told him there were not, he was shocked.

The expert was very interested and even amazed at the mix of chemicals contained within the plant site, and he told us that with the combination of DDT and chlorobenzene present, NAPL could continue to coalesce within the plant site, even for centuries to come.

Because of the various pathways leading from the plant site into the aquifer from which the city drew its drinking water, we began to ask nearly every month if the drinking water wells had shown any kind of contamination infiltrating them.

Our meeting minutes show that we regularly asked this question of MDEQ and EPA from 2002 onward. And our assumption was that if we asked the question, we would be given an honest answer.

During this time, our EPA Project Manager Stephanie Ball encouraged us to attend an EPA-sponsored conference in Albuquerque, New Mexico. CAGs and TAGs from across the country would assemble to share information with one another through presentations, panel discussions, and poster workshops.

To explain CAGs and TAGs, some groups in the country become Community Advisory Groups (CAGs), as we had done, and some become Technical Assistance Grant groups (TAGs). Our group was both, although the way we looked at it, we were a CAG that also had a TAG.

For our 10-minute presentation, Murray put together a fast-moving power point slide show with lots of pictures, and I read swiftly and steadily from a text.

We highlighted a few areas in which we had widened the territory for all CAGs and TAGs in using TAG grant monies for legal consultations and health advice. Our talk was divided into sections, with the first section entitled, "Who We Are," which was an ironic start to the year 2003, since many of our activities later in the year had to do with finding an answer for the question "Who are we?"

The positive feedback we received on our presentation helped re-energize us, and an EPA official told us we were one of the largest and most active CAGs in the country. The compliments were nice to hear, but also disturbing.

Why weren't the other groups as active and as successful? Perhaps from getting bogged down in battles with their city councils, responsible parties or competing CAGs. We certainly understood how those kinds of wars sapped vitality from a group.

We were still in that situation, although we had decided (at least for the time being) to no longer try to placate the city people, but to act separately from them in doing our activities to the best of our abilities. We believed that we had done all we could to reconcile with the city, and for the most part, our efforts had failed.

Meanwhile, after winning the Supplemental Environmental Project (SEP) four years previously, which brought some of the Total Refinery penalty back to our community, excavation began in Horse Creek. Valero, which now owned the defunct refinery, built a concrete pad near the river to hold the dredged sediments from Horse Creek and the confluence area of the Pine River. Those dredgings smelled horrible!

For that entire summer, the area on the west side of St. Louis reeked, and the hydrocarbon smell could give a person a headache in a short time.

As I had said to Mayor George Kubin over and over, things had to get worse before they got better. This was the perfect illustration. The sediment hadn't stunk while it was in the creek, and digging it out made the air smell unbearably bad for a time, and then, when the waste was drained and hauled away, the smell went with it, plus the creek was clean.

By November of 2003, Horse Creek had a new lease on life.

Now, the two miles of cleaned creek looked and smelled like a creek should, with life returning to it naturally. The workers had shaped the banks to help guard against erosion, and had planted native grasses and other vegetation. People who lived in the Evergreen mobile home park cleared excess brush at the backs of their lots to give themselves a view of the pretty creek, and of the cleaner river. Over 280,000 square feet of the confluence area had been cleaned, deepening the river in some places from inches to five feet. People could now get their boats to float in the water.

Having the creek and confluence area cleaned of petroleum sludge was one of our first achievements in overseeing the cleanups of all the contaminated sites in the Pine River watershed. It was a good start. We were pleased to remember that it was our letter writing that had brought $9 million into the community for this cleanup and also $900,000 for the city of Alma to help re-locate Alma Iron and Metal from off the shores of the Pine River.

Later in the year, when the Clarke Historical Library, located at Central Michigan University, asked to house our "archives," we were astonished to think of ourselves in that light. Were our piles of documents, reports, letters, and notes "archives?" Even though we were careful to keep past, present and future in focus as we dealt with one activity after another, we hadn't really thought of ourselves, or of our CAG, in terms of *becoming* the past. We hadn't really thought about our CAG as something someone might want to study someday.

I received a letter from Jennifer Wood, an Archival Assistant at the Clarke Historical Library, saying she had read an article I'd written for the *Life in the Middle* magazine about our Community Advisory Group, and that our efforts were of significance to the continuing social, economic, political and environmental development of our region. Would we consider "placing our papers" with the Clarke Historical Library as on "ongoing collection?"

When Alma College heard that we were thinking of housing our documents in Mt. Pleasant, President Saundra Tracy wrote us a letter asking that the college become the archive for our materials. She said that the college was "exploring options" of how best to store the materials.

It was decided that some CAG members should tour the Clarke facility before we made up our minds. As far as proximity was concerned, Alma College seemed the better choice, but when considering the state-of-the art set-up in Mt. Pleasant, Clarke seemed a better choice. In the end, we chose Alma College primarily because of its locale and also due to loyalty on the part of some.

But the bigger issue for all of us was to see ourselves in a different way. Both the Clarke and Alma College librarians saw our papers as having historical significance. The Clarke librarians had emphasized that they were not only interested in our formal documents, but also informal, internal documents. We were amazed all over again to think that our e-mails back and forth to each other could be seen as having historical significance. I think some egos were boosted a little, and I know I started to save more e-mails, but for the most part, we were brought back to the question of who were we, anyway?

Another situation arose around that question. The year before, Rita Jack, an employee of the Sierra Club, had joined our CAG. She was friendly and knowledgeable, and had willingly taught fifteen community members how to search for and collect benthic macro-invertebrates, whose presence indicates the quality of life in a river.

Now, though, she wanted the CAG to sign a letter addressed to MDEQ that recommended a policy change. Signatories on the letter included Sierra Club, Michigan United Conservation Clubs, the Michigan Environmental Council, the National Wildlife Federation, and many other upstanding organizations around the state.

I asked members of the Executive Committee for their views. Ed pointed out that although it was good to have the support of the Sierra Club, we *needed* the support of MDEQ, and we shouldn't take sides by signing the letter.

Murray said he planned to sign it as a citizen, but he didn't think the CAG should sign.

Gary and others expressed similar views, which matched my own.

My letter in response to Rita helped define for ourselves who we were. I told her that our CAG had a very narrow focus and that our intention was to remain as apolitical as we could, believing this would aid us in cleaning up our sites. I said, "We do not stand against anything other environmental groups stand for. We simply choose to remain separate and to concentrate our efforts on the tasks set before us."

From then on, the CAG has written letters on policy issues only when we thought they would directly aid our clean up efforts, such as asking for a reinstatement of the Superfund Tax.

A summer Sesquicentennial celebration was planned for the town of St. Louis, and at that time, Stuart Hill decided to once again re-activate his role as Community Involvement Coordinator. Our CAG had planned a booth, and then Stuart announced that booths at fairs were in his job description, and we should let him do his job. Moreover, he owned a trailer that was designed to be a booth.

Gary Smith was in a convivial mood that spring, and he suggested to Stuart that both booths be next to each other, and Stuart agreed to that compromise.

Stuart also planned a presentation involving a man named Peter Alsop who was maybe a clown or maybe a guitar-playing folksinger, or maybe a storyteller. We couldn't quite figure out what Peter Alsop did and why Stuart wanted him to come.

We were all trying to work with Stuart, though. He had recently retired and had announced to us that he had convinced EPA to let him "keep" his two best sites, and we were one of them. Some in the group made sarcastic comments out of earshot, such as "lucky us," but we had hopes that Stuart was turning over a new leaf.

Murray certainly thought he was, and he tried to convince us to pay half the costs, along with the city, to bring Peter Alsop to St. Louis. Even though we would pay half the costs, we were going to get the man's services for only 25% of the time, and our other 25% was to go to Stuart.

Why were we paying EPA's costs for an entertainer out of our TAG grant that was meant for hiring consultants? Several of us kept asking Murray what does Peter Alsop *do?*

Well, he sings, he clowns, he tells stories. But why do we want a singer/clown/storyteller? How is an entertainer going to further our mission of cleaning up our sites? No one claimed that it would. So will his coming foster unity somehow with the city? Apparently it would somehow, some way.

Murray thought that if we talked to Peter Alsop ourselves, we could get the answers to some of our questions. He arranged for us to make a conference call to Mr. Alsop from a meeting room in the provost's office at Alma College. Several of us gathered for the call. Peter Alsop seemed as puzzled as we were as to why his services were being requested. He could do all the things we had heard about. And if we wanted him to, he could sing some environmental songs. It still made no sense

At least we were able to reduce his time commitment during that phone call, which would reduce our costs. He agreed to come for one day during the celebration instead of the three that Stuart had proposed. Towards the end of our conversation with him, there began to be some light when Alsop mentioned that he did facilitation work to help groups solve problems.

So *that's* why Stuart and the city wanted us to hire Alsop. They wanted us to pay half the costs for another facilitator to "help straighten out the CAG." Apparently they weren't going to tell us that Alsop was a facilitator, but just let him come and sing and clown and tell stories and work on solving problems at the same time.

We didn't quite understand what to do with Alsop after the light bulb went on. In order to use our TAG grant to hire him, he had to tie his performance in with Superfund and also as a consultant of some kind.

The whole idea seemed nutty to me. Why would we spend TAG grant money on a person whose skills we didn't really want? Would we go that far to placate the city and Stuart?

Murray was willing to go that far, and wanted to "find" something for Alsop to do. Gary was still in his convivial mood and was willing to go along with Murray. Carol and I couldn't see the point of any of it. Melissa, Ed, Jim and Joe were still trying to figure it all out, amid questions and differences of opinion.

When Murray reported the gist of the conference call at our next meeting, Stuart decided to make a speech. He said that hiring Peter Alsop was a viable idea, and that we had the authority to spend TAG money in that way, and that the CAG needed to use Alsop's facilitation skills. We didn't take any action on the plan that night. If someone had made a motion, we would have had to pursue it, but no one did, and that was all right with me.

At the next monthly meeting, the discussion on the topic led to a decision that the 150th birthday of St. Louis was *not* the time to bring Peter Alsop to town. The discussion centered on bringing him at some future date, since he was a facilitator. Bernie Bessert made a motion, seconded by Ed Lorenz, to forget bringing him to town altogether. The motion passed unanimously, and that silly situation was ended.

So much for thinking Stuart had turned over a new leaf. He was using the same old tactics he and Beth Reiner had employed in the beginning. Beth had tried to sneak us into being friends with Velsicol by bringing Chuck Hanson to meet with us, and she later inserted John Hock into the CAG. She and Stuart had also tried to finagle us into facilitation sessions with the city at an earlier time. And now here was Stuart trying to trick us into hiring a facilitator ourselves. All of this folderol using taxpayer dollars. For shame.

Some people wanted to write a letter of censure about Stuart, referring to him as a Community *Dividing* Coordinator, but after some talk, we got over that, and went back to ignoring him as best we could.

After the air cleared, Joe suggested we ask local historian Dave McMacken to give a talk at Penny Park on the history of the chemical plant. Joe's sensible idea tied in with the historical nature of the sesquicentennial, and directly with our Superfund site that sat on the river across from Penny Park. It also reunited our group around a good idea.

The decision was made, Dave agreed to speak, and Phil Hansen, the publicity man for the city, wanted to advertise Dave's appearance in all the publications for the 150th birthday party. So there we were -- united within the CAG and also working with the city around this plan that was generated from a local person, and not by an out-of town facilitator or an EPA Community Involvement Coordinator.

On the night of Dave McMacken's talk, the picnic shelter at Penny Park filled up with people in lawn chairs and the audience spilled out into the grassy yard. The attendees could view the deep excavation in the riverbed, the large, white temporary structure that housed the water treatment facility, the collection tank for NAPL, the heavy equipment, and all the other paraphernalia of the ongoing cleanup of the river.

Dave McMacken spoke about the first drillings for brine made in the late part of the 19th century, the early business failures, Dow Chemical's attempt to establish itself in St. Louis, and the years of the thriving business of Michigan Chemical. Dave had asked me to talk about the history of the CAG's work to get the chemical contamination cleaned from the river and the plant site, and I did that. The presentation was well received, with good questions following. Afterwards, we had eight new people join our CAG.

Even though city and CAG had united around this event, not all was well between us. Bernie Bessert had attended several of the city's Brownfield Authority meetings throughout 2002, but animosity expressed towards the CAG kept flaring up at those meetings, and Bernie announced that he wasn't going to go to any more of them. The newspaper reported a concern among the members of the Brownfield Task Force that redevelopment of the plant site would meet the same resistance as plans to develop the Smith Farm site did, stating "Pine River Superfund Citizens Task Force stalled and perhaps halted reuse of the former chemical dump site." Chad Doyle was quoted as saying the former plant site was too important to the community to become "bogged down in environmental mish-mash."

The fact was, we had mailed even more "environmental mish-mash" to the State of Michigan about the Smith Farm Site. A new director of the MDEQ had come on board, and Murray wrote a concise letter bringing Steven Chester up to date on our concerns about the proposed "interim response" at the Smith Farm Site. We don't know if it was the result of our letter, but soon after that the plans for Smith Farm expanded with a dredging of the pond sediment added into the plans, which drastically reduced the mercury contamination in that little body of water.

As mentioned earlier, Smith Farm Project Manager Kim Sakowski had been attending our meetings regularly since our showdown with her in 2002. If not yet warming up to us, at least she was thawing. She actually began answering e-mails, and occasionally offered information at meetings instead of having it dragged out of her.

In fact it was Kim who told me the name of the MDEQ project manager for the Gratiot County Landfill Superfund Site. In our 5 ½ years as a CAG, we hadn't once discussed the Landfill. I had put it on my list of priorities for 2003, and when Kim gave me the name of the project manager, Matt Williams, I contacted him right away.

Matt came to our meeting and gave us a power point presentation on recent cap repair, the installation of a methane monitoring system, and a report on the slurry wall, which Matt described as a "colander." In one area, a large break had occurred with contaminated water running out of the site and onto private property. The State had replaced the drinking water wells of the two families who lived near the site. They had also installed a pumping operation that was pulling back the contaminated groundwater beneath the site. Like the plant site, this site had been built with no liner, and without even the presumption that a natural layer of clay till would serve as a barrier. The Gratiot County Landfill had been built on a swamp.

Originally, the Landfill had been a typical county dump, which Vesicol and other companies began to use for their industrial wastes. After the PBB Disaster in the 1970s, Velsicol dumped tons of leftover PBB into the landfill. Also buried there were carcasses of slaughtered cattle and chickens which had eaten the PBB in their food and sickened. Due to the cover up that followed the accidental mixing of the fire retardant into animal feed, PBB-ridden animals had been sent to market, and PBB-laced milk, meat, eggs and butter were placed on store shelves for people to buy. In that way, the 9 million inhabitants of Michigan unwittingly ingested PBB, leading to the largest food contamination accident in our nation's history.

From Matt's presentation it seemed the site was contained for the present, and we put the Landfill on the back burner once again as we moved forward with the river clean up and the plant site Remedial Investigation and Feasibility Study.

Even though Scott had predicted that we would have a remedy chosen for the plant site by the end of 2002, the discovery of NAPL had led to more testing, and now MDEQ was also testing the Golf Course Superfund Site, which was located across the river from the plant site. During its operations, Velsicol had piped or trucked wastes over there and set them on fire.

Weston Solutions, MDEQ's contractor, gave us a presentation on work being done at the Golf Course Site, and the aquifer that it shared with the plant site. It was during this presentation that we were told to change our vocabulary. We were to refer to the aquifer under the city as the "upper outwash unit" and the "lower outwash unit." I'm sure these name changes were meant to reduce panic should contaminants be discovered in the aquifer. Ordinary newspaper readers wouldn't make the connection between the aquifer from which they drew their drinking water and the "upper outwash unit" and "lower outwash unit."

As for the Golf Course Site, that title had been objected to for years by former owner Dick Green, because no one played golf where the Golf Course Superfund Site was located, even though the site lay within the boundaries of the Edgewood Hills Golf Course. We were now instructed to call it the "Burn Pit Site," and the name fit the former activity of that location.

During this presentation by Weston, we also learned that the lower outwash unit contained "contaminants of concern" in amounts greater than drinking water criteria allowed. The eight wells that St. Louis drew its water from were not compromised, they assured us, and they were being tested every two weeks.

Meanwhile, Stuart was able to help the city procure a $75,000 Superfund Redevelopment Initiative grant from EPA to make future plans for the plant site. We learned about the grant through the newspaper, which reported, "... council members were concerned that local input be considered and that the city council be the lead agency in contact with EPA and E2, rather than the Pine River Superfund Citizen Task Force. Collison assured them they would be..."

Since the CAG was an EPA-sanctioned organization set up as the official community liaison between EPA and the wider community, we questioned City Manager Dennis Collison's statement.

It was our understanding that EPA had a mandate to deal directly with us at each stage of the plant site cleanup process from the remedial investigation to redevelopment plans. That meant we would be the "lead agency," to use the city's words, which was the opposite of Collison's understanding. Bolstering our claim was a clause contained in the Fruit of the Loom Consent Judgment stating that the agencies of the U. S. government, including EPA, would keep the CAG informed of any actions proposed for the plant site and the Breckenridge Site.

As chair of the so-called "lead agency," I telephoned an associate of EPA's contracting company, E-squared. James Wilkinson told me that E-squared would pull together a land-use committee, develop a re-use plan, and then turn the plan over to the city to be carried out. I asked how the Custodial Trust would fit into the picture, and he knew nothing about the Fruit of the Loom settlement and the fact that the Trust owned the plant site property. He thought the city owned the property. I invited him to attend our next meeting, and told him I would invite Jay Steinberg, president of the Custodial Trust, to answer questions in person.

There was another point that needed clarification in James Wilkinson's thinking, and in clarifying it for him, it helped us to better understand who we were.

I wrote to Wilkinson and said I had noticed some wording in his outline that I hoped he would allow me to correct. I pointed out that he had an understandable misconception that the CAG was a "St. Louis organization," since we held our meetings in St. Louis. I said, "The fact is we are not a St. Louis organization, or even a Gratiot County organization, or even a Michigan organization... We are...a federally mandated group of United States citizens, and we represent not only the people of our immediate community, but the entire community of the United States of America.

"Your wording, then, in the aforementioned memo, must include the third party of the Pine River Superfund Citizen Task Force Community Advisory Group (CAG). We are not part of St. Louis, nor are we part of EPA. We are a third entity with direct responsibility to oversee any activity concerning the plant site."

Wilkinson wrote that he appreciated my explanation.

He and an associate came to dinner with us and Jay Steinberg, and E-squared made presentations at both of our meetings. They told us that the land-use committee would meet over the course of four months, and that they would not formulate a redevelopment *plan*, but only a set of recommendations.

Jay told everyone that the plant site property was being held in trust for the state and its citizens. The Trust would look into the recommendations for redevelopment that came from the land-use committee, but some proposed uses might not be feasible or financially possible. He said once the property was remedied and money was in place for redevelopment, then a plan would be made.

James Wilkinson sent me a thank-you note for the dinner and asked me to choose two people from the CAG to serve on the land-use committee. Ed Lorenz and Joe Scholtz agreed to serve, and I sent those names to Wilkinson. Meanwhile, I learned that Dennis Collison had given Wilkinson the names of two other CAG people for the committee. We ignored Collison's actions and kept on dealing directly with Wilkinson.

Through many of our activities and encounters in 2003, we learned much about ourselves as a CAG. We learned that our activities were forward-looking and our achievements commendable in the eyes of EPA and MDEQ. We learned that our documents had historical value. And even though we disliked the unpleasantness that had occurred in our challenging encounters with Rita over our refusal to sign on to bigger environmental causes, with Stuart and the city over the Peter Alsop deception, and with Dennis Collison over the question of our standing in regards to the plant site, each of these encounters were good occasions for self-examination and refinement of how we perceived ourselves. In the long run, these challenges served to strengthen our unity as we better understood who we were – of who we are – in this struggle to restore the land and water of the place where we live.

Chapter 9
(2004)
Caught in the Crossfire

When we formed our CAG in 1998, most of us had never heard of NAPL. Now the acronym was a part of our vocabulary and discussed at every meeting.

The former Velsicol plant site contained two kinds of DNAPL (dense non-aqueous phase liquid) and one variety of LNAPL (light non-aqueous phase liquid), and if the NAPL expert we had consulted was correct, the chemical contents of the plant site would continue to coalesce, generating new NAPL for centuries to come. EPA objected to this scenario, saying it would not occur. To us, whether it would or wouldn't was not worth arguing about. To our way of thinking, the best thing to do was bring in excavating equipment, dig everything up, and move it away from the river or incinerate it. Why did we need more tests? Why did we need to track down the source of NAPL? Why not simply get to work and dig it up?

We had contacted another NAPL expert, Dr. Michael Annable in Florida. When our EPA project manager, Stephanie Ball, suggested that he take part in a technical discussion with a "think tank" of EPA scientists from Oklahoma to discuss the NAPL issue, we withdrew money from our TAG grant to help pay for Dr. Annable's services.

Out of these discussions came a plan for MDEQ and EPA to conduct a Joint Sampling and Analysis Plan (JSAP) in which EPA and MDEQ would work together to find the source of NAPL, and would also share test results to fill in data gaps. At least that's what we were told. From the FOIA'd documents that we received several years later, we could see that Stephanie and her bosses at EPA had devised the JSAP idea to force Scott and his MDEQ contractors to finalize the data gathering and complete the writing of the Remedial Investigation and Feasibility Study. In other words, they wanted Scott to get the show on the road. Instead, Scott resisted the JSAP plan and organized his own Phase 3 Remedial Investigation which would require further sampling of soil, water, the outwash units, and the Burn Pit area.

As the disagreement escalated, Stephanie asked the EPA Region 5 Director of the Superfund Division, Richard Karl, to write a letter to the Chief of the Remediation and Redevelopment Division of MDEQ, Andrew Hogarth, in an attempt to resolve the contention between the agencies. Instead, it solidified the dispute, since Karl agreed with Stephanie's views and Hogarth agreed with Scott's actions.

The CAG was caught in the crossfire of this exchange between the agencies. Nothing was said to us, but we easily picked up on the strained formality between Stephanie and Scott at our meetings. We also were not receiving data. Previously, both agencies had quite freely shared sampling results with us, knowing that the members of our Technical Committee could correctly interpret it, and often could spot trends and anomalies, or ask questions that helped Scott and Stephanie and their contractors spot data gaps.

But the data flow stopped. Murray joked, chided, pleaded and complained about no data, but neither Scott nor Stephanie heeded him.

Now, with the letters of that time period before us, we can see that EPA didn't want MDEQ to learn anything new at our meetings, and vice versa.

Carol Layman let both agencies know what she thought about the "testing, testing, testing." She felt that this duel between the agencies was wasting another whole season when excavation could have been taking place. How many more years would this go on? Carol wondered out loud. It was a good thing she didn't know the answer to that.

We talked among ourselves about what might be the problem between the agencies, but we couldn't put our finger on it. We kept hoping they would move past it. Being caught in the middle worried us. For awhile it had seemed as if the CAG, MDEQ and EPA were the three legs of a stool, with one aim to clean up the community. Now, two legs of the stool were fighting, and the community would suffer.

We had noticed that Scott seemed to be working his way through the members of the CAG on a one-on-one basis trying to lower our expectations for the kind of cleanup to take place at the plant site. That was worrisome.

Then we noticed that Stephanie spoke up at meetings to tell us about other Superfund sites that had not received funding in the past year, and how children were dying who lived near them. She seemed to be trying to lower our expectations for receiving enough money for a complete cleanup.

At one of our Executive Committee meetings, we decided that we would refuse to feel guilty about receiving the funding necessary to clean the plant site up to our standards. When Stephanie brought up the issue of money at our next CAG membership meeting, telling us that the cleanup we wanted would be very expensive to implement, I said, "We don't have to be concerned about how much it costs. You and the EPA have to be concerned about that, but we don't. We are not interested in hearing about money issues anymore."

After a few repetitions of our refusal to listen to the money woes of EPA, Stephanie gave up trying to make us feel guilty for wanting an expensive cleanup.

After all, the community was not to blame for the expense of the clean-up. The State and EPA were guilty for having avoided a responsible cleanup in the 1980s, a cleanup that could have been paid for by Velsicol if EPA and the State had not let the chemical company off the hook.

Another situation arose in which we had to set some ground rules. Robert Kennedy, Jr. was coming to Alma College to deliver the Honor's Day address, and environmental groups such as Sierra Club and the Natural Resources Defense Council began trying to orchestrate his visit.

Ed worried that those groups would use the community for their own agendas, exploiting our misery for their gain. After some discussion with the Executive Committee, he wrote a long e-mail to Rita Jack and Rob Perks who were in positions of responsibility in the local chapters of those groups, urging them to be "sensitive to the concerns of the St. Louis and Alma communities" in their plans to use Kennedy's presence for their "bigger issues."

He said, "These communities have suffered exceptional environmental stress over the last two generations..." and that the communities did not want to serve as "poster children" to showcase environmental degradation. He asked that the environmental groups refrain from exploiting our community, and, instead, to celebrate it as a place that has fought for justice.

Through Ed's leadership on this issue, we were able to "take back" most of the visit of Robert Kennedy, Jr. In addition to the Honor's Day address (at which representatives from some of the environmental groups also spoke), Ed arranged a press conference for Kennedy at Penny Park located across from the plant site, and on the brink of the cells of the river that were being excavated.

In addition, Ed planned a breakfast for Kennedy and the Executive Committee of our CAG for the morning following the address. We also invited a few people from the City of St. Louis to join us. To have face-to-face time with Kennedy and the lawyers accompanying him boosted our morale. Kennedy was very interested in our Superfund-site-ridden community and the work we had done so far.

And he and his law firm would later prove to be a fruitful contact for the city.

As time passed and the city did not make a move to acquire the Smith Farm Site, we began to assume they had changed their mind. We were a little surprised, then, when Kim told us the city was on track to take ownership of the property once the state had finished its interim response measures.

The State of Michigan had torn down the house on the property and had plugged the drinking water well. Among the rubbish cleared from the site were 1500 old tires, 2,820 tons of metal trash, and another 25,000 tons of other non-hazardous material.

The pond was divided by a chain link fence crossing from one bank to another, essentially drawing a line in the air. We jokingly said the fence was put there to prevent contaminants in the pond from crossing from the uncleaned, privately owned side to the cleaned side. The private side of the pond and property still contained 3,000 old tires, dozens of old refrigerators and unknown other kinds of junk. Kim said she was trying to "educate" the private owner about recycling some of his metal trash. The state had also removed over 400 intact barrels of waste from the Smith Farm Site, with some of the barrels marked with the Velsicol and Michigan Chemical names, and some with C&C Chemical, a company that none of us knew anything about.

There were also the remains of rusted-through metal barrels and cardboard barrels, whose contents had most likely mixed with the sediment and water of the pond and with the soil on the site.

Plans called for installing a chain link fence around the entire Smith Farm property, with a monument erected to warn people that it was a former chemical landfill.

The prospect of yet another tombstone was like the last straw. Here we were trying to get the plant site freed from a fence and a tombstone, and here was the State of Michigan fencing and putting a monument on yet another site in our community. Kim hurriedly assured us that the monument would not be a purchased tombstone, but a nice big rock excavated from the property. They would affix a brass plaque to it with the warning engraved on it. We were not mollified.

The geo-textile fabric described in the cover-up plans for the Smith Farm Site had disappeared and now orange snow fence was going to be laid down as a "marker layer" with 18 inches of soil placed overtop. The snow fence would serve to warn people to stop digging and that they were nearing the chemically-contaminated waste, Kim told us.

And would the rock with the plaque tell people about the "marker layer?" No. And would animals stop digging when they came to the "marker layer?" That was the kind of question that did not get an answer.

Our CAG decided it was time to gather more facts about the Smith Farm Site and to express our disapproval with it being termed "remediated," even on an interim basis. Ed and Murray compiled a history of the site, including reports of inspection by the Michigan DNR, the Michigan Department of Agriculture, the Michigan Department of Public Health, the EPA and the MDEQ. Murray also made a topographical map with overlays showing recent test results of VOCs, heavy metals, PCBs, vinyl chlorides, and so forth, all exceeding direct contact criteria, and also mercury in the groundwater.

The conclusion of the report was that much more excavation was needed, and that it was of paramount importance to test to determine the extent of the contaminated groundwater leaving the site.

Kim didn't disagree with any of the facts or conclusions, but kept repeating that this was the only kind of cleanup (cover-up) that Clean Michigan Initiative money would pay for.

We also urged her to get the state attorney general's office to pursue the PRPs who were still in business to help pay cleanup costs. She said this was being considered.

We specifically mentioned Oxford Automotive (formerly Lobdell-Emery) because they had said publicly they were thinking of moving out of the area. Later, when the attorney general's office approached the head of that company, he said they couldn't afford to chip in for a clean-up, and the state quit pursuing them.

Meanwhile, Phil Hansen, Director of the St. Louis Downtown Development Authority, called Murray Borrello and asked to know the CAG's concerns about the Smith Farm Site, since he hadn't been around during the big meeting we'd had with Kim the year before.

Murray met with him, taking a copy of our report. After that meeting, Phil asked Murray to meet with the city manager, Dennis Collison, city council member Jerry Church and Kim Sakowski. Apparently Kim and Murray clashed over the issue of groundwater contamination in terms of whether or not it was migrating off site. Murray kept urging for tests to settle the question.

Apparently his insistence worked, because later Kim told us she had found some money within MDEQ to pay for tests to determine the spread of the contaminants underground. The subsequent testing showed, as we had feared, that the plume contaminated with vinyl chloride, 1,2-dichloroethylene and benzene had moved off site and had crossed under State Road. The extent of the plume was unknown. Since a city drinking water well was located a block or so from State Road, there was definitely cause for concern.

Murray wrote reports on the nature of these contaminants and shared them with the city.

We had thought this new information would surely convince them to steer clear of ownership. Instead, we learned from Kim that a final site inspection was due at the end of the year, and then the city would be given clear title to the property.

At least we, as the CAG, had done all we could to persuade the State of Michigan to abandon their interim response at the site, and perform a complete cleanup. We had also pushed the state to go after the responsible parties. And we had repeatedly tried to persuade the city to not take ownership of the site. The story wasn't over yet, but that was all that happened in 2004.

Ed Lorenz had decided it was time once again to try to get a comprehensive health study for the community. Fred Brown and Gene Kenaga had emphasized endocrine disruption as a consequence of exposure to DDT and PBB. Ed looked back at data given to Dr. Wilfrid Karmaus when one of the NIEHS grants for a health study was being written, and he zeroed in on non-diabetic thyroid cases, data for which had been collected by our local hospital. These kinds of thyroid problems were a possible indication that the endocrine system in a person's body was being disrupted by a chemical that mimicked human hormones.

Ed also mentioned that his wife, Marilyn, had developed a thyroid problem. When she went to a dentist in the next county, and responded to his questions by saying she had the condition, he remarked, "That's funny. Every woman patient I have from Gratiot County has a thyroid problem."

Ed wrote a letter to ATSDR (Agency of Toxic Substances and Disease Registry) to try to bring in a health study. He received a response stating they would come to town, but not to do a comprehensive health study, or even a health assessment, but a health consultation.

At a strategy meeting, the CAG Executive Committee decided to show our own power point presentation prior to ATSDR presenting their information to us. In this way, we could make it clear as to what we already knew so that ATSDR wouldn't waste our time. Our experience with federal and state agencies had taught us they could spend most of a meeting flooding us with facts known to us, rather than listening to what we had to say.

Apparently, in their conversations with Ed, Mark Johnson from ATSDR and Brendan Boyle, the ATSDR person with the state of Michigan, learned about our strategy. I received a team phone call from them the day before the meeting, and they pressured me to put them on the agenda ahead of our power point presentation.

I had to decline at least three times, explaining that we believed it was important for the community members at the meeting to hear about the data that we had already gathered on health concerns so that everybody would be up to speed before hearing the ATSDR presentation. We followed through with our strategy, and in this way the agency didn't monopolize the conversation.

Our hope was that this "health consultation" by ATSDR would lead them to conduct a health assessment, and perhaps a comprehensive health study, but they said they saw no new pathways of exposure for people since they had previously assessed the community.

Even our little survey about how people ate the fish was met with the response that the river was cleaner now than it had been, so that the eating of fish was less of a pathway than it had been in the past, despite the fact that the state health department still maintained a no-consumption advisory about the fish.

The most they could offer was to provide the State of Michigan with a health education grant that would buy new "Do Not Eat the Fish" signs. It was quite a letdown, and more so for the former Velsicol workers who had attended our meeting, and for two attendees who were still in the State of Michigan PBB Registry study that had begun after the 1970s PBB Disaster.

The Registry of 4,545 people had been set up to track health changes experienced by farm families, chemical workers, and others who had suffered greater exposure to PBB than the rest of the population. In the 1990s, however, the workers were dropped from the study in part because of their extensive exposure to other chemicals at the chemical plant. The scientists were afraid the final results might be skewed by their participation. And because of a shortage of money at the state health department, the rest of the cohort was not being tested regularly to study the long term effects of PBB exposure.

We continued to work with ATSDR liaison Kory Groetsch, through the designing of the "Do Not Eat the Fish" signs. We didn't want cardboard posters or laminated posters attached to bridge abutments with duct tape this time around. Kory suggested plastic signs, but we wanted metal signs of a good size (we settled on 15 x 17 inches) with raised lettering, mounted on steel posts.

In addition to the "no consumption" message written in both English and Spanish, we wanted a positive message on the signs, indicating that catching and releasing fish was safe.

After many e-mails to Kory, and after his negotiations with the Gratiot County Road Commission to legally post the signs, finally, in November of 2005, a group of our guys, along with Kory, installed 21 signs downstream from St. Louis. The cities of Alma and St. Louis were each given 10 signs to post within their city limits along the Pine River. This was a far cry from a comprehensive health study, but at least it was something.

Meanwhile, Ed became aware of a 1979 law regarding landfills that he thought might push EPA to dig up the whole plant site. The law required landfills to have a double liner, with a leak detection alarm system between the liners. Since this law had been in place when the chemical plant had been demolished, we began to think that the plant site was an illegal landfill.

We knew that EPA would argue that it was not a landfill, but a burial site, yet we could argue that because the contents of the Golf Course/Burn Pit Site had been carted across the river and dumped onto the plant site, that made it a landfill. After some investigating, we found that when the old St. Louis sugar beet factory had been demolished, that debris was also hauled to the plant site and buried there. Later, a backhoe operator told us that he had been paid to bury waste at the plant site, including veterinary medical waste. So it was definitely a landfill, and not a burial site.

And if they argued that the gravelly clay at the bottom was the liner, we could argue that it was not a double liner, and it did not have a leak detection alarm system.

When we raised the issue at one of our meetings, there was no immediate response from Scott or Stephanie.

A clue to their non-responsiveness lies in the internal documents we later received through a Freedom of Information Act request. Apparently Scott already had been using the term "landfill" to describe the plant site, which rankled Stephanie.

In January, 2004, Stephanie took Scott to task for "continuing to use [a] municipal landfill presumptive remedy approach or language."

116

Later in her comments, she said, "As was stated in our comments on the draft RI, the site should not be referred to as a landfill, as that implies specific construction requirements that were not adhered to during design and implementation of the OU1 RA in the early 1980s."

Most likely Scott and Stephanie's lack of an immediate response at our meeting had to do with the fact that landfills and liners had been a part of their contentious discussions for several months prior to Ed's legal argument.

Once again, we were in the middle of their crossfire, and we had placed ourselves there. Even so, we brought up the lack of a liner at the plant site every chance we got. We wanted the whole community to know that the leaking bottom of the plant site had to be dealt with.

One remedy was to dig everything up and haul it away, thereby creating a Lake St. Louis. Another was to dig up half the site, lining it, putting the contaminated dirt back, and then doing the same to the other half. In some way, shape, or form, the bottom of the site had to be addressed, or the site would not be remedied.

In the middle of the year, St. Louis hired a new city manager, Bob McConkie.

Before we had time to introduce ourselves to Bob, another newspaper article caused dissension between the city and the CAG. It was a long article in the Detroit News about the lack of Superfund money at the state level. People from MDEQ, Sierra Club, the National Association of Manufacturers, and others were interviewed, as was Murray Borrello from our CAG.

Mayor George Kubin was angry once again about St. Louis being seen as a toxic town. While the CAG accepted pollution as a reality until it was cleaned up, George hoped if it wasn't talked about, it wouldn't really exist. There's not a lot of meeting ground with such differing viewpoints.

It wasn't the best reception for a new city manager to be caught in the crossfire between the city and the CAG.

About that time, an opportunity arose to perhaps get the clauses about the tombstone removed from the original 1982 consent decree.

We had received notification that EPA and the State of Michigan would be filing a joint motion in court to amend the 1982 judgment in a very small way – the name "Custodial Trust" would be substituted for the name "Velsicol," to reflect the ownership by the Trust of the chemical plant property.

In Ed's view, if the 1982 Consent Decree was finally being opened, it was time to remove the requirement that the granite marker remain on the site. The Consent Decree had even spelled out the exact wording to be written on the marker:

WARNING

DO NOT ENTER

THIS FENCED AREA WAS THE SITE OF A CHEMICAL PLANT. THE GROUND CONTAINS CHEMICALS WHICH MAY BE TOXIC OR HAZARDOUS. THE AREA HAS BEEN CAPPED AND SECURED.

TRESPASSING IS STRICTLY PROHIBITED

For awhile the tombstone had been stashed behind the EPA trailer in a pile of rocks on the plant site, but now it was standing upright, placed even nearer the roadway so that it could be seen and read. It remained a humiliating reminder that a 52-acre parcel of prime downtown riverfront land was considered to be dead and dangerous. We thought it would do a world of good for the community as a whole to have the tombstone gone.

When we found out that the Stipulated Order had been lodged with the DOJ, the comment period was nearly at an end, and Ed rushed our comments into the mail. The judgment was amended, however, only in regard to the name change. Even so, our comments received a response and were now a part of the record. If posterity should look to see if we had attempted to get the tombstone off the plant site when this opportunity presented itself, they will see that we, indeed, tried our best.

In the bed of the river, much work was taking place. In addition to the cleanup going on in St. Louis, Eric van Riper from MDEQ was conducting an historical survey and sediment sampling upstream in the Pine River within the Alma city limits, and Scott and his contractors from Weston Solutions were collecting samples of sediment, floodplain soil and biological specimens downstream from the chemical plant.

In the impoundment area behind the dam, the Emergency Removal that had taken place in 1998-99 had removed about 30,000 cubic yards in the highly contaminated hotspot, costing the taxpayers $8 million.

Phase 1 of the sediment removal project (1999-2003) had removed about 350,000 cubic yards of contaminated sediment from the south side of the river at a cost of about $50 million.

Phase 2 was now underway and was expected to last through 2009, removing about 300,000 cubic yards of material and costing about $47 million.

The water treatment plant was processing about 2,000 gallons a minute and returning the clean water to the river. Up to 70 trucks a day were carrying stabilized sediment from the plant site to five locations around the state for disposal.

Then a change was announced. Stephanie said that the cleanup of the river sediment was ahead of schedule and that the project would end in 2006 instead of 2009. This caused great concern, because we had expected the river impoundment cleanup to fold into the plant site cleanup, which would allow the Superfund dollars to keep flowing.

If the river project ended before the plant site project started, that could mean that the plant site would go to the bottom of the National Priorities List and be years away from receiving dollars for a cleanup.

But perhaps this was a bluff, another barrage shot from EPA across the bow of MDEQ to get Scott to complete his testing and write the RI and FS. We didn't know for sure, but there we were, again, caught in the crossfire.

Our Executive Committee brainstormed, and the consensus was that we needed to get our elected representatives involved. We contacted Jim Turner, aide to Senator Carl Levin, and found that the senator would stop by to see the site for himself on a quick pass through our part of the state.

We asked both Stephanie and Scott to give brief talks at Penny Park during the senator's visit, describing both the cleanup underway in the river and the one being planned for the plant site. We all met at the park, Senator Levin arrived, and Scott and Stephanie both spoke concisely and well.

Ed and Murray also spoke from the legal and scientific angles, and then I said something from the community angle. We each expressed, in different ways, our concern about the EPA's artificial separation of the river and plant site into two Operable Units, and the further concern that funding for the plant site cleanup might not be forthcoming if the river cleanup ended too early. Levin understood, and turned to say to one of Stephanie's bosses that he didn't see any reason for the river cleanup to be separated out from the plant site cleanup. The EPA official said it was simply for funding purposes, and Levin said, "That's my point."

Afterwards Theo of CH2MHILL said to me that our CAG was "awesome." I asked him what he meant. He said he had been impressed with "how we had our act together with Senator Levin," with each of us presenting a different angle. I told him we had not planned that part at all. One of the benefits of having worked with the same core group of people for seven years was that by now we all knew the same story and we each knew when to join in with our part of the narrative to make sure the whole story was told.

Meanwhile, the money from the Fruit of the Loom bankruptcy settlement earmarked for the Breckenridge Site had flowed into the proper account, excavation had begun, and in November it stopped. The contractor, Environ, had run out of money.

More accurately, workers had found "more waste present at the site than was previously known," contractor David Heidlauf wrote to me in an email. It was an "I told you so" moment. At the Fruit of the Loom bankruptcy hearing when the NRC people had declared that $700,000 would be enough to dig it all up and dispose of it in Utah, our CAG members had reminded them that usually Velsicol's estimates for amounts of waste were low. Yet NRC had assured us that the $700,000 would be sufficient to get the job done. If only they had listened. If only agencies would learn to tap into local knowledge, rather than assuming that their expert knowledge is enough.

Later Environ used the last bit of money in the Breckenridge Account to go back out to the site and make tests to determine more precisely the extent of the contamination. And then the site sat unfinished for many more years.

At the very end of 2004, we heard through the grapevine that Oxford Automotive, with a factory in Alma, was filing for bankruptcy protection. This was one of the companies we had urged the State Attorney General's office to go after for dumping at Smith Farm. When the company had pleaded off due to a shortage of funds, we had kept our eye on them, and when Gary Smith heard that one of their large contracts from Ford Motor Co. had been withdrawn, we wondered if they would continue in business.

It was our policy to not go after companies that were providing jobs in the area, since our economy was suffering with high unemployment. But once a company filed for bankruptcy, they were fair game. Ed tracked down an Oxford bankruptcy claim form and filled it out, explaining in a letter to the judge that we wanted restitution from the company for the dumping of chemical and heavy metal waste into the Pine River.

Ed mailed the claim form and the letter on Dec. 24, 2004. We were hoping for a present from Santa.

Chapter 10
(2005 Part 1)
An Unexpected Result

One of our founding CAG members, Jim Hall, attended fewer meetings and took off many days from work as he and his wife traveled to and from the C.S. Mott Children's Hospital in Ann Arbor with their baby girl who had been born with multiple defects. Jim wondered if his lifelong exposure to chemical pollution had contributed to the difficulties his daughter was born with. His was one more story of a person wondering and never getting any answers.

Still seeking a comprehensive health study for our community, Ed had kept in touch with the federal ATSDR people, and planned a Health Symposium for January. A number of sessions would take place throughout the day, centering mainly on PBB and DDT and their health consequences, and allowing time for questions from the participants at each session. We hoped that something further would result from the symposium, namely an ATSDR-sponsored comprehensive health study, but we had no assurances in that direction

The Health Symposium workshops started in the afternoon at various locations on the Alma College campus, with the large meeting held in the evening in a small auditorium. We had a good turnout from the community. Despite the long hours, there is very little to say about this portion of the Symposium. Nothing new was said by ATSDR, and no pledges were made by them to do any kind of follow-up work in the community.

Our Executive Committee held a session the following morning with Alden Henderson, a PBB expert from ATSDR. This session focused on our idea of using infant blood spot cards as a possible way to gauge DDT and PBB exposure in humans in the 1970s and 1980s as compared with today.

Alden liked our idea. During our session with him, he put through a conference call to Dr. Dana Barr at CDC in Atlanta, and we brainstormed with both of them about how to get started with such a study.

Dana had new analytical technology that she was eager to use in this capacity. Furthermore, she would do the initial testing of the blood spot cards without expense to us. That was a welcome surprise.

Alden offered his help as a technical advisor to get us through the first step, which was to obtain anonymous samples from the state health department, and send them to CDC for the initial testing to see if DDT and PBB could be detected in the tiny spots of blood. If that step was successful, he said he would offer the services of ATSDR to help with a pilot study linking the names on the cards with the individuals in a follow-up survey of health, again without expense to us. Again, we were surprised and pleased.

Even with the expense-free assistance graciously offered by these two people, we had a difficult time getting the study underway, and the snag came with our state health department. I'll pick up the thread of the story when I write about the events of 2006, because it took that long before the study moved forward at all.

Surprisingly, our claim in the Oxford Automotive bankruptcy lawsuit had not been thrown out. When some paperwork arrived in the mail, Ed Lorenz said it would be a waste of time to fill it out since unsecured claimants rarely receive anything in a bankruptcy settlement. Also, he had heard that Oxford had moved all its assets to Europe to escape paying the claims, if possible. Gary Smith argued that it might not be a waste of time to submit a claim because someone "out there" might benefit from our efforts, even if it was not us. He thought Ed should file the proper response and "see where it goes." And I reminded the group of our past "shots in the dark," namely Horse Creek and the Fruit of the Loom claim. Why not give it a try?

Ed filed the paperwork, and the Pine River Superfund Citizen Task Force became an unsecured claimant.

Next, we received a ballot in the mail that was sent to all those who held unsecured claims against the company. The ballot offered three options:

1) Anyone with an unsecured claim could opt to receive $500 and release Oxford from all further claims. This option gave persons and businesses a small remuneration who might

otherwise have received nothing, and cleared the field for the Oxford lawyers to move ahead with the claims from large creditors.

2) We could vote to accept the general outline of the settlement, and hold out for the unlikely event that Oxford would have enough assets left after paying the secured claims to pay something on our unsecured claim.

3) We could vote to reject the settlement.

Ed said if our primary reason for filing the claim was to get EPA and other government agencies to intervene, as they had in the Fruit of the Loom bankruptcy case, then we should vote to reject the settlement to buy the agencies some time.

That's what we did, and very soon after that, the EPA attorney for Region 5, Gaylene Vasaturo, sent emails to me and to Ed, wanting to talk with us about the Oxford bankruptcy. Ed also received a letter from an attorney at the Department of Justice, thanking us for our letter sent with our initial claim form. It seemed as if things were percolating within the government.

The DOJ attorney also asked for documents that would help them build a case to show that the river contained unacceptable levels of chromium and other metals that Oxford may have dumped.

We knew we had one report from the late 1960s from the state DNR saying they had found hexavalent chromium coming from the factory into the river. More recently, Melissa Strait and her students had found that compound while sampling sediment, but her report was not official. We began a search to find more up-to-date documentation showing that the chemical was still present in the river sediment.

A hearing took place at the bankruptcy court in Detroit at the end of February. We didn't go.

Afterwards Ed received a phone call from an attorney representing legitimate creditors who were unhappy with the size of our claim of $100 million. We had chosen that number since it was costing almost that much to clean up the 36 acres of the river bottom near the chemical plant, and would likely cost that much to clean up the two-mile stretch of the river from the Oxford factory down to the chemical plant site.

The same lawyer called me, and tried to reason me out of our claim by remarking that no one had ever received the amount they claimed in a bankruptcy settlement. When that didn't sway me, he tried to shame me out of our claim, saying that others would get nothing if we were awarded that much. When I still didn't acquiesce to his view, he got angry and ended the conversation.

The next phone call Ed received notified us that a motion would be filed by the other unsecured claimants asking that our claim be dismissed. We fully expected that the judge would throw out our claim at this point, and that would be the end of it. We had the right to challenge the motion to dismiss, but in the end, we decided to let the motion be filed without a challenge.

The motion to dismiss our claim started out by calling us a "watchdog" group (their quotation marks), and ended up referring to us as "nothing but a watchdog group." Those were just the personal criticisms. The substantive criticism was that we had no claim.

- We were not a creditor or a real party of interest, and had no standing.
- The real party of interest was the State of Michigan who had already filed a claim.
- We were not a government entity so we had no right to a priority claim.

We couldn't argue with any of that.

They also said that only the Velsicol Superfund Site was within our purview, and that we had no business filing a claim against Oxford, since it was not part of the Velsicol Superfund Site. That was worth arguing about.

Ed wrote a response to the motion that made it clear that we, as a CAG, were not precluded from entering into any matters of concern that impinged on the Pine River, and we cited our interventions into the Total settlement and the Fruit of the Loom settlement. Then he argued that even though we were not the "real party of interest" as pointed out in the motion, we remained concerned about costs to the community, such as the loss due to the total fish-consumption ban on the Pine River, and the loss to the Saginaw Chippewa Tribe, whose treaty rights had been violated by the fishing ban.

In the motion to dismiss, the other party had said there was nothing to tie Oxford's wastes to the Velsicol Superfund Site. Our response referred to the 1970 dredging of the river that mixed the heavy metals from Oxford with the pesticide wastes on the Velsicol site. We also referred to the fact that the NAPL now found in the Velsicol site contained five metals above safe levels, including chromium.

In emphasizing that there was nothing to tie Oxford's wastes to the Velsicol Site, the motion to dismiss stated, "The only commonality between the Debtor's property and the Velsicol Site is that they both are located in the same county and border on the Pine River." The sentence was written to be dismissive of our claim, but in my view, it was an argument *for* our claim. Hello! We live in Gratiot County where both Velsicol and Oxford are located, and we want the river that both of them polluted to be cleaned up!

Still trying to buy time for DOJ or any other federal agency that chose to enter the fray, we requested that the court delay decisions concerning the Oxford bankruptcy until the RI/FS and the final ROD for the chemical plant site were issued by EPA; or that the other attorneys enter into negotiations with us to resolve our claim.

With this written response to the court, Ed enclosed copies of the old hexavalent chromium report, a New York Times article about the 1982 Consent Judgment, a copy of the letter from the Saginaw Chippewa Tribe to Velsicol about the 1819 Treaty, a report on the dredging of the river, and a number of more up-to-date letters and reports to support the arguments laid out in our response.

We had felt that the "watchdog" label was a little insulting, but more insults were yet to come. The other side's response to our response contained language that was meant to be scathing. It was as if the writer had flown into a temper and thought she could slap us down. I use the pronoun "she" because later we met her.

Ed felt somewhat deflated, because he'd done his best to make our response fit into the legal format, and the belittling tone in the Oxford response bothered him. The rest of us cheered him up, and we noted that our opponents had the capacity for temper tantrums, which encouraged us to continue the fight with calmness and patience. After all, we still had nothing to lose!

A hearing was scheduled for the motion to dismiss at the bankruptcy court in Detroit. We tried to line up some pro bono help, or even a lawyer who would represent us for the $900 we had in our CAG checking account, but we couldn't find anyone to help this time around.

Gary Smith and I were the only ones available to go the hearing. Neither of us felt prepared for the court appearance, but it was imperative that someone from our CAG be there. Gary said he wanted to arrive at the courthouse early to "get the lay of the land."

After the 2 ½ hour drive, we parked, went through security, and found the room where our hearing would take place. We sat down for awhile and watched and listened to other cases.

They came and went rapidly. These were not Perry Mason trials, that's for sure. A case would be called, the lawyers would go forward, they would say a few words, and the judge would ask one or two questions, make a quick statement, and that would be it. Next case.

We left the courtroom and went to the ground floor to the cafeteria. Rosemary Horvath, a newspaper reporter from our local paper, showed up, and she ate lunch with us. Then we returned to the hearing room.

As the time for our case drew closer, we figured out who the Oxford lawyers were when they came into the room. We knew that one of them, named Judith, would be there, and we picked her out. She was very animated in her conversations with other lawyers, and we overheard her wondering out loud if "they" knew about a certain statute, and it sounded to us as if the "they" was our CAG. Chances are we didn't know about the statute.

I felt very shaky and I tried to pray, but I didn't know what to pray for. Finally I said, "Dear Lord, surprise us!"

Our case was called.

Three lawyers for Oxford went forward, and Gary and I did, too. Judge Steven Rhodes asked each person to introduce him- or herself, and we did that. Gary said his name and that he was with the Pine River Superfund Citizen Task Force, and I did the same.

Judith talked very fast, and with an attitude of complicity with the judge, as if he were already on her side in the matter.

She began telling him how we had no standing as claimants of any sort, and essentially launched into her argument against us, saying that the $100 million was an absurd amount of money to ask for, and that the deadline for the federal government filing claims on our behalf had ended in June, and…and the judge stopped her.

Then he turned to us. He said to Gary, "Are you an attorney?" and Gary said, "No, sir, I'm not." He asked me the same question, and I said, "No, sir, I'm just a citizen." Then he asked if the Pine River Superfund Citizen Task Force was a non-profit corporation, and I said we were. The judge asked if we knew that any corporation must have legal representation to appear in federal bankruptcy court. We didn't know that, and Gary apologized for having wasted the judge's time.

The judge assured us that we had not wasted his time, and that he wanted to resolve our problem. Would we be amenable to having him assign us a pro bono attorney? We said "yes," and thanked him.

That's when the fireworks started.

I was glad that big, tall Gary was standing between me and Judith when she burst out with one angry protest after another. I saw her arms flailing around, and I think she stamped her feet. I was shaking hard, partly from nervousness, but mostly because I couldn't take it all in, and yet I had to stay up at the podium while the clerk came to get my contact information. I could hear Judith, behind me now, yelling at someone, and then I heard the door slam. After I'd written down my name, address, telephone number and email address for the clerk, I found Gary, who'd already gone to where Rosemary was standing, and then the three of us left the courtroom.

Rosemary told us it was when she identified herself as a newspaper reporter and asked a question that Judith had shouted and slammed out of the room. That was very brave of Rosemary to even try!

The three of us lingered outside the doors of the courtroom. Rosemary really wanted an interview.

We could hear Judith the Angry going on and on, loud and upset, in one of the conference rooms, and male voices which were quieter, but not consoling. I doubt if anyone dared to console Judith the Angry when she was having a temper tantrum.

Finally Rosemary wrote one or two questions on a piece of paper, along with her contact information, and slid it under the door of the conference room. Then we took the elevator down and left the building. Needless to say, Judith never contacted Rosemary.

On the drive home, Gary and I kept remarking to each other about what had happened and how it had surprised us. What an unexpected result! We wanted the others to know as soon as possible. After several tries, Gary reached Ed on his cell phone. Ed was astounded to hear we'd been offered a pro bono attorney. Gary put him on speaker phone, and we could both hear him exclaiming that he'd thought the judge would have ruled on the motion to dismiss and thrown out our claim! He thought the judge would have ended it all at that hearing!

Well, he hadn't ended it, and he'd given us the opportunity to pursue it further.

I had been disappointed to learn, when Judith the Angry had stated it, that the date for filing claims had passed and neither DOJ nor any of the other governmental agencies had submitted one. We had hoped they might file one on our behalf, as they'd done in the Fruit of the Loom bankruptcy case. Gary saw it as a point in our favor. Since it was too late for the government to file, then it was up to us to press our claim for all it was worth.

We were assigned two young men as our pro bono attorneys, Tim Graves and Colin Darke. After completing all the necessary paperwork, we had our first conference call with them to determine the best approach for making a claim. They said to show that the Pine River Superfund Citizen Task Force had standing as an unsecured claimant, individual CAG members would have to write affidavits stating how they had been harmed. Tim and Colin said speculative injuries wouldn't get us any place, and that our thinking should take the form of "I used to do this, but because of Oxford, I don't do this anymore." For instance, "I used to go tubing. Then I read the report about the hexavalent chromium Oxford had dumped in the river, and now I don't go tubing anymore."

The affidavits would need to be written, notarized and in the hands of our attorneys before the next court hearing, which was less than two weeks away.

Meanwhile, Tim and Colin would write a supplement to the document we had already filed, and when they received the notarized affidavits from us, they would incorporate them into the supplementary response.

Murray Borrello, Arnie Bransdorfer, Lester Eyer, Norm Keon, Phil Ramsey, Gary Smith and Jake Stockton all wrote affidavits that ended up in the court papers.

Phil wrote about working at Lobdell/Oxford in the Plating Department, and how he had mixed the dry chemicals with various acid solutions, and how the excess ran into floor drains that emptied into the Pine River.

Jake wrote about working in the zinc-plating department at Lobdell/Oxford and how it was the company's practice to empty the solution out of the tanks once a month down the drains in the floor, which ran in a sewer line to the river.

Murray's affidavit was from the standpoint of a scientist having researched the various chemicals that Lobdell/Oxford had dumped, and how those chemicals had caused ecological degradation and measurable harm to the Pine River.

Arnie wrote about having often taken two of his sons fishing on the Pine River until the pollution got bad. He also recalled canoe races that were no longer held due to the pollution, and now his family had lost the ability to make use of the Pine River.

Les talked about his family's poverty when he was a 12-year-old in 1924, and how he had caught fish from the river, going door to door selling them to earn money for his family. Now, neither he nor anyone else could eat fish from the Pine River, due to the industrial contaminants.

Norm talked about the fear of swimming in the river due to the pollutants, and also the loss of aesthetic pleasure, since the river smelled bad due to the pollution.

Gary wrote that he did not let his children play near the river for fear of pollutants. He said he remembered when the no fish consumption ban was put on the river in 1974, and how people were even afraid to touch the fish for fear of the pollutants.

In their written document, Tim and Colin noted that the Bankruptcy Code had changed in 1978 to eliminate previous "concepts of provability and allowability."

They cited various cases in which an organization had been found to have a claim because the individuals in the organization had claims. They quoted from our Articles of Incorporation to show that it was our stated purpose to oversee cleanup not only of the Velsicol Superfund Site, but other related sites in the Pine River Basin, and to ensure that the sites were no longer hazardous to human health and the environment.

Even before completing the supplement to our response, Tim received a call from Judith the Angry. He said later that being on the phone with her was like going to the dentist, but Judith had made a settlement offer. She offered to let us say how much we would take to shut up and go away.

The others in the CAG Executive Committee thought we must come up with a number, with some saying $100,000 and some saying $1 million, but I suggested that the so-called settlement offer was backwards. An actual offer would be to have Judith name a price that we could accept, reject, or negotiate. It wasn't the right way around for her to ask *us* to come up with a number (and to call it an "offer" was an insult to our intelligence).

I advocated that we refuse this "offer" and go forward with the judge to prove standing. If Oxford made a genuine cash offer, then we would certainly need to consider it, but if we set the price, it would make it appear we were giving up our principles and rights as a harmed community for a few dollars cash.

And wasn't it the principle that mattered? The people who were left with the pollution from an industry *should* have a legitimate claim, *should* have legal standing, and *should* be expected to collect in the bankruptcy settlement of the polluting company.

The Executive Committee agreed, and I let our attorneys know that we wished them to go ahead with filing the argument.

That meant we had to hustle around and find more documents for them, including a map showing the river, the chemical plant, Lobdell/Oxford, and the refinery. The map also needed to show the two sewers used by Lobdell/Oxford that flowed to the river. Luckily Eric Van Riper of MDEQ had been collecting historical data on the Alma-area portion of the Pine River, and we were able to get what we needed from him.

We learned later that when Judith the Angry saw the affidavits from our CAG members, she had another temper tantrum. Tim and Colin told us about it in a conference call, and I could hear the anxiety in their voices. I suspect they may have been eager for us to settle quickly so that they wouldn't have to deal with her any more. I completely understood their reaction. They said the lawyer for the other unsecured claimants, the one who had called both Ed and me early on, also blew his top, and threatened "to bring sanctions against" Tim and Colin for illegally dumping contaminants. What? That seemed like nonsense, and of course it was an empty threat, but both young men were somewhat shaken by this encounter with the two Angry Attorneys. We, however, thought it boded well for us if our affidavits had upset the other side to that extent.

The hearing date was set back a week by the Angry Ones. Before that date arrived, we received an offer from Judith et. al. of $75,000.

In studying the arguments Judith had presented, Tim and Colin were finding them quite compelling, which was a worry. Another worry came from having found so few reports on what Oxford had discharged into the river. We felt that we could not produce enough evidence if we were to go to court.

Moreover, our attorneys uncovered in their research the fact that Oxford had filed for bankruptcy in 2002. We vaguely remembered having known about it at the time, but we thought the filing had been dropped or resolved somehow. Ed did some fast research on the first bankruptcy, sending the information to Tim and Colin, and also found a Consent Agreement that Oxford had entered into with EPA in which they agreed to monitor the aquifer under the footprint of the factory.

Despite Ed's belief that the Consent Agreement information would trump the arguments of the other side, Tim and Colin advised us to settle. Because the 2002 bankruptcy more or less had wiped the slate clean for Oxford, it meant that the individual members of Pine River Superfund Citizen Task Force had no grounds to bring a claim against the company, unless we knew of someone in our CAG who had been involved in dumping or other illegal activity *after* June 2002.

With this new information before us, we decided we had better get what we could and get out. It would be impossible to achieve standing through a court battle when this information about the previous bankruptcy was revealed. Apparently, the other side hadn't learned about it yet.

We gave Judith the Angry a counter offer of $100,000 cash.

She came back with two options:

1) a lump sum of $84,500

2) a claim of $1 million, with a payout of 7%-11%, which would mean an eventual cash amount of $70,000 to 100,000.

We chose option #2, because we were still more interested in achieving legal standing than in having perhaps as much as $14,500 more in cash. To have the courts recognize that our community had a genuine claim seemed like the true victory in our eyes.

I notified Tim that we would accept the offer of becoming a claimant with a claim of $1 million. I added that we were not interested in any further discussion of the matter with the Oxford attorneys, or with any other options or stipulations that they might propose. I said, "If those arise, we will reconsider everything."

As we had hoped, the negotiations ended, and we came to an agreement.

Rita Jack from Sierra Club wrote to us about our "precedent-setting" victory. I'm quite sure we were not the first community, but we are certainly among the first, to blaze this particular trail in the legal system.

In addition to our legal victory, we looked forward to possessing a CAG savings account larger than a few hundred dollars. The Oxford settlement money would not be paid into a DOJ Trust Account, or be regulated by EPA or MDEQ. Rather, it would go into our savings account, and be regulated by us!

There was more paperwork for our attorneys to write, and for us to approve.

Finally we received word that the last Order was entered by the judge which allowed the Pine River Superfund Citizen Task Force an unsecured claim of $1 million. Colin wrote, "I enjoyed working with all of you in resolving this matter—and I am very pleased with the outcome. Congratulations!"

All of our conversations with Tim and Colin had been via email or telephone. It was high time that we met face-to-face. We organized an Oxford Victory Celebration to acknowledge our CAG members who had written the affidavits, and to honor our pro bono lawyers who had performed so well for us. We held the dinner at the Heather Room at Alma College, and invited our various project managers -- Scott, Stephanie, Theo, Eric and Kim -- and several people from the City of St. Louis.

After dinner, various CAG members related the narrative about the Oxford claim, passing the recounting back and forth among us until the story was told and the whole group knew all the details.

It gave us great pleasure to meet Tim and Colin, and we appreciated their graciousness to travel up from Detroit to spend the evening with us. We wished them the best in their careers, knowing they were the kind of attorneys to go the extra mile for their clients. Since they had proved they could stand up to Judith the Angry, they would do fine in any legal battle!

After several months, the payments on our Oxford claim began to arrive, and altogether we banked almost $100,000. Yes, it was far short of $100 million, but it was a sweet victory nonetheless. And our hope was that other citizen groups would copy our efforts.

In 2009, we received correspondence from the Kalamazoo River Watershed Council who had been informed by Rita Jack of Sierra Club about our successful citizens' claim in the Oxford Automotive bankruptcy settlement. The spokesman for the group said their initial reaction in hearing about the award was disbelief as he had never heard of a citizens' group having gained status as a claimant. Now their group was seeking the court documents from our case in hopes of replicating our success. To hear from this group was a reward in itself.

Chapter 11
(2005 Part 2)
A Mutual Aim

A pressing concern for us was that the river sediment cleanup might end before the plant site cleanup began, thereby disrupting the funding flow, and perhaps delaying the plant site cleanup for several years.

Then we learned that the government had cut the EPA Superfund program by a third. For us that meant instead of $10 million a year for cleanup in the river, we would now receive only $7 million.

With that news, Stephanie and her bosses changed their plans. Instead of excavating the contaminated sediment in the mill pond in 2005, they would do a smaller project, which was to clean the area of sediment west of the Mill Street bridge in cell 8.

On the one hand, less money each year would slow down the river cleanup, perhaps allowing for the plant site cleanup to get underway. On the other hand, it could mean a much slower cleanup of the plant site in the years ahead.

We decided to write to our legislators, protesting the reduction in funding. Congressman Dave Camp took action and amazingly "found" a leftover $5 million in the Superfund allocation from the General Budget. The money was not earmarked for any project in particular, and Dave and his aide, Eric Friedman, redirected the money to our site. The additional money meant that the mill pond would be excavated in addition to cell 8 near the Mill Street Bridge.

For the downstream stretch of the river, our MDEQ project manager Scott Cornelius had received $500,000 from the Clean Michigan Initiative fund to help pay for sampling and lab tests on the biological material collected in 2003 and 2004.

In addition, he had received money to help pay back the state Superfund account for tests done on the plant site, to pay for more tests, and also to fund the Feasibility Study.

In the Alma-area portion of the river, Eric Van Riper had studied maps and books about early and modern industries.

Through sampling, he and his contractors, Weston Solutions, found two locations with elevated levels of PCBs, and the sediment samples tested well above regulated levels for semi-volatiles and metals. Eric was trying to determine sources of the contamination in hopes of tapping the shoulders of responsible parties to get them to pay for cleanup.

And Kim Sakowski had "found" some money within the tight state budget to pay for tests to determine the extent of the plume of vinyl chloride leaving the Smith Farm Site. Her sampling of the groundwater moved further and further from the site, following the plume under State Road and quite a distance in the westerly direction. A drilling rig was brought in to test both north and south of the site to see if they could determine how far the plume had moved in those directions.

By year's end they thought they had found its outermost perimeter, but they had no money to do anything about it. They also determined that the surface of the plume existed at about 20 to 24 feet below the ground surface, but they did not know how deep the plume itself extended underground. Kim said she would "put in" for more money for further tests, but didn't expect to receive it. She said likely nothing more would be done at that site.

Mayor George Kubin surprised me one day by saying he thought we should have a joint meeting to talk about the funding issue for the plant site. He wanted Murray Borrello and me to sit down with the new city manager, Bob McConkie, and himself. With what I know now, I'm sure both George and Bob wanted to get acquainted with Murray on their own, to see if their view of him was different than that of the former city manager, Dennis Collison.

The four of us talked about how fast the river project was moving and how slowly the plant site RI/FS was moving, with all of us agreeing that Scott needed to hear a message from us to pick up the pace.

We were also concerned that the downstream risk assessment that MDEQ had begun might slow down the entire plant site cleanup, since the projects were tied together. We agreed that we needed to raise this concern with Scott, as well.

In addition, Murray thought we should apply for an Emergency Removal Action through EPA for the plant site.

An ERA had fewer bureaucratic hoops to jump through than a regular remedial action plan, and it could perhaps begin before the river project ended. Murray thought he could use new data from EPA's Joint Sampling study (JSAP) to prove that the plant site qualified for an ERA. That's what he did, but even with the new data, EPA was not convinced that they should perform an ERA for the plant site.

Meanwhile, we had learned that EPA planned to convene a conference at the Keystone Resort in Colorado entitled *Collaborative Cleanups: Revitalizing America's Communities.* The blurb said the conference would focus on "multi-site" communities, of which we were one. Several of us found the money to register for the conference and pay our way there.

The conference wasn't at all what we thought it would be, however. Apparently, it was sponsored by the newer brownfield division of EPA, and was organized for EPA workers employed in this brownfield-style program. Their goal was to reverse the blight of contaminated sites quickly, and the conference highlighted pilot study projects.

These cleanups were actually beautification programs, with money given to groups to buy and plant pollution tolerant vegetation overtop of contaminated sites. At first it was very discouraging to me to learn that citizen groups around the country had agreed to these cover-ups, even seeming thrilled to have received the miniscule grants handed out to complete the projects.

Then I moved into a determined mode: this kind of cover-up *would not take place* in our community if I had anything to say about it. To even use the term "cleanup" when referring to the cover-ups described was a travesty, in my opinion. But if this was how EPA defined a "cleanup," then we needed to find a different word for ourselves that meant what we meant.

I began to write notes for a talk that I thought we should give during the free sharing time at the end of the conference. Gary, Ed, Murray and Carol scribbled notes for me to put into the talk. We were industrious note-takers at our large, round table.

A field trip by bus up to a new subdivision in the mountains convinced us beyond a shadow of a doubt that we would fight against that kind of clean-up with everything we had.

The houses were cute with kind of a 1950s neighborhood feel, built close together, and with green grass in the yards. Under the few inches of sod lay a geo-textile fabric, and under the fabric lay the tailings and contaminated soil of an old gold mine.

Murray whispered to us that he wanted to take a hike further up the mountain. Carol wasn't able to, because of her bad knees, but the rest of us went. We snuck away from the rest of the tour group, and hiked up to the back of the subdivision.

Sure enough, there we found a highly polluted stream with tailings all around. Yes, a fence divided the green-grassed subdivision from the mess up above, but is there a kid in America who wouldn't climb a fence to go exploring?

And they had the audacity to call this a "cleanup."

On the last day, when most of the people had left for home, we gave our mini-presentation with four slides to the remaining conference-goers. Very briefly we outlined our history and the 1982 failed burial and capping of the plant site in our community. Then we said the overarching theme we had observed at this conference was *resignation*. No one believed funding for full remediation would ever come their way, and they had become resigned to their fate, which made them happy to receive beautification grant money. I said, "Frankly, our CAG seeks *big* money," and told them about our efforts with Horse Creek, the Fruit of the Loom settlement, and the excavation going on in our riverbed. We were insisting on a full and complete cleanup of all our sites, which would be expensive.

Even as I used the word "cleanup" in the talk, I kept thinking, "we need a better word. These people think they have received a "cleanup" when, really, it is only a cover-up.

The response that followed our short presentation surprised us. First the assembly gave us a hearty round of applause, and then both EPA workers and a few community people stopped by to tell us how inspiring our talk had been. Maybe that's why we were meant to be there – to raise the bar for other communities, and also to learn the EPA definition of "cleanup."

Back home, the St. Louis City Council had written a resolution to be sent to EPA requesting excavation and removal of all the contaminated soil at the plant site.

When Mayor George Kubin read the resolution out loud to us at a meeting, I was struck by his choice of words. He wrote, "Now, therefore, be it resolved, that the City Council, after much consideration and research thereof, does hereby request a full removal and cleanup of the former Velsicol plant site by the United States Environmental Protection Agency and the Michigan Department of Environmental Quality.

"FULL REMOVAL." Those were the words I'd been seeking. I told George that both the city and the CAG needed to use those words in everything we said and wrote from there on out. *"FULL REMOVAL."* That described what we expected, and, so far at least, EPA had not re-defined either "full" or "removal." as they had "permanent" or "landfill" or "cleanup."

The war between EPA and MDEQ continued. It had been quite some time since both Scott and Stephanie had attended the same meeting. Was it coincidence that they each attended every other CAG meeting? Whatever it was, we wanted them both at the same meeting so that we could ask them the same questions and compare their answers.

The agency battle was also being waged on the ground at the plant site over levels of danger from a new chemical discovered in the mix, a chemical called 1,2-dibromo 3-chloropropane (DBCP). It had been found in the groundwater, the soil, and as a DNAPL. DBCP is persistent in the air and it causes male sterility.

Scott had his Weston contractors working in the DBCP area wearing full protective gear, including a self-contained, full-face breathing apparatus. In contrast, EPA had sent some CH2MHILL employees into the area wearing air sampling badges, telling us later they had determined the amount of DBCP in the air was below OSHA standards, so they did not have their workers suit up.

I guess in a few years we can find out who won this battle. I, for one, would rather have been on the side that believed in the adage "better safe than sorry."

Down in the riverbed, excavation was moving quickly. Again, it seemed as if EPA had speeded up the operation to finish as fast as possible.

Complaints from residents rose to the highest pitch ever, due mostly to the excessive dust blowing into their houses. It's true, the prevailing westerly winds were carrying dust to those who lived on the east side of the river more than it had to those who lived on the north and south sides.

Also, EPA/CH2MHILL were using much more beet lime to stabilize the sediments because they were excavating much wetter sediments, not waiting for them to drain and dry naturally. If they hadn't used the beet lime, the sediments would have been too goopy to remain in the bed of the truck to be brought up out of the pit and dumped on the drying pad. It all had to do with haste.

And even as they cleaned the river, NAPL was leaking back into the cleaned areas. At least that's what Scott's tests showed. When asked about the NAPL leaks, Stephanie was evasive, but implied that their findings hadn't shown re-contamination, and of course they had the "temporary, interim" NAPL collection trench in place to capture any leakage from the plant site.

As I mentioned, Mayor George Kubin had been attending our CAG meetings regularly for several months, and one evening after a meeting, he came up to me and said, "You were right and we were wrong." When I asked him what he meant, he said he now believed our group's way of making a big production in the press about the pollution in our town would ultimately help us to get the best cleanup. He said that Jim Turner, Senator Carl Levin's aide, had convinced him of the necessity of letting everyone know how bad things really were with the contamination in St. Louis.

George went on to suggest that a few people from the CAG begin to meet every two weeks with him, City Manager Bob McConkie and Downtown Development Director Phil Hansen to plan how to get more exposure in the press. Of course, I agreed.

As we were beginning this time of working together, a new circumstance arose. Our community was asked to forgive some of the debt Velsicol owed to the Trust Funds that had been set up during the Fruit of the Loom bankruptcy settlement in 2002.

The president of Lepetomane Trust, Jay Steinberg, asked for our approval of a legal document drawn up concerning the debt Velsicol still owed. Signatures were being gathered from DOJ, Velsicol, from EPA Regions 2, 4, and 5, and the states of Michigan, New Jersey and Tennessee.

This new Consent Agreement allowed Velsicol to hand over their AIG insurance policy in exchange for debt forgiveness. It seemed to us that this new Consent Agreement allowed Velsicol off the hook by freeing them from spending insurance money on remediation at the seven sites. Jay and the others saw it as moving Velsicol out of the way so that the states and EPA could directly collect the insurance money from AIG and spend it on the sites themselves.

Our CAG decided we needed a better understanding of the Consent Agreement, and we asked for a conference call with Alan Tenenbaum from the U.S. Department of Justice. We did get a better understanding, but we weren't happy about it.

During the Fruit of the Loom Bankruptcy Settlement, Velsicol had pledged to pay $30 million into the Trust Accounts for the seven NWI/Velsicol sites around the country by the end of 2004. By this time in 2005, they had paid in about $15 million, another $5 million was due to come in from another insurance policy, and, if everyone signed on to this agreement, they would pay $1.5 million out of their own pockets. That didn't add up, however, to $30 million.

Essentially, under this new Consent Agreement, we were being asked to forgive Velsicol a debt of $8.5 million that they had promised to pay in the DOJ brokered Fruit of the Loom settlement. In exchange, Velsicol was agreeing to give up its right to collect any money from the AIG insurance settlement for itself. Instead, the president of the Trust, Jay Steinberg, would negotiate with AIG and the money collected on the policy claim would be funneled into the Trust Accounts for the Seven Sites.

The fact was Velsicol, already a year late in living up to their former promise, was being let off the hook instead of being penalized for the money owed. DOJ and the Trust were polite in asking for our acquiescence, but really, there was nothing we could do, because the government entities had made up their minds to sign off on the deal. Once that was done, Jay Steinberg assured us his negotiations with AIG would be concluded by early 2006.

He was wrong, however. Suddenly, in December 2005, after Velsicol had the signed deal, AIG filed suit against the Trust, claiming they had known nothing about the 2002 Fruit of the Loom bankruptcy settlement, and were not obligated to honor it.

Our little Pine River was at the center of the dispute, with the insurance company arguing that the river was not part of the property they had insured. Even though Velsicol had used the Pine River as its disposal chute, AIG claimed it was not part of the manufacturing site and not part of their responsibility, and they were not paying out any money at all.

The insurance policy carried a cleanup cost retention clause that required $44.5 million to have been spent in cleanup costs before the $100 million policy would kick in. Jay argued that the $60 million EPA had spent so far in cleaning up the Pine River satisfied the cleanup cost retention clause. He argued further that the containment wall built around the Velsicol site had failed, allowing chemicals to leak into the river to contaminate it. He didn't try to argue that Velsicol had used the river in its manufacturing process, but only that the river had received leakage after the 1982 containment system was built, and therefore the policy applied. AIG contested his arguments, insisting that the river was never part of what they had insured.

In an attempt to settle the argument, Jay invited two environmental engineers for AIG, employees of Malcolm Pirnie, to tour the plant site and river in our town.

The morning of the tour, Jay called me and asked that I gather a few CAG members and meet the engineers at the Heather Room at Alma College. He wanted the representatives of AIG to meet the people and hear in our own words what we thought should be done.

Murray, Melissa and I spoke to them about the hardship the community was enduring due to the ongoing pollution from the Velsicol chemical plant. We told them it was for this very purpose that the parent company of Velsicol, Fruit of the Loom, had purchased the pollution insurance policy, and it was only proper for AIG to pay the claims.

We told them that the lawsuit was draining other money from our Trust Accounts, making our situation even worse. We needed that money to clean up the pollution. We told them if they dropped the lawsuit and paid up, it would be a nice Christmas present for our community, and we would let everyone know that AIG had behaved in an upright manner toward us.

Jay later said that we had spoken well and he was sure we had made an impression on the two engineers. That may have been true, but the lawsuit wasn't dropped.

Our Executive Committee began researching AIG and their subsidiary AISLIC (American International Specialty Lines Insurance Company), including information on how Fruit's purchase of the insurance policy had quelled a sell-off of their stock back when stockholders learned of the polluted NWI/Velsicol sites.

We were able to get a copy of the Fruit of the Loom insurance policy with AISLIC, and several of us eagerly read it. It was frustrating. One sentence would lay out a circumstance that would seem of benefit, and the next sentence would cancel what had just been said. It appeared to us that the policy had purposefully been written with enough cancellation clauses in it so that the insurance company would never have to pay out anything.

Maybe that's why Velsicol had been willing to turn over the policy to DOJ in exchange for debt forgiveness. If Velsicol knew the policy had been written to make it uncollectible, by turning it over they were only getting rid of a useless packet of paper, and in exchange received forgiveness of the $8.5 million they owed our Trust Accounts. That's the conclusion our CAG came to.

The war between Stephanie and Scott – between EPA and MDEQ – escalated near the end of 2005, when Mayor George Kubin received a quiet notification from EPA that a small amount of pCBSA (para-Chlorobenzene Sulfonic Acid) had been found in three of the city's drinking water wells. The unthinkable had happened. The drinking supply for the town was now compromised.

When George told us about the notification, Murray and Dianne Borrello and Melissa Strait went into research mode right away. Generally, there is a wealth of information on the internet about anything under the sun, but there was very little to find about pCBSA.

We learned that it is a by-product of the DDT manufacturing process, and is both toxic and corrosive, and that it is highly soluble and moves fast in groundwater. In terms of health, everything known about it was based on one 1985 study done with 20 rats for 28 days. In 28 days, the rats did not develop cancer or birth defects.

On this study, and only on this study, EPA based its assurances to the city and the community that pCBSA would not poison us even a little bit, even though the 28-day rat experiment took place in conjunction with a study in California that stated very clearly that humans were *not* drinking the pCBSA-contaminated water.

When Mayor George Kubin found out that EPA had known about the contamination in the St. Louis water supply for a year before telling him, he hit the roof. Not only had they kept the information from the city and its residents, but EPA also had failed to notify MDEQ. Most likely it was part of the war tactics, and was reprehensible. EPA's silence did not hurt the State of Michigan, but it hurt the community of St. Louis. Any trust EPA had built with the community came crashing down.

George set up a press conference. Representatives came from Booth Newspapers, Central Michigan Newspapers and three Michigan television stations. He opened the press conference by making a strong statement that the city wanted a *full removal* and cleanup of the plant site, and that they would not back down from that position.

Then EPA gave a power point presentation on pCBSA which seemed based around a pre-arranged agenda to undercut any worry about the contaminant. For instance, we were told that the highest levels of pCBSA found in any of the city's drinking water wells was 140 times lower than "current health criteria," which EPA said was 25,000 ppb for pCBSA. The presentation said nothing about the fact that pCBSA was not rated by the Safe Drinking Water Act or by the State of Michigan, and that EPA had chosen to base its health criteria on one 28-day rat study that emphasized the fact that humans were *not drinking the water*.

At the end of the press conference, George repeated his statement about the city wanting a full removal and cleanup of the plant site, which was the ongoing source of groundwater contamination, and he also said the city needed a new water system.

Stephanie stated that EPA had no plans to drill new water wells for the city. In contrast, a man from the state Water Quality division said that he expected the city would be ordered by the State of Michigan to shut down the contaminated wells.

144

So there we were. The war between Scott and Stephanie and their agencies had come to this clash over the city's water supply, and who was caught in the middle with the bad water and no funds to purchase a new well system? The City of St. Louis. The agencies fought and the community suffered the losses.

Soon after that, the city received a letter from MDEQ advising them to minimize the use of the three contaminated wells, and strongly advising them to find another source of water "as soon as possible."

Let's step back for a minute. We are talking about a town of 4,500 people who lost their tax base in 1982 when EPA and the State of Michigan made a deal with Velsicol, allowing the corporation to leave town without cleaning up its mess. Velsicol was allowed to shove most of its mess under the "rug" of a clay cap and wall, and was not required to lift a finger to clean up the river which had served as the disposal chute for their manufacturing activities since 1936.

So now this town that had been seen as expendable in 1982 by both the state and the federal governments was being kicked around by both governmental units again. The federal EPA said that there was nothing wrong with a little DDT by-product in the people's drinking water, and the state MDEQ was saying the city had better find a new water source. Did St. Louis have the money to build another system of wells? Of course not. And neither the federal nor the state governments offered to procure a new water supply for the city.

The fact is, both government entities were half the cause of the water supply going bad. If they had required Velsicol to clean up its mess in 1982, the contaminants would not have been allowed to travel through the groundwater for 20-plus years to foul the city water.

It was like a game of monkey-in-the-middle, with the city of St. Louis always in the middle.

Later, the mayor and city manager met with the aides of Senators Debbie Stabenow and Carl Levin and Congressman Dave Camp. Each of the aides agreed verbally at the meeting to support "total clean up and removal of the chemical site," according to George. They also pledged to seek funding for new wells.

Meanwhile, the city had shut down the two worst contaminated wells, and used the third contaminated well only when necessary, mixing its water with clean water from the other wells before piping it to homes.

Around town, the schools bought bottled water for their students, making drinking fountains off limits. A number of homeowners had private firms test their water, although it was unlikely that any of those firms had the special equipment necessary to test for pCBSA. In fact, our CAG had been told that only two labs in the country were capable of testing for pCBSA. A newspaper article interviewing various residents revealed that most townspeople were drinking bottled water, and that some people who had thought of buying a house in St Louis went instead to other towns when they learned of the contamination of the drinking water wells.

North of us, the city of Mt. Pleasant had been debating whether or not the fluoride additive in their water was safe, and an editorial cartoon appeared in the paper, playing off that debate. One person said he was in favor of fluoride in the water, the second argued against it, and the third person in the cartoon, with a badge saying he was from St. Louis, Michigan, said, "Drinkable water? I'll take whatever I can get."

The city, the CAG and residents had written to Senators Levin and Stabenow requesting help with the new problem of contaminated drinking water wells. In late October, we received a copy of a strongly worded letter that the senators had written to Thomas Skinner, the EPA Region 5 Administrator. In the letter, they took EPA to task for

- waiting more than a year to tell the city that its drinking water was contaminated
- failing to inform MDEQ that testing for pCBSA was taking place, and only informing them of the results after the city was informed, despite conference calls each week to discuss ongoing issues at the site.

They wrote, "This type of behavior erodes the public confidence and could contribute to making it more difficult for both the MDEQ and this community to trust information it is receiving from EPA."

Both the city and the CAG breathed a sigh of relief to have both of our U.S. Senators fighting for our community, as was our Congressman, Dave Camp. We were sick and tired of playing monkey-in-the-middle.

The EPA response to the senators excused EPA for not having shared the information with MDEQ by saying that pCBSA was not listed as a hazardous substance under CERCLA, and that EPA had determined that the amount of pCBSA in the city's wells "was not a problem." Not a problem? Maybe not to a bureaucrat in Chicago, but it was most assuredly a problem for a town whose municipal water supply was tainted with the compound.

The letter also stated that EPA had shared the data about pCBSA with MDEQ "during the normal report review and comment cycle," but later said, "Be assured that EPA will fully share all site-related information with MDEQ in the future." In essence, the letter-writer admitted that all site-related information had *not* been shared with MDEQ. In terms of the war going on between EPA and MDEQ, it was interesting to know this, but it didn't get the pCBSA out of the drinking water.

The old war between the CAG and the city, however, seemed to truly be at an end. George had told me about many instances when the Community Involvement Coordinator Stuart Hill had tried to divide the city from the CAG. The details he shared with me helped fill in the blanks about much we had suspected back then.

By the close of 2005, the CAG and the city were working together with the same mutual aim of letting everyone know how polluted St. Louis was, and together we were loudly insisting on a full removal and complete cleanup of the plant site.

Chapter 12
(2006 Part 1)
A Constant Battle

In preparation for receiving the Oxford settlement payout, we had set up a separate bank account, putting a little of our money saved from dues and contributions into the account to keep it open until the checks arrived. In April we received a check for $90,000, and in September we received the second and last check for a little over $8,000. To have on hand $98,000 with no strings attached gave us a sense of stability.

Between the time of receiving the big and small checks from Oxford, we ran into difficulties with the EPA TAG grant. Our treasurer, Gary Smith, had made an error, failing to file a report in March that he was preparing to file in September. This happened because in a previous transaction with the TAG grant, we had asked EPA for an extension of our old grant, but instead, they had actually given us a new grant, so the report filing dates were different.

Gary immediately telephoned to explain his error, and to ask that the grant not be terminated. Even though he was assured over the phone that the problem would be rectified, nothing happened, and the grant was terminated. With the Remedial Investigation report release date set for July 11th, it concerned us to not have access to grant money for hiring consultants to render second opinions on the data contained in the document.

Gary, Ed, Murray and I composed a letter that explained the immediate problem and also reminded the EPA TAG people that we had been frugal in our spending, having kept the bulk of the grant for when the Remedial Investigation report was released. Because the studies of the plant site had taken many more years than first expected, we had been slow in using the grant money, and therefore, had often asked for time extensions on the grant. We apologized for missing the report deadline date and asked that the **terminated grant be reinstated.**

A month later, more phone calls and another letter yielded words of assurance, but no money.

It didn't make sense to us that an error of filing a report on a certain date from a volunteer organization should be so difficult to sort out.

When silence followed Ed's second letter, I called the EPA TAG person, explained the situation again, and was told that our grant had been re-instated and that we would be receiving a letter to that effect. No letter came, and we still could not electronically access the grant money.

Two more months passed, and Gary wrote a brief e-mail to the woman I'd talked with, enumerating the times he had called her without reaching her, and without her returning his phone messages. No reply.

By now it was easy to think in terms of a conspiracy theory. It seemed odd that as soon as our CAG had banked the first Oxford check, the EPA TAG grant should dry up. Were they hoping we'd spend down our Oxford money on supplies and fees and so forth and not have money available for a lawsuit if they failed to clean up the plant site to our standards?

I'm going to move ahead into the year 2007 to finish this story. Yes, it took more than a year to get our grant re-instated, and yes, we had to draw down on our Oxford money to pay our bills during that time.

We enlisted our EPA project manager in trying to resolve the roadblock with the TAG people, to no avail. Then we talked publicly at a CAG meeting in May of 2007 about getting our Congress people involved. Still nothing. Gary continued to phone and email without getting responses.

In August of 2007, a year after I'd been assured that the grant had been reinstated and that a formal letter of reinstatement would arrive shortly, I received a phone call from an entirely different EPA person saying she needed certain reports from us to close out the TAG grant that had expired more than a year before. I explained that we had submitted the reports back in 2006, and I gave her the name of the person we had sent them to.

Apparently she tracked them down, because finally EPA managed to close out the old grant, enabling us to apply for a new grant. Gary re-copied all the financial information, letters, reports, plus new reports for the past year, and sent them to a third entirely new TAG person. By the end of 2007, we were finally able to access TAG grant money again.

We couldn't help but contrast our error in filing a report on time and Velsicol's "error" in failing to pay $30 million on time into the Trust Accounts for the seven NWI sites. In Velsicol's case, EPA and the other government entities did not penalize the corporation, but quickly forgave Velsicol the $8.5 million still owed, while our volunteer, non-profit group was not forgiven, but instead punished by having to wait a year and a half before the grant was reinstated.

Then a double whammy came from EPA when they assigned us both a new project manager and a new community involvement coordinator. The amount of volunteer time to bring a new project manager up to speed on a site like ours is immense, and the same goes for a new community involvement coordinator. I could see how this set of circumstances of no grant money and new EPA personnel could cause a less cohesive CAG to crumble.

After Stephanie was removed as our project manager, most likely because of her tardiness in reporting pCBSA in the drinking water, Becky Frey came on board. We did our best to inform her about the facts and to have her get to know us as people. She seemed reluctant on the second part of the equation.

We began to wonder if she'd been sent to deliver bad news about the Remedial Investigation report, and that she preferred to not know the people who would have to live with the bad news.

On her first evening with us, she described the EPA Remedy Review Board process that takes place on any orphaned site that will cost more than $25 million to clean up.

From 2003 to 2006, we had listened to programs on the Remedy Review Board process three times, being assured that the RI was due any day. We had prepared for the Remedy Review process that many times, spending many hours collecting data and our thoughts and putting them in written form. All of that sincere, heartfelt effort our volunteers had expended, and yet we had no RI yet, and no shovel in the ground at the leaking plant site.

As a CAG, we spent far too many of our precious volunteer hours in listening over and over again to the same descriptions, the same reports, and in preparing the same letters and documents to support our firm resolve to have the plant site fully removed and completely cleaned up.

It was in the middle of our TAG grant crisis when Stuart Hill announced that he was stepping down as Community Involvement Coordinator and leaving the area. In his eight years as our CIC, he had been, at best, a puzzle to us, and at worst an antagonist. Nevertheless, at the end of Stuart's last meeting with us, I led the group in giving him a round of applause, because it was the right thing to do.

So now we had a new project manager, a new community involvement coordinator, no grant money, and yet it was time to hire an outside consultant, and on top of that, the river impoundment cleanup was winding down without the plant site work beginning, and without even a Remedial Investigation report in place to tide us over and to keep the funds flowing for cleanup.

Moreover, the Fruit of the Loom insurance policy was due to expire in the summer of 2008, and no work was taking place at the plant site that could be charged as expenses to add up to the necessary $44.5 million before the insurance policy could be accessed. The tension was high.

Meanwhile, Theo von Wallmenich, project manager for the EPA contractor CH2MHILL, was overseeing the extraction of the giant sheets of steel that had formed the coffer dams in the river. In the spring of 2006, his workers dewatered the cells for the last time to dig out the road they had built across the river for hauling excavated sediments from the north side of the river to the staging area on the south side.

As they finished the last excavations, and the drying and hauling of the last loads of sediment, and when they had finished cleansing the last gallons of run-off water and returning them to the river, then they removed the large, white structure that had housed the water treatment plant, took down fences they had put up to keep people away from the river, repaired sidewalks and road surfaces, and removed their trailers.

All that was left behind were the fence around the perimeter of the plant site with its signs alerting of toxicity and radioactivity, and the tombstone to warn people away.

It was good to have the job finished, and yet it was an adjustment to have the work crew gone.

Always before when we had felt frustrated at how little we were accomplishing as the years went by, we could point to the ongoing river sediment cleanup and remind ourselves that at least that site was on its way to completion. Now, with it finished, we had nothing ongoing to point to.

The Breckenridge Site that we had hoped to cross off our list had come to a complete halt when the Fruit of the Loom bankruptcy settlement money had run out. Smith Farm had received its "interim response," which was a cover-up with orange snow fence laid down on the chemically contaminated soil with a sparse layer of clean dirt spread on top. MDEQ had ceased the pump and treat operation at the Gratiot County Landfill and had contacted the Gratiot County Board of Public Works to tell them they now were in charge of maintenance of the site. The Golf Course/Burn Pit Site had been rolled into the Plant Site Remedial Investigation, and we were not comfortable with that decision. And the Plant Site RI had been delayed at least a dozen times in the last several years. Nothing was getting cleaned up. And as Carol Layman told EPA and MDEQ at almost every meeting, "We are losing another construction season!"

Maybe the lack of headway at any of the sites, and our feelings of restlessness, help explain why both Ed and Murray took on other projects during this time. They had become involved through the college with a planning committee for what was called an Energy Research Park. They were, apparently, sworn to secrecy by the entrepreneurs who hoped to build their research park on the site of Total Refinery in Alma. The City of Alma, Greater Gratiot Development, and Alma College were taking part in the initial thrust to help the entrepreneurs bring their concept to Alma.

When the first article came out in the newspaper, it sounded good, because the plan included research and development of wind, solar and hydrogen power. The research park was to employ 700 to 1,500 highly skilled people and cover a total of 1,200 acres.

The entrepreneur told the newspaper that he likened his project to "a university or scientific approach to research in the field of energy." That's why he had drawn Alma College into the planning stage of his development.

When the second article came out, two little red flags waved at me. Supposedly Gratiot County was the perfect place for the energy research park because it had underground *oil pipelines*. Furthermore, the article said that the research park would "encompass bio fuels, along with *fossil fuels*, wind, hydrogen and solar energy. Fossil fuels? Could it be that another oil refinery was coming to town?

When I asked that question in an e-mail sent to members of our Executive Committee, Murray wrote back, "Shhh...No one is supposed to know at this point that a refinery is part of the project."

It seemed that the entrepreneurs' strategy was to start out talking about solar and wind power, and then work up through bio fuels to finally revealing their true intention, which was to bring another oil refinery to our community. By using the words "energy research park" people were being manipulated into a receptive mood. The word "park" brings up an image of a green space that should be a safe place for children to play, and the word "research" brings up the image of precise, clean investigation, and not factory production with the inevitable sights, sounds and smells of the processing of crude oil.

Gary's reaction to the proposed "energy research park" was to say, "Hey, maybe I can get a job there." He had worked at Total Refinery for years, and now that it had shut down he had to drive to Midland to work at Dow Chemical Corporation. My reaction was to say that we needed to discuss this proposed "park," even if Murray was reluctant to reveal his secret knowledge, and wanted to swear the rest of us to secrecy as well.

Next we learned that the "energy research park" planned to build an ethanol plant and also a clean coal plant. What happened to solar, hydrogen and wind research? They were never mentioned again.

Murray and Ed did not want us to scare jobs away by raising concerns about the end goal of the energy research park.

I was of two minds about that. Yes, we wanted highly skilled jobs in a research park that was developing clean, alternate energy sources, but we didn't want the fumes that made your eyes water, the stinky smells, the noise, and the polluted surface and groundwater that oil refineries brought with them.

Both Ed and Murray tried to assure me that in this day and age, a refinery would have to be run much cleaner than Total's operation had been run, and I was sure they were right about that. Cleaner still, though, is no refinery at all.

When I told Murray that I feared he and Ed had compromised themselves by taking part in a secret committee designed to bring an oil refinery to Alma, he said he appreciated my point of view, and that he wished I had been at the meeting to interact with the developer, because my fears would have been assuaged. He felt it was essential that we not be "hostile" to this new economic opportunity for the community.

Ed felt the same way. He said it was time for "enthusiastic, if watchful, support for the energy park." He remonstrated, saying that the CAG needed to be "mature, responsible participants in this process."

Neither Ed nor Murray had told the secret committee they were CAG members. Some of the people on the committee knew they were, but the developers did not. I suggested they make it clear when they attended the meetings that they were wearing two hats. I also encouraged them to openly share information with the rest of the CAG members and not keep secrets from us. I said in an e-mail, "Divisiveness, disunity, and resentment are the only fruits I can see coming from the act of withholding knowledge and information on a project of this magnitude, and of such vital concern to the CAG."

All of our discussions took place prior to the entrepreneurs publicly acknowledging their plans for a refinery. It was about a month later when the newspaper reported that the "Great Lakes Energy Research Park" would have a coal gasification plant, an ethanol plant, a bio diesel fuel plant, and, when questioned, the entrepreneur said he wouldn't rule out an *oil refinery*. All of this was to be in addition to the research center, run by "really smart people," the paper quoted one of the entrepreneurs as saying.

A few days later, the paper reported that instead of producing electricity with a clean coal plant, the "Great Lakes Energy Research Park" would now produce motor fuel, since it was more profitable than making electricity. It would also mean that a bigger plant – *"more of a refinery"* – would be needed, the paper reported.

There was silence for almost two years, and then the paper reported that the Energy Park's plans had changed again.

Now the coal plant would become a "coal-to-liquid plant, manufacturing synthetic gas and then gasoline – specifically, jet fuel." Gasoline and jet fuel were what Total Refinery had produced. We had gone full circle. No wind power. No solar power. No hydrogen. No electricity from coal. The "energy research park" was to be an oil refinery after all. Luckily, when the 2008 financial crisis arose, it quashed the entrepreneur's plans.

Meanwhile, in our efforts to help St. Louis compile evidence that it needed a new water system, we were still pursuing a 90-day rat study to accumulate up-to-date information on the health effects of drinking or bathing in pCBSA-contaminated water. We had asked Stephanie to apply for the rat study on our behalf, and then we asked our new EPA project manager, Becky Frey. Senator Carl Levin and Senator Debbie Stabenow wrote letters supporting our request.

When pCBSA was found in California's groundwater, then that state set an allowable daily intake (ADI) for humans of 35,000 ppb the contaminant, based on the single 28-day rat study. Later, USEPA set an ADI of 25,000 (why 10,000 less, no one seems to know). The State of Michigan did not have a criterion for pCBSA, but when the chemical was found in the St. Louis water supply, they used the same 28-day rat study to establish a residential drinking water criterion of 7,300 ppb. It was our view that, at the very least, a new rat study of 90-days should be undertaken.

As we worked on getting the rat study, Mayor George Kubin worked to get a new water supply.

He invited our Congressional representatives (both state and federal), several upper management officials from EPA and MDEQ, as well as project managers Becky and Scott, and also Murray and me from the CAG. Tables were set up in the city council chambers in a very large square, and every seat was filled, with others seated behind them. Senator Debbie Stabenow "attended" the meeting via speaker phone.

The greatest success of the meeting, in my opinion, was that Stabenow, Camp and Levin's aide, Jim Turner, all said in different ways, and in firm tones, that the entire plant site needed to be removed.

Congressman Dave Camp made the point that the pCBSA found in drinking water wells showed that a pathway was in place for worse chemicals to follow. He likened the pCBSA to a canary down the mineshaft. Richard Karl from EPA Region 5 agreed that pCBSA had been used by EPA as an "indicator."

EPA, however, said they did not have a reason to fund new drinking water wells for St. Louis since the pCBSA in the water was not an "imminent and substantial danger." In contrast, from across the table the MDEQ people pointed out that the city needed to find another water source as soon as possible.

It was the scenario we had seen for decades, with the city of St. Louis caught in the middle. This time, though, St. Louis was not going to get trampled on. As Council Member Jerry Church said in a no-nonsense tone at the meeting, "We've been jacked around enough."

City Manager Bob McConkie made it clear at the meeting that the city had a right to sue both EPA and the State of Michigan, because each of them had violated their own safe drinking water rules. The state's rule required a minimum distance of 2,000 feet from a public water supply for a chemical disposal facility, which is what the plant site had become when it was buried on site and capped. EPA had violated the Clean Water Act, and the state had violated its Safe Drinking Water Act, Bob maintained.

To see the city manager and council members standing up for themselves and for their residents pleased me very much.

Several years earlier when I'd covered the St. Louis city council meetings as a reporter for the Saginaw News, an aura of defeat had tinged each sentence spoken by the council. At this meeting, I didn't hear any of that despondency. Despite the tombstone still standing within the fenced plant site, the city itself was reviving.

As the year went on with dates for the release of the plant site RI changing from July, to September, to November, we began to say to each other, "You watch, they'll wait until December when we are getting ready for Christmas, and then they'll release it." We made that prediction because it seemed as if every major report came out when the volunteers in our group had the least time to consider it and write comments and responses.

Sure enough, between Thanksgiving and Christmas the eight volumes of the RI report were delivered by Federal Express to my house. We had about two weeks before the public meeting to read and digest five years' worth of data, much of which we had not seen due to the war between the agencies.

Tensions ran high among the members of the Executive Committee. The long RI delays and now the short time to absorb the immense document, and having this crucial responsibility placed upon us at this particular time of year made tempers short. Despite all this, we rallied together and focused on the upcoming public meeting.

MDEQ had handled all the arrangements for the meeting place, putting up flyers and placing ads in the paper.

As soon as we learned of the meeting date, we contacted the city to see if their utility bills had been mailed yet. They hadn't, and we were able to enclose a notice of the meeting in those bills, which went to all the city residents.

Ed wrote handouts to give to citizens who attended the public meeting, including a timeline of the plant site, starting in 1935, and the pertinent events for each of those years. He also made sample letters for the people to send to the governor, our Senators and our Congressman.

The turnout was good, with the St. Louis Middle School cafetorium quite full.

The presentations were boring, with little information that was new to me, since I'd read the RI beforehand. The risk assessment speaker didn't even make sense to my ears. After such a long wait for this presentation, it was a massive letdown.

After most of the people had left, EPA Project Manager Becky Frey came over to where I was talking with others and said something like this: "I don't know if the people got this, but I was really hoping they'd take away with them that the upper part of the plant site is not very contaminated, because it's the clay cap."

Well, yes, we knew about the clay cap that ranged in depth from 18 inches to three feet. Was she suggesting the cap made the plant site a safe place to inhabit?

In response, I emphasized how worrisome it was that most of the contaminants were down deep, only one or two feet from the water table, and how the whole thing had to go. The cap, the debris, the wet and dry soils, the whole mess had to be dug up and hauled away. I went on to say how insane it was for an unlined, illegal, hazardous waste landfill to be located next to a river. She didn't reply.

Later, in an email exchange with others in our group, I commented, "Good grief, was she doing a Chuck Hanson?" referring back to the Velsicol vice-president's suggestion to just build a parking garage over top of the plant site, and not worry about what was underneath.

Or maybe she was thinking in terms of the EPA *Collaborative Cleanup Conference* housing development we'd seen in Colorado. Perhaps she envisioned a geo-textile fabric spread over the clay cap, and houses built on top of it, and then a thin sod lain throughout the new neighborhood to make green front yards.

Dianne said she came away from the meeting with a sick stomach. She wrote, "Joe asked the question, 'when do the trucks pull up and start shoveling it out' – and I got the distinct impression that is not even being considered. EPA's remedy will be to repair the cap and put in a pump and treat system for the groundwater."

Gary wrote, "If you cannot stop the crap from continuing to go down and you don't want it to go down, you have to remove everything you can that is above. I see no other way to be certain of stopping movement of new contamination. Try the pump and treat on the stuff that has already gotten away from us if you want. What else is there to say or do? If you cannot guarantee it will work, we don't want it. If you are leaking water on the floor, do you just let the leak continue and mop it up for the rest of your life, or do you turn the damn leak off? I graduated from St. Louis High School. I know what I'm talkin' about."

Ed said what happened to us at the RI public meeting was intended to discourage questions. "The experts presented a 90-minute power point that was designed to be hard to see and difficult to interpret and make us feel foolish for wanting to ask the obvious – 'When is it going to be taken out?'"

Carol agreed about the power point. She said, "People who read power points out loud to us drive me up the wall. We're too stupid to read? The fact that they have totally ignored the health issues is also irresponsible. I think the data that has been gathered and the types of health issues in the area prove that all of the chemicals have had a detrimental effect on the community, especially for those living in the plant's backyard."

Ed added that EPA should "do less research and more digging."

That's how we all felt. Why the years of delay on the RI? What a waste of taxpayer money to have all those people year after year study, study, study (and bicker, bicker, bicker) when they could have been hiring excavating companies to dig it up and haul it away. I graduated from Alma High School. I know what I'm talking about!

Chapter 13
(2006 Part 2)
A Trip Together

With EPA saying it was not their responsibility to find St. Louis a new water supply as part of the plant site cleanup, and with the State of Michigan telling the city they *had* to find a new water supply, and with St. Louis refusing to be the soccer ball for the two agencies to kick around, life got interesting.

At our monthly dinner meetings which Mayor George Kubin had set up with a few of us from the CAG, Bob and George said they had a lawsuit on their minds as a way to get a new water supply for the city.

We gave them the name of an environmental law firm in Traverse City, and Bob and George set up a free consultation with one of the attorneys about their options. Ed and I were invited to sit in on the discussion.

The lawyer concluded that the city had a viable lawsuit, but he didn't think his firm would take the suit on a contingency basis. Since the city had no money to buy a new well field, and no money to pay for a lawsuit, they needed to find a law firm that would take them on a contingency basis.

We reminded Bob and George about Robert Kennedy Jr.'s visit to the Velsicol site two years before, and suggested his law firm as a possibility. Also, Ed and I informed them about the "other" insurance policy as a possible money source, the Velsicol policy with AIG that we'd heard about but never seen.

Soon after our discussion, a resident of St. Louis called a radio show that had been interviewing Robert Kennedy, Jr., commenting about the plight of St. Louis. Kennedy remembered his visit to our community and contacted City Manager Bob McConkie to see if his law firm, Kennedy and Madonna, might be able to help. Kennedy's firm then connected the city with a California law firm, Sher-Leff, which specialized in litigations involving municipal water supplies. With the information about the two $100 million pollution insurance policies, Sher-Leff took the case on a contingency basis.

The two pollution insurance policies were contracted by Fruit of the Loom and Velsicol through AIG's subsidiary, American International Specialty Lines Insurance Company (AISLIC). The Fruit policy had been part of the 2002 Fruit of the Loom settlement, and it covered the seven worst contaminated Velsicol sites that NWI had "owned," including the plant site in St. Louis and the Breckenridge radioactive site. The Velsicol policy covered the 161 other Velsicol contaminated properties, including three in our county: Smith Farm, the Golf Course/Burn Pit Site, and the Gratiot County Landfill.

Recently our attention had been on the Golf Course Superfund Site, now known as the Burn Pit. It was a five-acre area situated across the river from the plant site where Velsicol had burned waste. The waste had been transported to the Burn Pit either by truck, or by a large pipe that spanned the river to spill liquids directly onto the site. A photo taken in the 1960s, and given to me by CAG member Norris Bay, showed black smoke billowing up as waste was burned. The cloud of smoke would then move east over the residential neighborhoods, spreading its fallout as it traveled on the prevailing westerly winds. In its path were Saginaw Street, where a cancer cluster had been located, and the village of Breckenridge, where a mysterious outbreak of non-Hodgkins lymphoma had occurred while the chemical plant was in production.

During the shutdown and 1982 burial of the Velsicol plant, the Burn Pit area had been scraped and 68,000 cubic yards of unburned waste and contaminated soil trucked around to the plant site to be buried under the clay cap. In a 1981 letter written by a Velsicol lawyer to the EPA and Michigan's Department of Natural Resources, Velsicol argued that the wastes at the Burn Pit Site were non-hazardous, non-toxic, and even "non-ignitable." Velsicol was concerned that the agencies might view the plant site as a "reactivated" hazardous waste management facility when wastes from the Golf Course Site were brought there and dumped.

The letter says, "We would request that EPA and DNR both confirm that our removal of the non-hazardous golf course materials to the main plant site will not cause the plant site to be classified as an activated hazardous waste management facility under RCRA laws or Act 64."

161

That sounded as if they were concerned the plant site might become an illegal landfill.

The letter showed once again how the agencies bent over backward to give Velsicol what it asked for. EPA and the State of Michigan wrote an all-encompassing release for "Velsicol Chemical Corporation, its subsidiaries, parent companies, predecessors, affiliates, successors and assigns, and their officers, directors, agents, and employees, with respect to and from all violations of civil law and any and all claims for civil fines or penalties, damages, reimbursement, injunctive or other legal or equitable relief resulting from or otherwise relating to the disposal or presence of chemicals or other substances at the Golf Course Site or any migration or discharge of chemicals or other substances therefrom to the surrounding environs which has occurred, is occurring or may occur as a result of such disposal or presence of chemicals or other substances at such site."

Because the Golf Course/Burn Pit Site fell under a different pollution insurance policy than the plant site, we were concerned that the community might be losing access to a claim against the Velsicol policy by having EPA and MDEQ fold the Burn Pit into the plant site remediation plan. The agencies had decided that combining the sites would allow them to cover both in the same RI/FS. We understood their thinking, which was to acquire the necessary funding for both at the same time, and accomplish the cleanup of the whole area at once. Previously, it had seemed to us to be an effective and desirable plan. Now, though, with our better understanding of the two insurance policies, we theorized that keeping the Burn Pit separate might give our CAG an avenue for litigation that neither EPA nor MDEQ could take, because of having signed off on all the documents that released Velsicol from harm.

When we raised this issue at our meetings, our MDEQ Project Manager Scott Cornelius found the idea so interesting that he said he was going to talk with every attorney he knew to find out the answer. The CAG suggested that Ed write a letter on this issue to Alan Tenenbaum at the U.S. Department of Justice, and send copies to Gaylene Vasaturo at EPA, and James Stropkai at the Michigan Attorney General's office, which he did.

Almost immediately after receiving the letter, Gaylene called Ed and said that from now on she would insist that the Golf Course/Burn Pit Site be identified in all RI documents as a separate Superfund site.

She and I also talked, and when I asked if she had a copy of the Velsicol policy, she said she knew one existed, but she had not seen it, and doubted that she would be able to get a copy of it. This began our intensified two-year quest to get a copy of the Velsicol insurance policy to read for ourselves.

In the course of our investigations, Ed found a strange anomaly. He found that the Golf Course Site had been de-listed even before it was listed.

At that time, every Superfund site in the nation was placed on the NPL (National Priorities List) and rated as to its urgency for cleanup dollars. Once a site received a remedy, it was removed from the NPL, or "de-listed." In the case of the Golf Course Site, EPA and the State of Michigan had signed off on its supposed cleanliness after Velsicol's scraping and hauling work in 1981, in effect de-listing the site before it had been listed on the NPL.

Ed told the CAG that this was an error on the part of EPA, and that it could hurt the final cleanup, because with the Golf Course Site having been officially declared clean, it was conceivable that the upcoming Record of Decision would recommend nothing more be done at that site, despite recent testing which showed high levels of many chemical contaminants.

In fact, the site may still have been "ignitable" because of the high levels of benzene left in the soil.

We wrote a letter to EPA Project Manager Becky Frey asking that the Golf Course/Burn Pit site be put back on the NPL list.

Finally, in 2009, the matter came up for comments. Scott worked through his channels at the State of Michigan, and subsequently, Governor Jennifer Granholm wrote a letter to the EPA Region 5 Administrator asking that the site be placed on the NPL list. Murray and I also wrote comments in favor of re-listing the site that had been de-listed before it was listed. In 2010, the site made it onto the NPL.

An internal issue came up for the CAG when we became aware of severe agricultural run-off into tributaries of the Pine River, as large Concentrated Animal Feeding Operations (CAFOs) sprang up in Gratiot County. When we learned that a group from Grand Rapids planned to buy an entire section of land in Gratiot County and put in a hog CAFO, several people in the CAG sounded the alarm.

A few of them attended a meeting organized by another citizen group named ECCO (Environmentally Concerned Citizens Organization), to which county and state agricultural officials had been invited. Ed reported that when the citizens learned that local authority over the activity of CAFOs had been undermined and deleted through new legislation passed at the state level, they were upset and angry. They also learned that CAFO owners were allowed to keep secret the environmental reports about their operations that were compiled by state officials.

It put us in mind of the many old reports we'd read of state officials allowing corporations such as Velsicol to get away with environmental atrocities without the local citizens knowing what was going on until much later.

Ed and Marilyn Lorenz, Murray Borrello and Phil and Lois Ramsey got involved in the new anti-CAFO group, helping to organize it and providing it with information. A newspaper reporter contacted me and asked my views on CAFOs. I gave her my views, but I asked her not to print them, as I didn't intend to pour my energies into the CAFO issue, having only enough time and energy to keep up with CAG issues.

Soon after the first anti-CAFO meeting, the newspaper published an editorial that discussed "transplanted city folk" clashing with farmers, yet that was not the scenario in our rural county. Rather, the clash in our county was between well-rooted rural and small town folk, many generations deep, who were objecting to big factory farm owners moving in with a style of food manufacturing that is entirely foreign to rural and small town living.

Frankly, CAFOs could be set up in downtown Chicago as well as in a rural county such as Gratiot.

CAFOs do not require land. They do not require acres for hayfields, pasture, or for growing grains. They do not require good husbandry habits of crop rotation, allowing fields to lie fallow, and moving herds of animals from one grazing area to another so as to maintain sturdy pastures

We brought the CAFO issue up to the CAG membership, wanting them to decide if the CAG itself should become actively involved, since tributaries of the Pine River, and ultimately the river itself, were being compromised by the CAFO discharges. The membership voted that as a group, we didn't have the time, although we encouraged individual members to take part if they so chose.

I agreed with that decision, yet I worried that Ed, Murray and Phil would not have as much time for CAG issues with all the time and effort they were putting into anti-CAFO issues. And they worried that I *wasn't* actively involved in advocating against CAFOs, telling me that CAFOs were the new Velsicols, and implying that I wasn't stepping up to the new dangers as they felt I should.

One of our ongoing CAG projects, the blood spot study, had slowed to a stop, with the holdup occurring at the Michigan Department of Community Health. Once again, it was the legislated privacy statute causing the problem.

No one had ever before applied the new privacy law to drawn blood samples in which the person from whom the blood was drawn (the infant) did not sign a waiver for research to be done on the blood. That was the gist of the explanation given to us. For many months, Dr. Dana Barr of CDC had not found a way to satisfy the requirements as set forth by the state health department, and had not been able to acquire any blood spot cards for analysis.

We wrote letters to Senator Debbie Stabenow and Senator Carl Levin, who had championed so many of our requests, asking for their assistance. It wasn't until 2008 that Dana Barr finally had some cards to test, and she said the letters sent by the senators had expedited the process.

In a way, the bloodspot study was our fifth full-strength try for a health study, following the grant proposals submitted three times, and then the ATSDR Health Forum

Another CAG issue that had come to a standstill was the cleanup of the Breckenridge radioactive site, and we had no prospect of moving forward until the AIG vs. Lepetomane Trust lawsuit was settled.

I learned from a newspaper article that a group of citizens from Breckenridge had organized themselves to insist on a complete cleanup of the radioactive site, and they wanted Jay Steinberg to appear before them in person.

I recognized the name of the spokesperson for the group. I called her and offered to loan her my file of documents, letters and newspaper clippings about the Breckenridge Site. At that time, as she and I talked, I gathered she felt betrayed because she had thought the site near her home had been cleaned up years ago. She was angry to find out that radioactive materials were still buried there.

In thinking about this new group focused on the Breckenridge Site, it seemed wise to try to incorporate them, and their passion, into our CAG. I invited the group to attend our next meeting. I told them we never had enough volunteers, and if they were willing to be a committee focused on the Breckenridge Site, that would be a plus for us. They were favorable to the plan.

I also arranged for Jay Steinberg of LePetomane Trust to come to our next meeting to describe in person the latest dealings with the Nuclear Regulatory Commission over the Breckenridge Site.

David Heidlauf of Environ, Jay's environmental contractor, gave a power point presentation about the site to help bring the new people up to speed. David explained that after excavating only two of the nine confirmed contaminated areas of the site in 2004, more material had been found which was "wider, thicker and of a more wide-spread volume" than had been anticipated. When David was asked how much it would cost to clean up the rest of the site, he explained that more testing was needed to determine the actual amount buried there, but that remediation could cost anywhere from $1 million to $4 million.

Then Jay went to the front of the room and explained that the Trust was seeking additional funding for cleanup of the site in its negotiations with AIG over the Fruit of the Loom pollution insurance policy.

The woman leader of the Breckenridge group began to question Jay, and seemed to have the intention of pinning the blame for the insufficient funds on him. She demanded to know how he had spent the $700,000 awarded in the 2002 Fruit of the Loom settlement. I understood her frustration, but the level of her anger was high, and began to escalate

Gary Smith spoke up and said maybe she should direct her anger at the Nuclear Regulatory Commission, since we had questioned them in 2002 about whether $700,000 was enough to complete the job, and they had said it was. The atmosphere cooled, and we moved on to other business.

The woman from Breckenridge wasn't finished, though. After the meeting ended, she cornered Jay. I was dealing with other people, but my awareness was on her body language, and then the loudness of her voice. I learned later that Jay had tried to reason with her, but when she kept accusing him with verbal attacks, he responded in kind. Things had certainly become loud and angry in that corner of the room. During the argument, I had asked David Heidlauf for a copy of his power point presentation, and we walked out to his car to get it.

While David and I stood talking by his car, Jay strode out, livid with anger. One of the men from Breckenridge exited right behind him, caught up with him, and said, "Don't let it get to you," and Jay said, "I bet she's done that before," and the other man nodded. Jay said, "All the time?" and the other man said, "Pretty much."

We'd dealt with a lot of people challenges over the years, but this was the first one quite like this. As Jay and David drove away, I went back inside.

The woman from Breckenridge was telling her side of the story to Gary and to others who would listen. I gathered papers and folded up extra chairs and put them away. It took awhile for her to wind down, and she was one of the last ones to leave.

As I locked the door, I spoke to her about the further testing planned at the Breckenridge Site and, when the land was fully cleaned, how it would meet NRC standards that freed it for any use, even for the planting of crops. She was glad to hear what I had to say, and we both went home, but she never attended any more of our meetings.

The NRC came through with the necessary review of Environ's proposed sampling at the Breckenridge radioactive site, and by November 2006, the contractor was out on the property to further determine the extent of the contamination so that when money became available to continue the cleanup, the characterization of the site would be complete.

As Jay had told us at our meeting, the Trust and AIG were locked in a suit and countersuit over the Fruit of the Loom insurance policy, and since the Breckenridge Site was part of the squabble, it meant no action could take place at the site until a settlement was reached. To think that the money in our Trust Accounts was being spent on this endless litigation instead of cleaning up our sites infuriated us, and our blame was focused on AIG, the giant, prosperous insurance company.

Other than their ads on TV, most of us had not paid much attention to AIG until the name came into our purview through the 2002 Fruit of the Loom Bankruptcy Settlement. Even then, they were one of several insurance companies with which the Custodial Trust would negotiate the settling of claims for Fruit of the Loom/NWI in the bankruptcy settlement. With the other companies, negotiations had been a challenge, but settlements were reached and the funds flowed into the Trust Accounts for the seven former NWI sites. We had expected the same from AIG.

Jay had filed the claim with AIG in 2003, and soon after that, negotiations began with an exchange of letters that continued over the next two years. In 2005, Jay was able to schedule a meeting at the AIG office in New York, and he expected that that the rest of the issues would be ironed out at that meeting. His goal was to start formal negotiations for a settlement in early 2006.

Then, unexpectedly AIG/AISLIC filed suit in federal court in Chicago to block the payout on the pollution insurance policy they had issued to Fruit of the Loom in 1998.

Since the filing of the claim, our EPA and MDEQ project managers had remarked often about the quantity of time their agencies had spent in providing documents and reports subpoenaed by the AIG lawyers. And we also kept Jay supplied with information about our CAG activities.

So not only was our Trust Account money being used up in the litigation, but also our volunteer time, plus thousands of dollars of taxpayer money with the work EPA and MDEQ were putting into the lawsuit. And why? All because AIG did not want to live up to its contractual promise to pay for pollution cleanup at the sites covered under their policy. The giant insurance company probably hoped to drain the Trust of money so that the suit would be dropped.

When the lawsuit began, three of the eight drinking water wells in St. Louis had been contaminated with pCBSA. The most highly contaminated well had been taken off line. By late 2006, five of the six still operating wells contained measurable amounts of pCBSA in the drinking water. Jay had asked the CAG's opinion on which should be at the top of the list – money for the Breckenridge Site or money to replace the city's well field. None of us hesitated in saying that the city's well field needed to be at the top of the list.

The Executive Committee of our CAG tried to discover the motive for the owners of Fruit of the Loom to buy the pollution insurance policy in the first place, and for AIG to sell it to them when they knew the seven Velsicol sites were highly polluted. The policy was purchased in 1998, sixteen years after the St. Louis chemical plant had shut down, ten months after our CAG had formed, and four months after the Emergency Removal Action had begun to clean up sediments from the Pine River. Of course, AIG benefited immediately, because Fruit paid them $3.6 million for the policy.

As for Fruit of the Loom, Ed discovered they had been in financial trouble at that time in 1998, with their stocks falling precipitously. The reason for the policy purchase seemed to hinge on concern among their shareholders that the company owned the seven highly contaminated NWI sites that were not producing any revenue and that could become a liability. The purchase of the pollution insurance policy in mid-1998 seemed to reassure shareholders, since the stock went back up.

Soon after this, the shareholders voted for a reorganization of the company, and moved the headquarters to the Cayman Islands. William Farley, Fruit's owner at the time, owned over 2 million shares in the company, so he benefited directly from this scheme.

169

In our research, we found out that on April 3, 2000 a class action suit had been filed on behalf of purchasers of Fruit of the Loom stock who had made their purchases between Sept. 29, 1998 and Nov. 4, 1999, charging fraud and misleading statements. We wondered if we could prove insurance fraud, or at least gather enough facts that pointed to fraud, to cause AIG/AISLIC to settle out of court with the Jay Steinberg and the Trust. We contacted an expert on insurance fraud, and learned that insurance fraud is exceedingly hard to prove. We were advised to let the Trust continue its legal sparring with AIG, and most likely a settlement would be reached without going to court.

In the midst of our investigations, Murray and Ed learned that a good portion of their Alma College pension money was invested in AIG. Ed wanted to file a claim in the class action suit, and Murray thought it was a bad idea.

They clashed openly on this, and seemed intent on embroiling the entire CAG in the issue. I said that filing a claim in a class action suit was something for each of them to decide, and they didn't have to decide in the same way. Murray thought it might hurt the CAG if he or Ed filed a claim, but I couldn't see how it would if the CAG wasn't named.

In June of 2006, Jay let me know that the U. S. Department of Justice had intervened in the AIG/AISLIC vs. LePetomane Trust lawsuit. Jay said even if AIG managed to drain the Trust money through the lawsuit, the government would continue the lawsuit against them, because their funds were endless (thanks to us taxpayers). He thought this change of circumstances might get AIG to the table to settle with the Trust. On the other hand, the intervention by the government might cause AIG to head to the courtroom.

One day in November Jay called to ask if I would consider coming to Chicago to testify at a court hearing planned for the middle of December, and would I bring some of the other CAG members with me? He wasn't certain that the hearing before the judge would actually take place, but he would keep us informed right up to the time of our departure. Because of our indignation, and because we were ordinary citizens, Jay and his legal team thought we would make excellent witnesses.

Sure enough, by late November, the lawsuit was headed to court. We got the call that a status hearing was scheduled to take place in federal court in Chicago on Wednesday morning, December 13th. Already tired from our big push for the December 6th RI public meeting, I was surprised that several of us were still willing to make the trip to Chicago, and, yes, right before Christmas.

Murray, Dianne and I drove to Battle Creek to catch the train into Chicago. Ed planned to come on a later train. Gary was hoping to work things out to be able to catch a 6 a.m. EST flight from Lansing to Chicago and be there in time for the 9:30 a.m. CST hearing.

About halfway between Battle Creek and Chicago, Murray received a call on his cell phone from David Heidlauf, Jay's contractor, saying that the status hearing had been "continued" to a date not yet set. AIG had asked for the postponement right after they learned that the citizens from Michigan were on their way to attend the hearing. We called Gary to let him know not to make the flight. We also reached Ed, but he was already on the later train traveling to Chicago.

Since we were on a train and not in a car, we couldn't turn around and go home. Also, our hotel rooms were paid for and non-refundable. We went into Chicago, had a delicious dinner at an Italian restaurant, and planned what we would do the next day before the return trip on the train. We arranged for a visit to David Heidlauf's office to look at some old reports he had on the Golf Course/Burn Pit Site.

The next morning, after some conversation with David about AIG, our group sat at a large table in his office, divided up the Burn Pit reports and began reading, calling out interesting details to each other, and scribbling notes. Jay stopped in to thank us for having made the trip.

Traveling home on the train, the four of us had a constructive and lighthearted brainstorming session about some of the various CAG activities, including a rehash of the public meeting for the RI. We also talked about how we might make use of the Golf Course/Burn Pit documents, and then we conversed about our families, religion, and justice.

I believe our time together helped deepen our friendship. Ed and Murray had distanced themselves from each other after disputing about filing claims in the class action suit against AIG. Murray and I had pulled apart over his time spent on CAFO business and the proposed energy park.

Riding the train and talking as friends about a variety of other subjects was a good tension reliever. Our immediate goal had been to go to court and testify, but what turned out to be the truly important part of the trip was traveling together on the train.

Chapter 14
A 5-Year Review
(2007)

It was time for EPA's third 5-year review of the plant site containment system. And in a sense, it was the second 5-year review of our CAG because we were now in our 10th year. Our first 5-year-review would have occurred in 2002, and at the time, we noted that five years of hard work had passed since our formation, and we were still without a clean river to swim in and without DDT-free fish to eat. The year of 2002 had been busy, though, with excavation going full tilt in the river, the dredging of Horse Creek soon to start, and the Fruit of the Loom bankruptcy settlement supposedly going to stream millions to the seven NWI sites for thorough cleanups.

In contrast, at the time of the 2007 5-year review, and the tenth anniversary of our group, cleanup at all our sites had come to a standstill. Even so, we kept busy.

At Joe's fishing derby the previous year, a videotape made by Hunter's Exchange TV aired on nine different television stations before the year was out.

Joe and Murray were interviewed by Duran Martinez on AM Outdoors on WJR Radio – Joe about the fishing derby, which had grown to about 500 participants, and Murray about the river and plant site.

I handed out awards at both the Fishing Derby and the Bass Fishing Derby that year (and had the experience of a largemouth bass flapping around my bare ankles when he escaped the scales).

Carol attended as many St. Louis city council meetings as she could, including a Zoning Commission meeting when the city rezoned the plant site property to residential in hopes that EPA would clean it up to residential standards.

Ed and Marilyn took a trip to the EPA Conference in Jacksonville, Florida, at which they found an emphasis on conflict resolution, reminding them of Beth Reiner and Stuart Hill.

Murray, Melissa, Ed and I wrote comments on a dioxin report assessing the Tittabawassee River downstream from us.

I was interviewed by a sociologist from Michigan State University about our CAG, and learned that a group organized around a social cause to have lasted as long as ours was highly unusual.

John Baker was interviewed in the newspaper, and David Eldridge organized a canoe race on the Pine River.

Melissa Strait gathered information on how our CAG and Alma College had been working together for many years and submitted an application for the Carter Partnership Award.

Murray and I gave a presentation about the CAG and the cleanups to the Gratiot Historical Society.

Norris Bay brought in photos, maps, booklets, and newspaper articles about Velsicol for us to pore over after our monthly CAG meetings.

Rita Jack organized a trash pickup day in the river.

The Knight School of Journalism from Michigan State University put up a website about our CAG, and interviewed Joe, Ed and me.

Still nothing was happening with the blood spot study, and to the best of our knowledge, more cards containing blood spots were due for destruction. Our MDEQ Project Manager Scott Cornelius wrote a letter to the Michigan Department of Community Health requesting them to cease destroying blood spot cards, saying that he was "very concerned that valuable data that would give us a better understanding of the contaminate migration and exposure pathways at this site is being lost due to the destruction of these blood spots samples."

Also, the Executive Committee authorized me to see a lawyer about getting an injunction to stop the destruction of the blood spot cards. The lawyer told me that the legislature had passed a statute authorizing the systematic destruction of the cards due to privacy laws, so the courts would not intervene.

Again, we wrote letters to our Michigan legislators, explaining our concerns, and it turned out that a number of universities had also asked for a cessation of the destruction because of the value for research that the blood spot cards represented. A hold was authorized while the legislature figured out what to do. To know that the cards were safe for a time eased some of our anxiety.

It wasn't until 2008 that some blood spot cards were released to Dr. Dana Barr at CDC. Her initial results showed elevated DDE in all of the samples, and PBB was also detected. Later we learned that even though the DDT breakdown was identifiable in the samples, the blood spots were too small for statistical analysis. Finally, we gave up on the idea of initiating a more extensive health study by using the blood spot cards. We had taken our good idea as far as it could go.

In terms of the sites

- We wrote detailed comments on the RI report and submitted them
- Murray wrote another letter again requesting an Emergency Removal Action at the plant site, and it was again rejected
- Ed wrote a resolution for the Michigan Senate and Federal Senate to adopt asking for a full removal and complete cleanup of the plant site
- Gary designed "EPA HAUL IT AWAY yard signs and buttons and arranged to have them made
- A banner appeared on the fence around the plant site saying "EPA HAUL IT AWAY"
- Jenni Palmer designed T-shirts for us to buy for ourselves and to sell to others with a nice logo on the front and on the back saying "EPA HAUL IT AWAY"
- Some of the guys began to plan a camping trip on the plant site wearing Tyvek suits for a photo op, and Jay Steinberg, the property owner, said if any camping took place on the site, no one would be charged with trespassing
- We lined up a legal person to investigate the idea of suing the agencies because the plant site didn't have a liner
- Dianne Borrello and I scoured old reports made when the Golf Course Site was cleaned up, learning lots of new details

As for reading reports, that leads me to Appendix F.

While I was reading the inch-thick Final 2006 Cleanup Status Report on the river remediation, a paragraph in Appendix F floored me. It discussed a plan to *enlarge* the plant site containment system by leaving sheet piling from the coffer dams in the river, connecting them to the plant site slurry walls, and then hauling excavated waste from the Burn Pit Site across the river and burying it in the new landfill, making the whole polluted pile extend even further out into the moving water of the river.

It astonished me to think of such a thing even being contemplated. We knew a 1500-foot stretch of sheet piling had been left out in the river north of the plant site, and we had wondered why a *liner* had been laid down that extended almost 100 feet out into the river to that sheet piling. When we had asked about the liner previously, EPA Project Manager, Becky Frey told us they had laid it to hold the river bank and slurry wall in place on that end of the plant site. When we asked why it extended so far into the river, she said it was necessary to protect the NAPL collection trench. Now it looked as if they were preparing to implement Appendix F.

At the CAG meeting that night I brought up Appendix F to Becky and Theo from CH2MHILL. I wish I could remember the sequence of sentences I spoke. I remember feeling coldly rational as I put into my own words the outrageous suggestion made in that memo. I spoke directly to Becky. I remember that Theo made some quick comments as I was speaking, but I didn't let him distract me.

I held Becky's eyes and told her that such an idea should never have entered the minds of people in EPA. And I said, "Shame on you." She looked down but didn't say anything. Theo said some more things and Murray and Gary talked with him. I'd said my piece. There was no more to say.

The next day several people in the group wrote impassioned emails about various topics discussed at the CAG meeting, especially Appendix F. I still had some of that cold rationality left in me when I wrote this to the Executive Committee: "We are at a point in this process that has moved beyond academic discussions with our fellow colleagues from the agencies. The time for diplomacy has come and gone. We are entering a battle, and ...WE CAN'T LOSE THIS WAR.

"In my personal time of living near St. Louis, I have seen the town live, die, and now it is struggling to be resurrected to new life. It went from a thriving town to a run-down, has-been town, and is now coming back to life. The economic resurrection is great. The emotional resurrection is vital. When I sat in the city council meetings year after year as a reporter, I heard and reported the facts, but I also perceived the truth of their despondency, their hopelessness, their death. To now perceive their spirit fighting to revive is enough all by itself to keep me in this battle to get the right thing done at the plant site."

Then I suggested that we suspend the Technical Committee meetings until it was time for the Feasibility Study to come out. Before the Remedial Investigation had been completed, talking in detail about the science and the technology had been necessary. Now we were in a time when rhetorical, political and historical persuasive tactics were needed to get EPA to do the right thing. The group agreed to forego Technical Committee meetings for awhile.

During this time, we were not only trying to get used to having Becky as the new EPA Project Manager, but we were also working to understand Bob Paulson as our new Community Involvement Coordinator.

Gary suggested having Bob engage elementary school children in the community with projects that tied in with the site cleanups. His said now that we had a new Community Involvement Coordinator, why not see what he could do for us out in the community? Why not give him some direction so that he wouldn't go off on his own tangent? We encouraged Gary to approach Bob about the projects for school children.

At our next CAG meeting, Bob Paulson reported that he had placed a packet of "general environmental information" in the St. Louis library, which turned out to be coloring books about recycling. He said if enough interest was expressed in the material, he would consider adding something that was more "site specific." When asked if he'd contacted any local schools, he said he had to "go through channels." This is how he talked, kind of in a code that didn't quite give you the answer to your question, but seemed to do so.

No one thought much of his outreach effort with coloring books. That wasn't quite our idea of community engagement by a Community Involvement Coordinator.

Ed wanted to get Bob to do some PR work for the CAG, with us looking over his shoulder. He thought we should try to make Bob's job "fun" for him. I told Ed to go right ahead, but I wasn't the right person to make the job fun for Bob. I found his "lingo" difficult to follow, and, frankly, I would have been content to let him sit silently at the back of the room.

Both Ed and Gary tried to draw Bob out in conversation, and then later commented that whatever they said, he had a way of talking that led the conversation onto other things, including his adventures in the army, his life in Alaska, and sundry other things that had nothing to do with the start of the conversation. At an Executive Committee meeting, we speculated on what the role of an EPA Community Involvement Coordinator might be. With Stuart, it seemed to be causing division. With Bob, it seemed to be doing as little as possible. The group asked me to write a letter to Bob asking him to supply us with an informal job description to help us better coordinate our efforts with his.

I did so, and when more than a month had passed with no reply, I sent an email to him and asked for a written response to the letter we'd sent. He e-mailed back a three-sentence response, saying that his position at this site was as a member of the EPA team, and it was his job to advise the EPA team on community involvement, and an important part of that effort was to ensure site information was presented to the public in a language and form they could understand. I smiled at the irony of the third item, since I had such difficulty in understanding Bob's code-talking.

We decided to leave it at that. Carol wanted us to write to Region 5 and get him replaced. I was content to leave him at the back of the room. If Ed and Gary wanted to help make his job fun for him, fine, but leave me out of it.

Meanwhile, the city of St. Louis had filed a lawsuit against Velsicol, NWI, LePetomane Trust, Edgewood Hills Golf Course and Hidden Oaks Golf Course. They were seeking damages to pay for the cost of removing harmful chemicals from existing drinking water supplies, or the cost of finding an alternative water supply and constructing a new system.

By suing the LePetomane Custodial Trust, the city was going after all of the money that had been put into the Trust Accounts for cleanup of the plant site. A newspaper reporter called me to see if that surprised us. I explained that the city had told us in advance they were going to go after the Trust, and we understood that they had to do what they had to do. We hoped that the filing of the lawsuit might encourage AIG (who held the insurance policies for Velsicol and NWI/Fruit of the Loom) to go to the table with Jay Steinberg and settle the other lawsuit, the one between AIG and the Trust.

I pointed out to the reporter that AIG was the real adversary in this situation, and everyone simply wanted the company to pay out on the policies as they had promised to do when they accepted the purchase-price money from Fruit of the Loom and Velsicol in the late 1990s.

One of the items that kept recycling on my to-do list for the Executive Committee was to find a way to bring some of the $100 million in the Velsicol pollution insurance policy to our community. We knew we would need to sue Velsicol in order for Velsicol to tap into the money in the insurance policy. We couldn't sue them for contaminating the river because the 1982 Consent Judgment had let them off the hook for that cleanup. We knew we couldn't sue them for the plant site contamination, since that site was covered by the Fruit of the Loom/NWI bankruptcy settlement. We could perhaps join the city's suit for pCBSA contamination in the drinking water, but as a group we would have to show the damages we had suffered, and, really, the city had the better case with having to replace their well field. We knew it would be best to sue Velsicol for one of the smaller sites not considered to be one of the seven main sites.

Maybe the Burn Pit Site? Were our chances ruined because EPA had included that site with the plant site cleanup project? Maybe the Smith Farm Site, even though the state had given it an "interim response" cleanup? What about the Gratiot County Landfill? We were quite sure that all three of these sites were covered by the Velsicol policy, because a page listing them had been included in the Fruit of the Loom policy. These smaller sites were designated A & I (Assumption and Indemnity) sites.

If we could get our hands on a copy of the Velsicol policy, then we would know for sure. Jay had told us that the Velsicol policy was a "twin" of the Fruit policy, and he encouraged us to file a claim of some kind to try to get money from it. Since the policy hadn't been named in the Fruit of the Loom bankruptcy settlement, he had no clout in asking for the policy or trying to get money from it.

Gary, Joe, Melissa, Murray and Ed all thought it was a waste of time and energy to go after the Velsicol policy. Carol didn't have an opinion one way or the other. I was the only one interested in following this trail. I told the group that at the moment, I had time to try to acquire the policy, and they agreed that I should go after it.

I called James Stropkai, the environmental attorney in the Michigan Attorney General's office. He didn't have a copy of the policy, but he was willing to come and talk to us about it. Our stated goal was to get Stropkai's ideas, and to let him know we were seeking a way to tap into the policy, and our secondary reason for engaging him was to encourage MDEQ to make a claim against Velsicol that could tap into the policy. Since the state was required to come up with 10% of the costs to clean up the plant site, why shouldn't they try to put some money in their treasury from this insurance policy?

We wrote out questions to ask Jim Stropkai, especially about the Burn Pit Site, and sent them to him in advance. At this point in time, the site was still de-listed without ever having been listed, and we needed to find out if it would be in our best interests or not to have it re-listed on the NPL list.

It was interesting to me to watch Stropkai's demeanor the night he attended our meeting. At first he was answering our questions one by one, and, without really doing so, counting the minutes until he could leave the meeting. Then Ed came up with his "donut hole" theory, and the lights went on in Stropkai's eyes.

The "donut hole" theory described what was inside the Burn Pit Site and what was outside. If the Burn Pit was seen as the donut hole, and was unavailable for a lawsuit under the Velsicol policy, because it was being cleaned up as part the plant site, which was under the Fruit policy, then what about the donut area around the donut hole? Could we use that area, which contained contamination, to sue Velsicol?

Stropkai thought our idea was worth investigating, but the state couldn't help us. He said that the state had no standing to file a lawsuit against Velsicol, because they'd signed off on the 1982 Consent Judgment. Once again, that original consent decree served as a blockade. We asked Stropkai if he had at least seen a copy of the Velsicol policy, and he had not, although he thought it was identical to the Fruit policy. Stropkai's final advice was that the EPA attorneys should be looking at the Velsicol policy and also at Ed's donut hole theory.

So I invited Region 5's EPA attorney Gaylene Vasaturo to come to a meeting, sending her the same list of questions. She thought Jay Steinberg, president of the Trust should also attend, and that was fine with us. Neither Jay nor Gaylene had seen the Velsicol policy, but Jay said he thought he had heard that the drop dead expiration date on the Velsicol policy was not in 2008, as was Fruit's, but in 2009.

Gaylene said Ed's donut hole theory was very creative, and that she would discuss the idea with her staff.

Meanwhile, our main cleanup mission showed no forward progress. The contaminated sites we had tasked ourselves to oversee sat empty, with no trucks, no excavators, and no workers digging up the messes. It was enough to make us want to get out our shovels and go to work.

Woven orange snow fences had gone up in some residential yards on the west side of town, near the plant site, marking areas in citizens' front and back yards that contained levels of DDT and PBB above the direct contact level that regulations said were safe. At first it seemed that EPA would come in and excavate the yards right away, but plans changed. Those mini-sites also came to a standstill. Later we learned that the residential yards were another area of disagreement between MDEQ and EPA, and once again, ordinary people living in St. Louis were caught in the crossfire. Can you imagine trying to sell your house and having to explain that the orange fence in your front yard is there to keep children and pets away from poisons in the ground that would hurt them if their skin came in contact with them? And how do you mow that part of your yard with the sign on the fence that warns you not to enter?

Once again, our CAG wrote to EPA and requested an Emergency Removal Action for the residential yards. Surely they could dig up those yards right away, and not make the residents wait until the plant site Feasibility Study was released, the Remedy Review Board process gone through, and the Record of Decision signed. Yet, we were turned down. Their only concession was that once everything was in place for the plant site remediation to begin, the residential yards would be first on the list for cleanup.

Again, we were left in a holding pattern.

Our CAG member and DDT expert Gene Kenaga broke his hip just before he turned 90. He had a hard time recovering. From the hospital he was moved to an assisted living home, and within a couple of months he passed away. That was very sad news for us. I went to the visitation in Midland and there I had a good chat with Gene's son, Dave. Both our dads had been active in the Michigan Audubon Society, with Gene president and my dad vice-president during the late 1950s when concerns about DDT were being raised by Dr. George Wallace at Michigan State University and later by Rachel Carson. Both our dads had helped sound the alarm about DDT even before Carson's book *Silent Spring* was published.

People from the Knight School of Journalism at Michigan State University, who had come and interviewed several of us for their Great Lakes Wiki website, made a television documentary about Dr. Wallace and his research with the dying robins on the campus of Michigan State University. The impetus for the documentary was the 100th birthday of Rachel Carson, author of *Silent Spring*, who had passed away more than 40 years before.

Because it was Carson's birthday, much about her was in the news, and much of what was written blamed her warnings about DDT for the spread of malaria in the world. First Bernie Bessert, and then Norris Bay and Phil Ramsey spotted newspaper articles that were pro-DDT. Ed began tracking the trend in articles and editorial columns, concerned that if sentiment turned back to supporting the use of DDT in our country, EPA might not feel an urgency to clean up the former site of DDT production in our town. He tossed around a number of ideas at our Executive Committee meetings about how to counteract this propaganda trend that was taking hold.

First he wrote a letter to the New York Times in response to a science columnist who had said that Carson's voice "drowns out real science" on the question of DDT. The columnist may have not known this, but his criticisms of Carson's science denigrated the efforts of dedicated scientists like Dr. Wallace from whom Carson had drawn her knowledge of the issue.

Finally Ed told us that he thought we should organize a DDT conference and bring scientists together to talk about the proven effects of DDT on endocrine disruption, neurological problems, liver damage and genital abnormalities. Also, it had been proven scientifically that insect resistance to DDT could show up in as few as four generations of insects. There was also the proven fact of the persistence of DDT in the environment. Studies of our own Pine River fish had shown an increase in DDT levels between 1985 and 1997, even though production of DDT had ceased at the chemical plant in 1967.

Ed began to contact DDT experts worldwide and found a high level of interest in such a conference. As we talked about this, both Ed and I had the idea of naming the conference after our own DDT expert, Dr. Eugene Kenaga, and with Kay Kenaga's approval, that's what we did.

Meanwhile, it came time for the EPA's 5-year review of the plant site. Under CERCLA law, data about a Superfund Site must be reviewed and reconsidered in light of any changed circumstances that might allow the contaminants contained to cause harm to humans or the environment. No new data is gathered for these pro-forma reports.

When the newspaper published a notification regarding the 5-year review, our EPA Project Manager Becky Frey asked me in an offhand way if we had any interest in giving oral interviews during the review process. I thought it would be a good idea, and I assumed she meant the members of the Executive Committee would be interviewed.

Later, since our Community Involvement Coordinator, Bob Paulson, seemed to be the person organizing the 5-year review interviews, I asked him if he was planning to talk with the CAG members in a group or singly, and he said "groups tend to make speeches." He said things are kept in "generic states," and that he was looking for the "thrust of the community."

I'm quoting the phrases he used, which I wrote down during our telephone conversation, because, frankly, I had a hard time understanding what he was saying.

I asked Becky if the interviews would be used by EPA in the writing of the Feasibility Study, and she said they would be considered. When I reported back to the Executive Committee on this last piece of information, they decided that we should rally the entire community to come and give interviews and written comments. Ed designed a flyer, made copies, and we delivered them to churches, tacked them up on bulletin boards downtown, left some at the libraries, and gave them to St. Louis City Manager Bob McConkie to send out with the city's utility bills.

The interviews were to take place in the St. Louis public library. I got there early and sat down at a table in the meeting room with Bob and Becky, preparing to take notes. Bob informed me that privacy laws would not allow me to be present when the interviews were taking place. I thought that was strange, and later I learned from Bob's boss that this was not the usual way for the 5-year review process to proceed.

I didn't argue with Bob and instead went out near the entrance door to greet people as they arrived, and handed each of them a campaign-style pin that said "EPA Haul it Away." Almost everybody wore the pin when they went in for their private interview.

The line of people waiting to give interviews grew very long, so I stepped into the room to ask Bob and Becky to try to speed things up. If anything, things slowed down more. Many of the people left to go back to work and never gave an interview. Some stayed to fill out a sheet of written comments. Some said they would write a letter. I felt that Bob had sabotaged the interview process.

The form that was used by EPA for the interviews seemed odd. The interviews were supposed to be about the effectiveness of the EPA efforts at the plant site, but many of the questions asked silly, almost personally insecure things, such as "Do you think this EPA/DEQ team is truthful?" and "Is the EPA and/or the Michigan [sic] doing the right thing in St. Louis?"

After her interview, Rita from Sierra Club sent an email sharing her impressions of the odd session. She said that some of the questions were unprofessional, and all the questions, except for one, were subjective. Moreover, Bob Paulson had asked Rita what the people in the CAG were telling her about EPA. She thought Bob was probing to see if we were contemplating litigation. She wrote, "I almost felt as though the sessions were meant to try to divide and conquer the community, to figure out who would accept a less-than-thorough cleanup just to get it done, vs. who might fight them tooth and nail."

Most of the 60-plus people who were actually interviewed were the usual crop of polite people who populate our community. One came with a more hostile attitude. I wasn't there when it happened, having run home to let my dogs out. Apparently our hostile community member frightened Bob enough during the interview that he later told Gary Smith he wanted armed policemen attending our next CAG meeting, which was to take place the following evening. Gary assured Bob that he would see what he could do. And so at the meeting the next night, we had a St. Louis police officer sitting at the back of the room.

We decided to put in a Freedom of Information Act request for the written comments of the people interviewed, because we were told that we wouldn't be able to see the comments otherwise, due to privacy laws. When the package of comments arrived, all the personal information had been blacked out, but the information we were interested in was there in black and white. All but one of the written comments was in favor of a full removal and complete cleanup of the plant site.

In addition, about half of the interviewees felt that EPA was trying to do its best, which perhaps helped EPA feel less insecure.

As for the bizarre process that Bob conducted, we can only hope that he finally found his job to be fun.

In October I received a welcome call from Jay Steinberg saying that in the AIG vs. LePetomane Trust lawsuit, it looked like a settlement had been reached. The settlement document had been signed by Michigan, Illinois, the DOJ, the Trust, AIG, FOL (Warren Buffet's Fruit of the Loom company), and, later New Jersey.

We grew hopeful once again that money might soon flow to the Breckenridge Site for a complete cleanup, and that before long we would cross the site off our list. Maybe the standstill was at an end. Maybe cleanup at all our sites would begin to move forward again.

The last item in my 5-year review of our Pine River Superfund Citizen Task Force is a sad one. At the very close of 2007, on December 29, Fred Brown passed away. Fred's technical expertise and his political savvy were invaluable to our CAG. His strong sense of right and wrong upheld us when we sometimes felt roughed up by the whole process. I treasured his phone calls, when he would ask, "Have you thought about..." this or that, and when I already had, he'd say, "Good, that's good. You're doing well." To have his approval was high praise.

Murray and Dianne Borrello, and Kay Kenaga and I attended Fred's funeral at the Methodist church in Midland. On the back of the bulletin was a note from Fred. It was a farewell message to us and to the other environmental and conservation groups to which he had given his expertise and love over the decades.

He wrote, "I appreciate all the efforts throughout the years by many of you to win major environmental wars. We have made substantial gains, but much more needs to be done. Thanks very much for all your efforts. I hope you can keep fighting and winning. Sincerely, Fred Brown."

Yes, in the 10 years of our CAG's existence, we had made substantial gains, although much more remained to be done.

It was easy to list those projects that remained to be done:
- The Velsicol Plant Site
- Upstream and downstream in the river
- The Golf Course/Burn Pit Site
- The Breckenridge Site
- Smith Farm Site
- The Gratiot County Landfill
- A health study

And it was also important to list our substantial gains:
- The Horse Creek SEP cleanup
- The clause in the Total/UDS settlement allowing further action

- The upstream sampling in the Alma-area by MDEQ
- The Fruit of the Loom bankruptcy settlement language changes and money for cleanups
- The Oxford bankruptcy settlement
- The first phase of the cleanup at the Breckenridge Site
- The city/CAG relationship reconciliation

Lists can only show so much. The explanations of how we had achieved our successes were also important to us, and it seemed that our methods might be useful to other citizen groups. That thought led me to begin writing this memoir in an attempt to describe those things that aren't easily listed. It takes many more words than a list can hold to describe the challenges faced by a group of people working together to change the very landscape of where they live, and to change the perception of that landscape. In fact, it takes a whole book.

Chapter 15
(2008)
A Lack of Trust

Ed brought his idea for the DDT Conference to the CAG membership, and they voted to sponsor the event to be held on the Alma College campus in the spring. Suddenly it seemed like the floodgates opened and along with planning the DDT conference, we were suddenly busy with a possible settlement in the St. Louis drinking water lawsuit, possible leads to obtaining a copy of the Velsicol policy, and a possible settlement between AIG and the Trust.

The AIG vs. Trust lawsuit dealt with the Fruit of the Loom pollution insurance policy. If agreed to, this settlement would bring $12.5 million into the trust fund for the St. Louis Velsicol site and $2.1 million to finalize the cleanup at the Breckenridge Radioactive site. Also, money would go into the trust funds in Toone, Tennessee and Bergen County, New Jersey.

The public comment period was underway, but Jay called to request that we wait to express our views. He said he expected objections from us as to the terms of the settlement, and with the St. Louis drinking water litigation at a crucial phase, he didn't want anything we said to nix that deal.

When I relayed his request to the others, suspicious e-mails circulated. We were being asked to trust that our interests in making timely comments were not being overridden by other interests, yet Jay couldn't give us the whole story, because it entailed unresolved legal issues. We were reluctant to acquiesce. Ed suggested we file for an extension of the comment period and also ask for a public meeting, but Jay responded by asking us to hold off on that, too, which created another flurry of emails, expressing concern that we were being used for some ends with which we might not agree. The level of trust plunged sharply.

Then Ed suggested we now had bargaining power. We could negotiate with the Trust and the government, offering to hold off on asking for the extension of the comment period, in exchange for a copy of the "other" insurance policy, the Velsicol policy.

He followed through with this plan by writing a letter to the Trust and DOJ, emphasizing the necessity of releasing the Velsicol policy to the public because the public was now being asked to submit comments on an agreement that discussed that policy. How could we effectively assess the meaning of the settlement without having access to the text of the insurance policy, when the policy was cited on several pages of the agreement document?

The response was silence.

In the middle of these considerations, Jay called to let me know about a court hearing for the St. Louis vs. AIG et. al. drinking water lawsuit to take place in Federal Court in Bay City. I was the only CAG member able to attend, and other than City Manager Bob McConkie and Council Member Jim Kelly, all the rest were lawyers, and lots of them. Even Jay, who was a lawyer himself, had a lawyer.

Before the proceedings began, I greeted those I knew (Jay Steinberg, David Heidlauf, Gaylene Vasaturo), and for the first time met Vic Sher, the city's attorney who specialized in cases dealing with municipal water supplies. Everyone wanted to know if we'd made a decision about sending in our comments or not. I told them we hadn't.

During a break in the court proceedings, I introduced myself to the lawyers for Velsicol. I told Eric Gotting that I was interested in obtaining a copy of the Velsicol pollution insurance policy. He said he knew about my request, but he didn't think Velsicol would share the policy with me, since it wasn't a public document.

I countered with Ed's argument, saying that with the policy cited in the proposed settlement, and with the public being asked to comment on the settlement, it was clear that the insurance policy had become a public document. He said he would ask his client if they would share it with us. He gave me his card, and later I e-mailed him to repeat my request, but he didn't respond.

In addition to AIG and Velsicol, St. Louis was battling the Trust, EPA and DOJ in the courtroom over their quest for uncontaminated drinking water. The two federal agencies had entered into the lawsuit to protect the trust funds set up during the Fruit of the Loom bankruptcy settlement.

They argued that taking money out of the trust accounts to settle with St. Louis on the drinking water issue would violate the entire system of how the U.S. brokered bankruptcy settlements with corporations. And because St. Louis was going after the trust fund money as well as the insurance policy money, the Trust had aligned itself with AIG and Velsicol in this proceeding. In fact all the parties present in court were adversaries of St. Louis in this matter.

When the judge asked DOJ's attorney, Arnold Rosenthal, why taxpayer money was being spent by DOJ to intervene in the case against St. Louis, since the government's argument was the same as the Trust's, Rosenthal said he was there to protect the interests of the United States of America. That remark startled me. Wait a minute. Who is the United States of America if not the people? And if protecting the interests of the people of a small town who are losing their water supply due to corporate negligence and government bickering is not protecting the interests of the United States of America, then take me back to a high school government class and teach me all over again, because I don't get it.

Soon after the hearing, which left the case still undecided, I couldn't see how it would impede the city from getting a new water system if the CAG was to send in its comments on the other case. When I relayed this message to the other Executive Committee members, we went ahead and submitted them. We never did learn why Jay had asked us to wait.

The next hearing in the St. Louis drinking water case took place in Judge Thomas Ludington's chambers, and, from what I was told, the judge first asked the Trust if it was prepared to settle, and Jay said they were. Then he asked Vic Sher if the city was prepared to settle, and Vic said yes. AIG was ready as well. Finally the judge asked Velsicol if they were prepared to settle, and their lawyer said no, and went on to say that Velsicol had no intentions of ever offering any money to St. Louis for well replacement. That was reminiscent of Chuck Hanson.

In our 1998 sit down meeting with the Velsicol vice-president, I had counted the negative comments that he freely offered. Apparently taking the negative stance had worked for that company for many years.

The Velsicol lawyer wasn't the first person I'd asked for a copy of the Velsicol policy.

In one of my phone conversations with Jay Steinberg, I said surely he now had a copy, since it was a document cited in the city's lawsuit with the Trust, but he hadn't. He thought maybe his environmental contractor, David Heidlauf had obtained it. I wrote to David, saying "Since the previously mythical Velsicol/AIG insurance policy is now referred to as real in the proposed settlement, we would like a copy of that policy to read over to aid us in making our comments on the proposed settlement." But David didn't have it, either.

I wrote to the Region 5 EPA attorney Gaylene Vasaturo, but she didn't have it. Gaylene said her contact person at Velsicol was Chuck Hanson, so I found a Memphis phone number for him on line and called and left a message, asking that he send us a copy of the policy. No response.

I wrote to Alan Tenenbaum at DOJ, and I learned later that both Gaylene and Jay had forwarded to him the e-mails I'd written to them, also.

From Tenenbaum I learned that the policy was under protective order, which meant DOJ couldn't share it with us. Jay then offered to speak to the city's lawyer, Vic Sher, to see if he could subpoena a copy of the policy for the city's lawsuit against Velsicol, but I had already contacted Vic, and he couldn't share it with us, because we weren't his client.

Jay said we had definitely gotten the attention of the DOJ by making our multiple requests for the document. Later, lawyers for DOJ told me that Velsicol was "paranoid" about us possibly getting a copy of the policy. The Velsicol lawyers hadn't seemed paranoid when I spoke with them at the court hearing, but they also hadn't provided me with a copy of the policy.

We continued to voice our complaints about being prevented from seeing the insurance policy that was discussed in an agreement that would directly affect our community. The local newspapers took up the issue in articles, and an editorial column compared the policy to Area 51, the experimental site kept secret by the government even after the public was sure it existed.

Then, out of the blue, a CAG member received a copy of the policy from an unnamed source. Success at last! The squeaky wheel finally got the grease.

When we read through the policy, we were surprised. We had been told it was a twin of the Fruit of the Loom policy, which was written with each clause canceling out the previous clause.

In contrast, the Velsicol policy read as if it were really intended to provide protection to the polluter. And the expiration date, December 22, 2009, when the policy would automatically conclude, was fast approaching

Even while we had been trying to obtain a copy of the policy for ourselves, we were also trying to get the State of Michigan to make a claim against it for Natural Resource Damages (NRD).

The Velsicol plant site was covered under the Fruit policy, but the downstream portion of the Pine River was not. With the extensive pollution in the river downstream of the plant site, the river had been reduced in value to our community and other communities downstream as a result of Velsicol's actions.

A proof that we had lost resources was the no fish consumption advisory on the river. There was also the damage done to the aquifer beneath St. Louis, and in that instance, the proof of Velsicol's guilt was that the chief contaminant found so far was pCBSA, a byproduct of DDT production from the Velsicol chemical plant. It seemed clear to us that Velsicol owed compensation for damages to our natural resources.

Ed, as chair of our Legal Committee, wrote a letter to Michigan Attorney General Mike Cox, describing our position in great detail, with many footnotes, and stating in the first paragraph that we believed it was irresponsible for the state to *not* pursue cost recovery from the company. The Alma and Saginaw newspapers championed our quest to get the state involved.

When no response came, Ed called the attorney general's office, and was told that in 1976 Velsicol had paid the state for natural resource damages to the river. That was a surprise to us.

Apparently the state had negotiated with Velsicol and subsequently received a check for $20,000, releasing Velsicol from all responsibility for cleaning up the tons of toxic waste they had dumped into the river.

The news seemed unbelievable to us. Why had we never heard about this document?

When we received a copy of it, several of us thought it wasn't even authentic, because it was short (just over one page), not written in legalese, and the typeface on the first page was different from the typeface on the second page. Also, those of us who had lived in the area for decades did not remember any newspaper reports about this legal transaction that had sold our river down the river for $20,000. Not $2 million, not $200,000, but a paltry $20,000.

The state, however, considered the document real and binding, and since they had already sought natural resource damages, and they couldn't do it a second time.

Meanwhile, it was time for our public meeting on the proposed AIG settlement with the Trust, trying to get insurance money to flow into our trust accounts. We invited the two DOJ attorneys who had worked on the settlement proposal, Steve Baer and Eric Albert, to a pre-meeting dinner at the Heather Room at Alma College, along with participants from EPA, the Trust, and the City of St. Louis. After the meal we congregated with other CAG members and townspeople at the American Legion Hall on Michigan Avenue.

The DOJ lawyers gave a brief explanation of the settlement, and then the audience asked questions and made comments. Why hadn't the DOJ insisted that AIG pay out the entire worth of the policy, the $100 million? The lawyers pointed out that a $42.5 million settlement was one of the largest settlements the environmental section of DOJ had ever won.

Why was AIG allowed to pay the settlement money in such small amounts stretched out over 10 years? The "why" of this question was not answered – that's just how it was set up, we were told. Several of us said in different ways that we wanted a lump sum payment deposited into our trust account. We didn't rely on the parties to keep to the payout schedule over a 10-year time period, remembering how Velsicol hadn't lived up to their agreement in the Fruit settlement.

The lawyers were asked why the policy said the Pine River was *not* covered along with the plant site, while the proposed settlement agreement said it was, listing the Pine River in its description of the plant site.

The answer had to do with the Fruit bankruptcy settlement having included the river as part of the St. Louis Facility, and also because the river was now on the NPL list. That didn't make sense to us. This proposed settlement with AIG required that $44.5 million be spent even before their insurance would be available to the policy holder. If the river was part of the St. Louis Facility, then surely the $97 million spent in cleaning it up would satisfy the $44.5 million requirement.

What I took away from the explanation is that AIG had wanted it both ways, and the government was allowing them to have it both ways.

We objected at the meeting, and in our formal written comments, to being asked to comment on the proposed settlement without having access to the Velsicol policy (which we didn't yet possess). The settlement not only cited the policy, but also discussed it in terms that sounded as if no one would ever be able to bring a claim that might tap into it. Eric Albert explained that only the signatories on the settlement would be prevented from bringing suit against the Velsicol policy, and that others (such as the CAG) would *not* be prevented from pursuing remuneration from that policy. That kept hope alive.

A follow-up question was asked: Was it in the public interest for our U.S. government to give up the ability to pursue claims under the Velsicol policy? Eric Albert maintained that the government had already given up that ability during the 2002 Fruit of the Loom settlement. This was news to us.

The major benefit for the community from this settlement was that $2.1 million would come off the top for the Breckenridge radioactive site. After that lump sum payment, then each of the sites named in the settlement would receive a first installment payment of $8.5 million. The rest of the money would be dribbled out over the next ten years in equal installments of a little over a million to trust funds that had been set up for the Velsicol-blighted communities in Michigan, New Jersey and Tennessee.

Our concerns about actually receiving the promised payout escalated during the 2008 stock market drop. The news reported that AIG was teetering on the edge of bankruptcy, and then it was reported that the government planned to seize up to 80 per cent of AIG and take over its management.

This worried us greatly. After all, we had ten years of payments due us from AIG, and the city was negotiating with them for millions of dollars for a new water system.

When the news reports of a government bailout were confirmed, and the citizens of the United States were on the hook for $75-$85 billion in AIG liability, Ed sent a Freedom of Information request for all records pertaining to AIG and its subsidiary AISLIC. Since the U.S. taxpayers were now a majority owner in the company, it seemed logical that the public should have access to the company's records.

The response to Ed's request was silence.

Next he wrote to our legislators, and Senator Debbie Stabenow responded that the insurance side of AIG was in good shape and their agreement to the ten years of payments would be upheld.

While we were juggling all of these AIG-related issues, we were also planning and carrying out the Eugene Kenaga International DDT Conference at Alma College.

Ed had invited DDT experts from South Africa and Canada as well as the United States. Traveling from South Africa were Dr. Riana Bornman, Dr. Henk Bouwman, and Dr. Tiaan de Jager. From Canada, we had Dr. John Giesy. And from the United States we had Dr. Aimen Chen, Dr. Barbara Cohn, Dr. Amy Dailey, Dr. Brenda Eskenazi, Dr. Diane Henshel, Dr. Suzanne Snedeker, Dr. Darwin Stapleton, Dr. Henry Anderson, and Dr. Christopher De Rosa.

The experts assisted us financially by asking only for their airfare and room and board to be paid. They gave their time and expertise gratis.

EPA and MDEQ personnel were invited, as well as our state and federal legislators, and city and county officials. Community residents were encouraged to attend. With the $50 registration fee, it was surprising to me how the conference filled up with many local citizens who chose to take part.

In addition to the usual power point presentations and question and answer times, small focus groups were planned during which citizens could interact with the experts.

I had helped arrange a bus tour to Penny Park, located across the Pine River from the Velsicol plant site, where our EPA Project Manager, Becky Frey and our MDEQ Project Manager, Scott Cornelius would give an outdoor presentation about the $97 million remediation of river sediment, and about the extensive and concentrated contamination in the soils and groundwater of the plant site

About a month before the conference, we had learned from news articles that a new ATSDR report entitled *Public Health Implications of Hazardous Substances in the Twenty-Six U.S. Great Lakes Areas of Concern* was being suppressed by the agency. We then learned that a pirated copy had appeared on a website. A quick look at it showed that our county was discussed in the report in terms of our higher than expected rates of infant mortality and breast cancer. We also learned that Dr. Christopher De Rosa at ATSDR had objected to the suppression of the report, and subsequently he had been "promoted" to an empty office with no work to do. We hadn't yet heard if Dr. De Rosa was planning to come to the DDT conference, but now that current events had brought his name into the news, we especially wanted him to attend.

Ed's students found a home phone number for him on line, and I called him. Dr. De Rosa said he was very much aware of the upcoming conference, and had submitted a proposal for travel expenses to his bosses. Then he said, "If it's approved, I would like to come," but something in his voice made me think he didn't expect his bosses to approve the trip. I let Ed know, and he called Dr. De Rosa, offering that the CAG pay his travel expenses, rather than De Rosa waiting for approval from ATSDR, and that's what we did.

The presentations about the uses and abuses of DDT were informative, and the pictures of genitally deformed children in South Africa sobering. The bus trip to the Superfund site was a success, and the afternoon round table discussions were enlightening.

During the last round table discussion, I was seated at a table with Dr. Chris De Rosa and Dr. John Giesy, among others. The topic of incineration came up, and De Rosa contributed ideas about the benefits of incinerating on site.

Since our group had raised the idea of incinerating the plant site wastes, rather than trucking them some place else, we were eager to hear Dr. De Rosa's thoughts on the topic, especially since his expertise was in the field of public health. Essentially, Dr. De Rosa echoed what we had been telling our project managers. Giesy joined in with his agreement that incineration, although often more costly, was the best plan in his opinion, because it accomplished "ultimate destruction of contaminated wastes," which was a benefit to everyone.

Gary Smith spoke about the incineration project that was underway at Dow Chemical in Midland where dioxin-contaminated river sediment was being destroyed. Both Giesy and De Rosa were very interested in his account and asked good questions.

I turned to Becky Frey, our EPA project manager for the plant site, and asked her if she was taking notes. She tapped her temple, letting me know that she was listening and taking it all in.

Another observation made by De Rosa was that we might not need a comprehensive health study in our community. He said it was already known and documented that the people in St. Louis had been exposed to high levels of DDT and PBB. If we could learn at what level health problems were triggered, we would have enough data to establish that the DDT levels were responsible for the various health problems in our community. He said we could not wait for "agreement on causality" but that we had to use "the stool with three legs." Those three legs were

1. biologic plausibility
2. the research findings of epidemiologists from similar communities
3. and the findings of toxicologists

We had hoped there would be a follow-up study using Dr. De Rosa's advice, but so far that hasn't come to fruition.

Toward the end of the conference, one of the presenters suggested that a Consensus Statement be composed by the researchers and academicians who had attended. They agreed, and over the subsequent months it was compiled and edited, and then published as "The Pine River Statement: Human Health Consequences of DDT Use" in *Environmental Health Perspectives* journal, May 4, 2009.

In one way of looking at it, this conference was another of our many attempts to obtain a comprehensive health study in our community. Some CAG members recalled our past history of researchers having come to town, gathering their data, and then never giving the community any feedback. The publication of the article was a fine thing, but it wasn't a health study of our town.

Following the conference, there were hard feelings caused when some bills we had thought the college planned to pay were presented to us for payment. And then the Alma College alumni magazine lauded the college for the conference, and failed to mention the Pine River Superfund Citizen Task Force, despite our sponsorship of the event and footing most of the bill.

In the midst of all this, suddenly our website disappeared off the internet, and Felicia Leipzig, who was managing it, received a notice that a Digital Millennium Copyright Act complaint had been filed against us, causing DreamHost to take down our website. We learned that an Alma College student had filed the complaint; in fact he had helped to build our website the previous summer. Felicia spoke with the student and I spoke with the college provost, and together we sorted out the problem. The student withdrew his complaint.

Several of the CAG members were upset at this point and feeling that the college was taking advantage of our willingness to work with them on projects.

This episode had been preceded by another problem with an Alma College student, and later the DDT conference left us with billing difficulties and surprises, with the CAG's portion of the costs approaching $14,000 and the college's costs barely over $1,000.

For years we had offered summer jobs and other projects to college students, and we had faithfully paid them. We thought it was great to have the help of the students, and we believed their involvement while they were in college might make them better citizens when they settled into a community. And, of course, the faculty members who were also members of the CAG were invaluable. But at this point, some CAG members were having second thoughts about our close ties with the college.

Ironically, at this time when we lacked trust in the college, an award was presented to both of us for having worked so well in partnership with each other!

The previous year we had been finalists for the Jimmy and Rosalynn Carter Partnership Award for Campus-Community Collaboration, and in 2008, we were the award winners. The $10,000 cash prize would be split between the CAG and the college. Several of us traveled to the Fox Theater in Detroit for the awards ceremony.

When we greeted Michigan Governor Jennifer Granholm at the dinner, Melissa gave her one of our campaign-style buttons that said "EPA, Haul It Away." At the ceremony, the governor presented us with two large trophies, one for the college and one for the CAG. As I accepted the one for the CAG, Governor Granholm grabbed my hand and said, "I'm so glad you applied for the award again this year." Thanks to Melissa's efforts, we had.

A yearly activity that we were proud to give our time and treasure to was the Free Fishing Derby organized by CAG member Joe Scholtz. And for that, we didn't use TAG grant money, but our own dollars.

During one of the first brainstorming sessions of the CAG back in 1998, while discussing how the townspeople avoided the river and were afraid to allow their children near it, Joe said we should find ways to promote the river to change the way it was viewed by everyone. He also thought it was important for EPA and MDEQ to see us using the river, underscoring the fact that we wanted the river to be a *real* river – to be enjoyed as a recreational resource. Among Joe's ideas was a plan to hold a fishing derby along the banks of the Pine River on the Free Fishing Weekend promoted by the Michigan Department of Natural Resources. On that weekend, people throughout Michigan did not need a license to catch fish.

Joe organized the fishing derby by getting sponsors, and collecting donations from businesses for prizes and giveaways, and provided a free lunch for those who registered for the derby. He had 86 people show up the first year for a catch and release fishing experience, even though many of the fish had lesions, bleached skin, and genital abnormalities. Over the years the number of people registering for the derby climbed, and the number of hotdogs that the CAG bought for the picnic lunch climbed also. In 2008 we bought 1,000 hotdogs.

Joe and Murray appeared on many radio stations prior to the derby, with Joe talking about the derby and Murray talking about the chemical contamination. They made a good team. TV specials were also produced about the fishing derby, and several outdoor magazines wrote about the most-attended free fishing derby in the state that took place on one of the state's most contaminated rivers.

During the derby, my job was to record on the registration tags worn by each participant the weight, length and species of fish caught. My partner (Jim Hall, Gary Smith and others over the years) did the weighing and measuring. I never had to handle the fish, which was fine with me. One summer I rode in a golf cart with Jim Hall back and forth along the banks at Leppien Park, ready to write down the statistics for any person who had caught a fish. Most years when I helped, I walked.

The length of bank to traverse had increased as private homeowners began to allow people to fish from their banks on Free Fishing Day. In addition to Leppien Park and the private yards, fishing took place in Penny Park, at the Barnum fishing platform below the dam (another of Joe's projects), at a site above the dam, and at the footbridge over the river that connected the high school to its athletic field.

In addition to CAG members and city council members, helpers included other townspeople, Theo von Wallmenich (the CH2MHILL project manager for the river remediation), local and state candidates running for office, magazine writers and fishing product promoters.

Phil Hudson, the local DNR officer, showed up in uniform to intermingle with the adults and children who were enjoying the river and its bounty.

The atmosphere was festive.

Council Member/CAG Member Bill Shrum always supervised cooking the hotdogs, which were given out free when the derby ended at noon, along with potato chips, bottled water, and cookies home baked by Winnie Kubin, the mayor's wife. At one o'clock the prizewinners were announced. There were different age categories, and in each category prizes were given for the heaviest fish and the most fish caught.

Joe's tireless activities in organizing the derby and carrying it out were recognized by the wider community in 2007, when he was given the Spirit of St. Louis Award, a citizen of the year prize. We were thrilled with his well-deserved recognition.

By 2008, the derby's tenth year, and two years after the cleaning of the river bottom, most of the fish caught looked healthy. We were pleased to see more species, and also younger fish. It seemed that visible results were beginning to show from our years of commitment to getting the river cleaned up.

And the river's reputation was improving as well. We looked forward to the day when the warning of "do not eat the fish" would be a thing of the past.

Meanwhile, we couldn't figure out the hold up at the Breckenridge Radioactive Site, since money was now available for the project, thanks to the AIG settlement with the Trust. I e-mailed Jay, asking to see some action at the site. The spring construction season was upon us, and still no work was underway.

In July David Heidlauf of Environ told us that a turnover in staff at the Nuclear Regulatory Commission was slowing down the Breckenridge project, and that he was looking for competitive pricing among contractors certified to remove nuclear waste.

A month later I was contacted by a representative from a company called Energy Solutions that wanted to contract to clean up the site. I invited the company to give a presentation at our September meeting, which they did. We learned they had hauled waste from other radioactive sites in Michigan, including Fermi 1, Dow Chemical, and Big Rock Point. They said they could clean up all the waste at the Breckenridge Site over the course of two or three months, for the $2.1 million won by the Trust in the settlement with AIG.

It sounded good. Then everything went silent. And it wasn't until 2009 that we learned why the project had come to a halt. Again, it had to do with a lack of trust, this time on the part of the Trust.

Chapter 16
(2009)
A Difference of Opinion

"Shovel ready" was a slogan put forth by the Obama Administration as it tried to jumpstart the economy after the 2008 financial collapse. We liked it and decided to use it on the fence around the Velsicol plant site. In addition to our "EPA Haul It Away" banners, the new "Shovel Ready" banners went up. We had a group picture taken under the slogan, with some CAG members wielding shovels

In reality, the only "shovel ready" project on our list was the Breckenridge Radioactive Site. We had the data, we had the money, the site was "shovel ready," yet nothing was happening.

In talking with the Trust's president, Jay Steinberg, I learned that bad feeling had arisen due to a change in the rates charged at the disposal site in Utah owned by Energy Solutions. In 2004, Environ could dispose of radioactive waste dug from the Breckenridge site at the government rate, but this time around, Energy Solutions was not offering them the reduced rate.

In addition to the business side of things, there was a personal side. Jay was not shy in telling me that he didn't like the spokesman for Energy Solutions and, because of that, he did not trust that the company would do a good job. We made our position clear: If Energy Solutions was capable of cleaning up the site quickly and thoroughly for the $2.1 million allocated in the settlement, we were in favor of hiring them. Finally Jay gave the go-ahead for Energy Solutions to submit a proposal to the NRC, in addition to the one his own contractor, Environ, had submitted.

All of that took place in 2008. By June of 2009, there was still no activity at our shovel-ready project, and Carol Layman pointed out repeatedly that we were losing yet another construction season. I felt the same urgency she did, and it seemed that foot-dragging was taking place on the part of the Trust.

I asked Murray to join me in a phone call to Jay Steinberg to see if we could tag team him and pin him down. Jay was always entertaining to speak with, and his distrust of Energy Solutions and its representative was expressed in colorful ways, but Murray and I didn't learn anything we hadn't already known.

Next Murray, Gary and I called Energy Solutions. The spokesman told us his company was willing to excavate to the NRC cleanup standards and haul the contaminated soil to Utah for disposal, all for $1.9 million. It sounded even better to us than when we'd last talked with him.

That afternoon I received a phone call from Jay wanting our approval to draw up a contract. He said he didn't want to be fighting with us over which company to award it to, and wanted our opinion on if he should to award it to Energy Solutions or Environ. After polling the others to make sure, I told him our preference was for Energy Solutions.

Despite all our efforts to set in motion work at the site, still nothing happened. I kept calling Jay, and the conversation was nearly identical every time, with his colorful language about Energy Solutions mixed in with non-information. I finally told him I didn't understand why he'd told me nothing new in the past six weeks, and he assured me he was still negotiating with Energy Solutions and Environ.

That surprised me, since I had thought Environ was long ago out of the picture. Obviously, since Environ was Jay's contractor for the Trust, he wanted contract dollars to go to it, but that's where we differed. To us it seemed that the company that offered the complete job at an affordable price was the company to hire. Environ could not guarantee to complete the job for the money available since their disposal costs would be much higher than they had earlier predicted. The community certainly did not want to have another *try* at cleaning up the site, only to have the money run out before it was done.

Finally, in October, a contract with Energy Solutions was signed, with oversight authority given to Environ which would bring some contract dollars into Environ's bank account, also.

Clauses in the contract spelled out that for $1.9 million Energy Solutions would clean up any and all radioactive waste found at the site, even if it had not yet been characterized. That meant if more was found buried, as was the usual case at Velsicol sites, then Energy Solutions would have to bear the extra expense of getting the waste dug out and carted away. That seemed like a good safety clause to us, and we were glad Jay had negotiated to get it in there.

With the proposed work plan under review by NRC and MDEQ, we invited everyone to attend our monthly meeting. Representatives from Energy Solutions, Environ, the Trust, NRC, EPA and MDEQ all agreed to come. I received a call from Jay asking how I planned to run "the circus" when everyone was in town, and he suggested that he should speak first at the meeting to "head off any baloney" from Energy Solutions.

I told him we had invited Energy Solutions to give a presentation, and that's how it was going to be. Jay then said he should go first to explain the history of the site and why it had taken so long to reach this point. I agreed that he could speak for three minutes, but I didn't want him to "cuss out" Energy Solutions in front of everyone, and he gave me his word.

There were no fireworks at the meeting. Jay spoke briefly about the history of the site and its stop-and-go cleanups, and held his peace about everything else. NRC spoke, too, and everyone seemed to think that if the next steps took place as planned, by the end of 2010 we would cross the Breckenridge Site off our list.

As for the chemical plant site, the news kept us on pins and needles. Every month or two we were given a date of when we would need to submit our letter to the EPA National Remedy Review Board, and when the date drew near, we were given a different date further in the future.

Ed wrote a 25-page letter, with footnotes, focusing on the injustice to the community when the 1982 Consent Judgment had been signed, and on the corruption between EPA and Velsicol at that time (which had sent one EPA official to jail), and how justice was now due this community.

Murray and Dianne Borrello expressed a different opinion on the best thrust for the letter, saying it should focus more on the present day circumstances and the science and technology intended for remediation. Ed urged that we not leave out the history of the site and its failed containment system that was allowing recontamination of the $97 million cleanup of the riverbed.

I asked Murray and Dianne to draft a letter emphasizing the science, and said I would try to meld it with some of what Ed had written about history and justice.

A few years earlier, we had approached EPA about submitting a video to the Remedy Review Board, along with the required letter. Since the RRB meeting was closed to the public, we believed a short video would put our faces and voices before the Board and help persuade EPA to do the right thing for our community. We were told that our request was a first, but it was granted. So work to produce the video began, too.

Before hiring a consultant to aid us in interpreting the soon-to-be-released Feasibility Study for the plant site, we thought it wise to read the draft FS document first, because how would we know in what area we needed consultation until we'd read the study? But our new EPA project manager, Tom Alcamo, announced that CAGs were not allowed to read drafts, but only the final document. We'd never heard that stipulation before, and we objected, but it did no good.

In order to determine in what area we needed the most professional help, we looked back at the Remedial Investigation study from 2006. Clearly, it was the risk assessment section that troubled us the most. Even though math is used in risk assessment, and attempts are made to quantify that which doesn't easily fit into quantifiable categories, the process is, at best, a soft science, and, at worst, the mere manipulation of numbers to achieve a pre-planned outcome.

We were still without TAG funds to pay a consultant, because of the unresolved dilemma over our grant from EPA, but when we found a candidate, he joked that as a risk assessor, he was willing to take the risk that we'd be able to pay him eventually. The man we hired was Dr. Peter deFur of Environmental Stewardship Concepts who had worked with citizen groups as well as serving as an expert witness in various proceedings involving chemical contamination.

Soon after Peter came on board, we organized a conference call with our MDEQ and EPA project managers to discuss the four plans that were under consideration for cleanup of the plant site.

We wanted to know if

- the 2002-2003 collection of data downstream from St. Louis would be used to calculate ecological risks for the plant site;

- how NAPL, which was heavier than water, would be drawn to the collection wells planned for the underground areas of the site;
- if changes in river dynamics or groundwater movement were being considered in formulating a remediation plan for the site;
- whether or not on-site incineration was under consideration;
- and, since almost every area of the site contained a "hot spot" of one chemical of concern or another, was the whole site a "hot spot?"

We also asked to have the entrance and exit gates moved to M-46 so that the trucks and other heavy equipment could go in and out of the plant site without traveling on Bankson Street.

First of all, we learned that the entire plant site was not considered to be a "hot spot," yet it all exceeded Michigan's Part 201 criteria in one way or another, and EPA had agreed to meet Part 201 standards, although that could mean capping and not excavating.

We learned that any contaminants in the groundwater that had travelled too far to be drawn back by the proposed hydraulic system would simply continue to move through the groundwater uncaptured. As they met with fresh water, they would become diluted and that is how they would be "remediated." Dilution as the solution.

The one exception would be the #30 intermediate test well on the plant site at which pCBSA concentrations had exceeded 100,000 ppm. Scott said they would "make a concerted effort" to collect and clean the groundwater in that area.

A proposed deep sump pump for NAPL located at 99 feet underground would be an experiment, we were told. They didn't know if the viscous DNAPL could be pumped from that depth, but they intended to give it a try.

The rest of our questions would have to wait for the Proposed Plan, we were told.

In addition to our work with the plant site and the Remedy Review Board submission, we were pulling together a presentation to give at an EPA conference in Seattle.

Our Community Involvement Coordinator, Bob Paulson, had encouraged us to submit a proposal to speak, and it had been accepted. By using some of our Carter Partnership Award prize money to help pay expenses, several of our CAG members were able to attend.

The conference itself was called *Community Involvement Training*, and we thought its purpose was to bring representatives from community groups together to speak about ways to involve their citizenry in dealing with Superfund Sites. Instead, the conference was a training session for Community Involvement Coordinators – the Stuart Hills and Bob Paulsons of EPA.

I figured that out at lunch on the first day when I was seated at a large round table, chatting with the gentleman on my right and found out that he was a CIC for several Superfund sites. He talked about his classroom projects for kids, about going door-to-door to survey residents, and other activities that impressed me.

I explained, without naming names, about how our first CIC had actively worked to divide the CAG from the city. My tablemate was shocked, and said that any of the Community Involvement Coordinators seated at our table would be unpleasantly surprised to hear my story. That's when I realized that the conference was intended not for community groups, but the EPA employees who were assigned to them.

The man next to me asked who we had now as our CIC. I gave him Bob's name and related how he'd contributed coloring books when we'd asked him to plan some programs for elementary school children.

The woman on my left had overheard our conversation, and she indicated a man across the table, and told me he was Bob's boss and that I should talk to him. So after lunch, that's what I did. Jeff Kelley said he would like to travel to our town later in the year to visit at length with members from our CAG, which he did.

When I told the other CAG members who the conference was intended for, some light bulbs went off over their heads. They now better understood the small group topics and why no other CAG or TAG groups were present.

Our program entitled "Empowering a Community to Reverse Environmental Health Mistakes" was completely different than others given at the conference. For that reason, we wondered if anyone would attend, or if they would find it meaningful. About 20 people showed up, and their questions following our presentation exhibited true interest.

Later, an evaluation sheet given to us showed that our presentation was rated quite highly, with several attendees commenting that they were glad to hear from CAG members. One person wrote that our story was a good precautionary tale on how EPA should listen more carefully to community knowledge. Yes, they should.

Our EPA Project Manager Tom Alcamo had attended the presentation, and he said he'd gained a better understanding of why we were slow to trust EPA officials. Since Tom had said often during our meetings "Trust me!" I wondered if he now would be more careful in using that phrase when talking to our CAG members.

One of the small group sessions that I attended focused on communicating risk to communities. Our exercise was to write a letter to a community leader in response to an environmental problem the community was facing. We were told to write it in such a way that the letter had a positive "can-do" tone, yet showed empathy.

I wrote a pretend letter to Mayor George Kubin about the pCBSA discovered in the municipal water supply. When we shared our letters with the group, the others in the class were amazed to learn that chemically contaminated water was a real issue faced by our community.

And in comparing my pretend letter with the real letters George had received from EPA, I think the EPA officials could have benefited from the small group session on how to write letters to communities.

Mayor George Kubin had announced that he wasn't going to run again for office. With the economic recession pressing hard on small businesses, he needed to spend full time at his furniture store, and employ fewer people.

He encouraged both Joe Scholtz and Gary Smith to run. Gary wasn't interested, but Joe thought it over and decided it was another way to serve St. Louis, and that he'd campaign for the office. His opponent was a retired military man and a Baptist pastor, another good man, but Joe had the experience of community involvement, not only with the CAG and the Fishing Derby, but also from having testified on community issues at 25 state congressional hearings and at 30 Natural Resources Commission hearings in Lansing.

When a reporter asked him why he was running, he said, "It's the right time. St. Louis is going to turn around and I want to be a part of that."

When the votes were tallied on election night in November, Joe had won 64% of the vote. After the celebrating was over at the River Rock bar, Joe wrote some heartfelt e-mails to the CAG Executive Committee, thanking us for our support of him over the years. The following January 1st, I attended his oath-of-office ceremony.

Now that he was the mayor-elect, Joe decided it could be a conflict of interest for him to continue serving on the Executive Committee of our CAG, so he stepped down and we elected former mayor George Kubin to Joe's place on the Executive Committee. With the two exchanging places, it was a beautiful reminder of how far we had come in our CAG/City relationship.

With the Velsicol pollution insurance policy in hand, thanks to an anonymous friend, and with the December 22, 2009 "drop-dead" date fast approaching, Gary Smith, Carol Layman and I pushed for getting some kind of legal action underway before the policy expired. The Executive Committee decided that I should contact an environmental law firm in Traverse City called Olson, Howard and Bzdok.

Also, Ed and I shared information about the Velsicol policy with the Gratiot County Administrator, Nicole Frost, thinking the county might want to mount a lawsuit against Velsicol over the Gratiot County Landfill, which contained chemical waste from Velsicol, including (according to Velsicol's reports) 269,000 pounds of PBB.

And I had also called Don Long, Supervisor of Bethany Township where the Smith Farm site was located. Years ago, the City of St. Louis had thought it might want to own the Smith Farm Site, but after learning how contaminated it was, had (finally) changed their minds. Instead, the Township had acquired the property in a tax reversion process through the State of Michigan.

Don didn't think his board would want to get involved in a lawsuit, but he asked to be kept informed.

When I called the law firm, I was told they would look at the insurance policy and our other documentation and render an opinion on whether or not a case could be built. The fee for this initial work would be $500. That seemed reasonable to me. I asked for a vote from the Executive Committee. I needed at least four yes votes, and it was like pulling teeth.

Ed, Murray, Gary and Melissa were against spending any money on lawyers even for an opinion. Later, Gary changed his mind, and then the others changed theirs, and we ended up with a unanimous decision to send the documents for evaluation.

Chris Bzdok called to tell me that we didn't actually have to file the lawsuit before December 22, but we would have to make a legal written demand by then. The demand would ask for a reimbursement for money spent by our CAG and/or Bethany Township in cleanup activities at the Smith Farm Site, and also what we expected to spend in the future on cleanup.

At that point I thought it was all over since we hadn't spent anything on cleanup, and didn't expect to. Chris said we could spend money by hiring an environmental consultant, and having him take samples from the site for analysis paid for by us, and then writing a formal work plan for the site, including the cost for future cleanup.

It was now November 11th. I didn't see how there would possibly be enough time to accomplish this work prior to the policy's December expiration date, even if the Executive Committee would be willing to give it a try.

I explained the necessary steps to Don Long, the Bethany Township supervisor, and he tracked down a person from Michigan Consulting and Environment, located in Mt. Pleasant.

Then Don and I and Joe, who still sat on the Executive Committee until his January 1st swearing in, met with the consultant, Robert Anderson on November 25th. Robert picked up on our situation very quickly, and we learned that he was experienced in working with MDEQ as well as with corporations and insurance companies. He said he could begin work right away and have a work plan in our hands in a week to 10 days.

The first stage of his work would cost $500-700 and would consist of his review of all the Smith Farm documents located at MDEQ headquarters in Lansing. He would then do field work and sampling at the site, the cost of which would be determined after he'd read the documents. The final work plan would cost an additional $3,000-5,000.

Joe and I looked at each other and agreed to pay the initial $500-700, even without a vote of the Executive Committee, because we wanted to keep this project moving forward. My thought was that I would pay the initial fee out of my own pocket if need be, and later Joe said he was thinking the same thing. Don had to get approval from his board, but we said the CAG would cover the costs for now, and if his board approved the expense, he could pay us back half the expenditure. Don hoped to get his board to agree to spend $5,000 to cover the entire process with the environmental consultant if need be. And later, he actually got them to agree to $15,000.

Thankfully, the Executive Committee agreed to the initial $500 for the environmental consultant, although Ed raised another issue. Other companies besides Velsicol had dumped at the Smith Farm Site, and he didn't want those employers to be drawn by Velsicol into a lawsuit. I remembered that in years past Alma Products had cleaned up their asbestos at the site and that Alma Iron and Metal had paid the state for their share of the cleanup, relieving them of liability. It was only Velsicol that was still liable.

On November 30th, Robert Anderson presented us with a proposal for the site visit and the work plan for a total of $3,500.

We still had no firm commitment from the Township, nor did we know what the county would do, although the commissioners had invited me to come to their December 1st meeting to talk with them about the proposal.

The whole expense, at least for now, rested on the shoulders of the CAG. With the signed proposal, we needed to give the consultant a check for $1,000 as a retainer. Gary, Ed, Murray and Melissa all reared up at that news.

Gary was against making a decision until we knew what the Township and County might do. He wanted us to slow down, and said that I was being too hasty.

I pointed out that it wasn't me, but the drop-dead date on the Velsicol policy that was the source of the haste. Here it was December 1st, and the policy expired in 21 days. I reminded everyone that the environmental consultant had to give MDEQ 48 hours notice before being allowed to do field work at the site, and that for him to have enough time to complete the field work and complete the work plan by Friday of that week, we needed to pay him his retainer now and sign the contract. If people wanted to vote "no" on the whole attempt, fine, but there really wasn't time for indecisiveness.

That evening I attended the meeting of the Gratiot County Board of Commissioners, and gave a short talk about the Landfill, which had been walled and capped in the early 1980s.

When I asked for questions, I learned firsthand about the frailty of institutional memory. Many of the commissioners had no idea they owned a landfill, let alone that it contained chemical contaminants. After I'd given them some history, I again suggested that they might want to enter into the legal action that we were pursuing, and that Bethany Township might pursue with us.

They were interested, but the speediness needed to make a decision was a deterrent to them. When they learned that the Bethany Township Board would make a final decision about their actions on the following Tuesday, December 8th, the county board decided to wait until then.

After the county postponed their decision, several Executive Committee members voted to pay the environmental consultant the $1,000 retainer -- four of us out of seven.

But that's all we needed. On December 3rd, Gary wrote the check and I picked it up and drove it to Mt. Pleasant with the signed contract.

Meanwhile, the attorney Chris Bzdok had told Don Long that it would be good for the Township to have an end use plan for their property. Murray, Melissa, Joe and I met with Don to help him brainstorm.

Brainstorming wasn't needed, though, because it turned out that the Township had paid a professional to compile a Recreation Plan the year before. It was perfectly suited as an end use plan.

On December 8th, with 14 days until the deadline, I returned to the Gratiot Board of Commissioners for their afternoon meeting. Their attorney was present, and he told the commissioners they needed to speak to both an environmental consultant and an environmental lawyer because he thought the county might actually be a PRP (potentially responsible party) for the Landfill, since they had allowed industrial dumping in the 1970s when the landfill was not licensed for industrial waste.

Later I learned that the county had been cited eight times and fined twice by the State of Michigan. I thought the attorney's caution to the commissioners was sound, and I certainly wasn't going to try to persuade them in their decision.

Don Long attended the county meeting, and one of the commissioners asked him what his board had decided. He said they would be taking a vote at their meeting later that evening, but he thought the board members would decide against taking part in the legal action.

After discussion, the county commissioners postponed their decision until they had their legal questions answered.

Next Don and I traveled out to the Bethany Township hall for their evening meeting. We answered the questions of his board members, and when a motion was made and a vote taken, they unanimously decided to move ahead with the work plan and field work at the Smith Farm site to find out if they had a viable demand for more extensive cleanup of the site by Velsicol.

This good news helped re-energize the CAG Executive Committee, both to know that half the costs would be paid by the Township, and also to know that others in the community thought the plan was feasible.

Still, some of the yeses from our group were reluctant, with Ed saying he thought it was a waste of our money, the money we'd received in the Oxford bankruptcy settlement. I reminded him and the others that we weren't saving the Oxford money for our old-age pensions. Our mission as a CAG was to see our sites cleaned up, and so what better expenditure of the Oxford money than to try to get the Smith Farm Site remediated?

On the 16th, the county board decided they would not pursue any legal action. I think they were wise to back down, once it was known they were a PRP for the Landfill. They might have ended up suing themselves.

On December 17th, I received an email from Chris Bzdok saying the drop-dead date on the Velsicol policy was sooner than we had thought. While re-reading it in preparation for writing the demand letters to Velsicol, he noticed that the policy period ended, as we had said, on December 22nd. What we hadn't seen was that it ended at 12:01a.m. on December 22nd, which meant that the letters had to arrive on December 21st. Thank goodness he had spotted that detail! He was able to get the final bit of information from Robert Anderson regarding the costs of a thorough cleanup of the site ($12 million), and send the letter to arrive on time.

The letter demanded money damages for nuisance, trespass, property damage, negligence, and recovery of past, present and future response costs. He also sent out two 60-day notices of intent to sue, one under federal CERCLA and RCRA laws, and one under the state laws Part 201 and Part 111.

Now the question was this: Would Velsicol reply with an offer to clean the site themselves, or would they offer us a monetary settlement (most likely out of their pollution insurance policy) so that we could pay a contractor to clean it up? Or would they say nothing and again outwait us until the new date of 2015 came and went?

Chapter 17
(2010)
A Monumental Task

We came to the conclusion that our new EPA Project Manager, Tom Alcamo, was avoiding "capture." His interruptions when others were speaking, his attempts to divert discussions, and his general rudeness were symptomatic, we believed, of his intentional avoidance to get to know us as people. If he could avoid knowing us, respecting us and, God forbid, *liking* us, then he could avoid looking at our situation from the viewpoint of the community. It would be easier for him to deliver bad news to us if he hadn't become our friend.

I've been told it's usually when EPA or other agency representatives interact with the nice guys from a polluting corporation that they are captured. The agency employees come to see the good qualities in the corporate people across the table, trust is built, and then the corporations exploit that trust for their own benefit, and to the detriment of the community.

A perfect example of that scenario took place from 1978-1982 when the nice guys from Velsicol captured EPA and the State of Michigan, gaining their trust, and then exploiting that trust by crafting a good deal for themselves, which relieved them of responsibility for the messes they had made in our town.

We further speculated that perhaps Tom viewed the CAG as the PRP (Potentially Responsible Party) by the way he interacted with us, when really the EPA more closely fit that description, since they, along with the State, had become the responsible party for the chemical plant site when they released Velsicol back in 1982.

I invited Tom (and all the agency people) to our July picnic, and he didn't attend. I invited him to the Christmas Potluck, and he didn't attend. In addition to the group-wide invitation, several times I personally invited Tom to the Mexican restaurant for supper between the afternoon Technical Committee meeting and the evening CAG membership meeting. He didn't attend. He had made it plain that he did not want to socialize with us.

A loud confrontation with Tom occurred over the EPA Appendix F memo that had proposed leaving the 1500-foot sheet pile wall in the river, extending sides from it back to the plant site, and then filling the new area with contaminated soil from the Burn Pit and residential yard excavations.

We had raised our concerns about Appendix F with our former project manager, Becky Frey. When the issue was raised again in 2010, Tom Alcamo refused to believe that such a memo existed, and even joked that using the wall for that purpose sounded like a good plan.

My patience left me at that point. I told him precisely what I thought of that viewpoint. Tom talked over top of me, saying repeatedly that he refused to believe the memo existed. Then his CH2MHILL contractor, Theo von Wallmenich, spoke up and affirmed that the memo did exist, and that he had a copy of it.

Gary began to explain to Tom that this was no joking matter for EPA to have a plan to enlarge the plant site out into the river. Tom kept interrupting him and Gary got loud and red in the face as he told Tom off. There was silence.

As the temperature level dropped, I reminded Tom that he could tell us right now that the sheet pile wall would *not* be used for that purpose. Tom said, "Trust me, we're not going to bring the Burn Pit wastes over there and bury them. Trust me on that."

Later, I sent him a copy of the memo, and he replied in writing, saying, "I expect the sheet piling to be removed sometime during the cleanup activities." I wish it had been a more definite statement. The words "expect" and "sometime" still left us with uncertainty.

One of the workshops I had attended at the EPA conference in Seattle dealt with language. It taught Community Involvement Coordinators how to *seem* to respond to people's questions and comments during meetings, yet to avoid being drawn into real conversation with the mutual give and take of information. Tom must have taken the workshop at some point in his career, because he avoided the give and take of information as best he could. Nevertheless, we kept pushing and pulling him into a semblance of conversation, even if it was against his bureaucratic will.

Despite the personality clash, we moved ahead with the business before us.

At one of our meetings, Tom explained how the proposed pumping system to hydraulically contain groundwater beneath the plant site would interact in a negative way with the city's pumping system for the municipal water supply. Tom said that once the remedial pump-and-treat system was established at the plant site, if the city's pumping system was still operational and working against the new EPA pumps, it would cost EPA an extra $5 million or more a year in O & M costs. To solve this problem, the city's wells needed to be shut down. That meant EPA would have to include replacement of the city's water system in their remediation plans for OU-1, the plant site.

This was big news! This is what the city's lawsuit against Velsicol and AIG was all about. And this was what we and MDEQ had insisted needed to be done -- to include new wells in the plans for remediation of the plant site. Tom emphasized that the decision was based solely on cost effectiveness, and not on risk to the community from the pCBSA in the water.

At the plant site, even though the regurgitation of NAPL had slowed, still about 300-500 gallons of the toxic brew was collected each year and incinerated off site. As for the contaminated groundwater pumped up, EPA disposed of about 82,000 gallons a month, which later climbed to about 100,000, with disposal costs mounting to almost $2 million a year.

Despite the quantity of NAPL collected on the north side of the site in the temporary trench, we worried that other areas of the site were still leaking into the river.

The State of Michigan decided to fund a bathymetry study of the river bottom, which would show if contaminated sediment was settling onto the cleaned floor of the river. The study would take soundings and convert them electronically into a diagram of the riverbed. Because the excavation in the river impoundment area behind the dam had deepened the river by 10 to 25 feet, both agencies were interested to see the new underwater contours of the river's floor.

Scott from MDEQ invited the CAG to take a field trip to Leppien Park in St. Louis to see the bathymetry boat and the pictures it had produced from the soundings.

The results of the study showed sedimentation was resettling into the bottom of the river at a slower rate than expected. Was that good news? Or did it mean that the contaminants from the plant site were flowing on down the river since there were fewer sand particles for them to latch onto? Since we were again seeing tumors and lesions on the fish caught during the Fishing Derby, we suspected that leakage from the plant site was causing the abnormalities.

Some good news came from upstream. We learned that an area beyond the Total Refinery property would be cleaned up during 2010. The sediment removal project would take place in a wetland adjacent to the Pine River, located on the former Midwest Refinery property, now owned by Valero.

The project went smoothly, and when it neared completion, the MDEQ project manager for the site, Eric Van Riper, reported that about 12,000 cubic yards of sediment had been removed, which was contaminated with heavy metals, principally lead and mercury, as well as petroleum sludge. We were pleased because we knew this would contribute to a cleaner waterway.

We wondered how the EPA's decision to provide a new water system for St. Louis would affect the drinking water lawsuit presently in Federal Court.

Even though he was on the other side of the lawsuit, I knew Jay Steinberg, President of the Trust, would be happy with EPA's decision, since he had wanted St. Louis to win a new water supply from the litigation with AIG and Velsicol. I called Jay and he told me the decision meant that the city would have its wells replaced within a few years, rather than the decades it would have taken to get AIG to agree to provide the money for them. He said he had told one of the AIG people that with EPA putting the well field into their plant site remediation plans, AIG might just as well give up the lawsuit now, instead of going on "screaming like tied pigs."

One of the results from having sponsored the DDT conference in 2008 was an influx of DDT researchers wanting to share their data with Ed. As a group, we were particularly interested in the link between diabetes and DDT exposure, since our CAG member, Mayor Joe Scholtz was fighting the disease.

Born and raised in St. Louis, Joe had been exposed to DDT his entire life, especially during his childhood and youth when the chemical plant produced it by the ton. At age 53, Joe was now experiencing greater consequences from his disease. In March he was hospitalized for blockages in his leg veins. The surgery seemed to go well, and he returned home with three stents in the leg. Almost immediately, he hemorrhaged, and suffered a heart attack. Back in the hospital he underwent heart catheterization and a blood transfusion.

It was a terrific scare. A very weak-voiced Joe called me while he was still in the hospital, and I told him how much we needed him. We reminisced about how he and I had signed up at the 1997 community meeting when the idea of a CAG was first put forth. We talked about how we had been in this fight together from the beginning, and that we wanted to see it through to its end.

Five months later, he was back in the hospital for more work on the leg. He had two hopes going in: that they would put a new vein in his leg; and that he would not have to lose toes. Apparently things had deteriorated too far for the new vein, but he kept all his toes. Again, he was sent home, hemorrhaged badly, and was returned to the hospital. He survived, though, and felt well enough later that month to invite some of us to go for a ride in his bass boat on the Pine River.

Gary and I went, and the three of us enjoyed the beauty of our river, the centerpiece of our 12 years of cleanup efforts, and which had been for each of us a priority long before the CAG's formation.

With the constantly changing date of the national EPA Remedy Review Board in Washington, D.C., our letter had not yet been submitted. I had edited Ed's 25-page letter down to eight pages, but the letter wasn't complete. Periodically, I had asked Murray and Dianne Borrello for input from the scientific side, because of their criticisms of Ed's letter, with nothing forthcoming.

Finally, I drafted the best 10-page letter I could, using what Ed had written, and sent it around for review. Most of the others thought it was good. Ed liked it, but thought it needed one more paragraph to make it explicit that we would accept no cost-cutting compromise on the thoroughness of the cleanup.

His paragraph was added to the letter, and another draft was sent around by e-mail.

This brought a response from Murray who thought the letter went beyond stating facts to "hammering the reader over the head." He offered to tweak it that weekend, but he never sent me a revised draft.

The 10-minute video for the Remedy Review Board also remained an unresolved issue. Murray and Ed had taken on the video project, planning to use college equipment and college students.

At first the students interviewed Mayor George Kubin, but later George told me he found it distressing that the students didn't ask relevant questions. Next the students asked him to simply talk in narrative form about the plant site and the town, and he told them he would do that only if he had a script. Ed came up with a script, and I edited it to make it better for the ear. Instead of George, Ed asked Mike Vickery, a professor in the Communications Department, to narrate.

After Ed's work on the project, Murray and his students took over. For several months in a row, Murray said he would bring the video to our meeting for a preview, but problems with the equipment, the editing process, and time constraints delayed him.

Melissa and I went to the video lab to see what was recorded so far. In my opinion, much of the film was good and useable, but there was no beginning, middle or end, and the editing was highly amateur. Not that I'm anything more than an amateur myself, but I thought it could look a lot better than it did.

Finally the video was brought to a meeting. At the end of the viewing, not one of the 30 people in the room said anything. And it wasn't a sense of awe that kept them silent. I think it was that we had expected more than what was delivered.

Gary and I both separately approached Murray to ask if maybe the project of making the video was too time-consuming for him. He wasn't ready to relinquish the project to someone else, though. Gary suggested that if the past and present mayors of the city, George Kubin and Joe Scholtz, could talk about the plant site on videotape, the resulting dialogue would be a good addition to what Murray had produced so far. Murray and I both liked Gary's idea.

Joe and George agreed to be filmed at Penny Park, across from the Velsicol Plant Site, with Gary on camera, and me as director. Beforehand, they asked me to write a list of topics for them to discuss, and I also encouraged Joe to bring some "props" to make the talk more visually interesting.

One prop Joe brought with him was a beautiful 100-year-old green bottle from the St. Louis Mineral Springs, a thriving business that had, ironically, brought fame to our community from the 1870s into the 1930s because of our healthful water. As I handled the green bottle, I thought an image of it and Joe's words about it would be the perfect beginning to our video.

When the DVD of the mayors was delivered to Murray, he said it could not be put it into a format that could be edited, and that we should buy a new camera that could be downloaded onto a DVD player without any editing.

I'd run out of patience with the college's equipment, and finally Murray was ready to turn the video-making over to someone else. I called a friend, Klay Watson, whose hobby was recording and editing programs for our local public access TV channel.

In re-making the video, Klay and I used the narration from the original, and pieces of footage from the first attempt, but then we tapped into many more sources. Joe provided us with video he'd taken during the river sediment remediation, others provided us with clips of the Fishing Derby, and we found photographs we could use. We shaped the story scene by scene, with Klay nimbly cutting and pasting electronically, and inserting video clips or still photos. As the story unfolded, visual gaps presented themselves. To fill them, Klay and I interviewed more people, took video footage of the Rachel Carson book, a Detroit News newspaper headline about Toxic Town (St. Louis), and of maps and aerial photos.

On another front, even as we were working to get DDT contamination cleaned up in our community, there were others in the world who promoted the use of DDT. One of them was a pro-DDT lobbyist who had begun to write e-mails to two of the experts who had attended our DDT Conference. The lobbyist found fault with the experts' recent publications and interviews, and asked them to provide him with scientific data to support their claims.

221

Within the e-mail exchange, reference was made to the *Pine River Statement,* the position paper published by the various DDT experts following our conference. Ed Lorenz's name had also appeared on it as an author.

When one of our local newspaper reporters published an opinion column on the e-mail exchange between the lobbyist and the experts, including quotations from Ed, she received a letter from the pro-DDT lobbyist, threatening legal action. To me it seemed that perhaps Ed had gone too far when he insinuated a connection between the lobbyist and Velsicol Chemical Corporation, but Ed came through, showing the link in published documents.

When we learned that the lobbyist had written a book promoting DDT, I ordered a copy, and was amazed to see the *Pine River Statement* discussed.

The book said studies published by the authors of the statement were "un-replicated, contradictory, or statistically insignificant." Later the book linked the publication of the *Pine River Statement* with a change in policy of the World Health Organization and the United Nations Environment Programme, which the author saw as a negative change. The organizations had issued a press release saying that to reduce their reliance on DDT for malaria control, they had begun to encourage the installation of window screens, the planting of mosquito-repelling trees, and the introduction of fish that eat mosquito larvae.

To us, that seemed a positive change, and indicated that our Eugene Kenaga International DDT Conference, which resulted in the published *Pine River Statement,* had made a difference in the world.

As for our local actions, our only hope for immediate achievement was the Breckenridge radioactive site, which was slated to be finished in 2010.

Work at the site got off to a slow start. The Energy Solutions employees lived in the south and were surprised at how winter lingered in Michigan. Even after most of the snow had melted, they couldn't mobilize until the weight restrictions on the county roads were lifted. Then, when the crew was able to get on site in May, a very rainy spring ensued, which slowed their progress and sometimes stopped it.

I had contacted Jay Steinberg and asked if CAG members could visit the site to see the work once it got underway. He agreed, as long as we signed access forms and someone from the Nuclear Regulatory Commission accompanied us.

On the designated day, a rainy one, Gary Smith and I drove out to Madison Road, east of St. Louis. We were met by Bill Snell and Mike McCann from the NRC, and Ken Coble, a physicist from MDEQ, as well as some crew from Energy Solutions. We stood outside the chain link fence and watched as the radiation detection machine with a built-in Global Positioning System picked up information while a crew member slowly walked a portion of the site. Both men from NRC were familiar with this site, and had worked on it years ago when Memphis Environmental (Velsicol's contractor) had been directed to find some answers for the regulators about the site's contents and levels of radiation. The men were pleased that it was now going to be cleaned up.

Later that season, I visited the site again to watch excavation underway and a crane lifting supersacks, as they are called, each filled with about 10,000 pounds of contaminated soil, onto a truck bed. Then the truck was driven to a railway siding in Hemlock where the sacks were loaded onto train cars owned by Energy Solutions. The railcars had lids on them to safely contain the sacks as they journeyed across the country to Utah to a licensed site owned by Energy Solutions, where they were buried.

The excavation process was quite exacting, with only 6 inches of soil being removed in each "lift." We were told that the back area of the site would need many more lifts, probably to a depth of 10 feet. They had already found double the amount of contaminated soil than what was expected. Later, we would learn that four times the amount reported by Velsicol would be dug.

Except for a few setbacks (a broken winch and dropped sack, and a derailed train car), progress was steady at the site during June and July.

Then, on the 6th of August, I received a phone call from Jay Steinberg saying the site had been shut down because barrels buried in a trench had been broken open by the excavator, spilling liquid. This was alarming. No chemical substances were supposed to be buried at the site. And Energy Solutions was under contract solely for the removal of radioactive waste, not chemical waste.

The crew was ordered off the site and representatives from NRC and the Trust converged on the scene. Later Bill Snell called me from the site with more details. The liquid that had spilled from the broken barrels looked like diluted antifreeze, he said, and it had a strong, sulfurous odor that made people in the vicinity nauseous. Three workers had been medically checked on site and then sent to their doctors. The smell dissipated when the liquid ran down into the trench where it oxidized into a grayish substance. Bill said the work site would be shut down until the liquid and oxidized substances were identified, and then NRC and the Trust would determine how to proceed.

While the lab tests were underway, no excavation took place for three weeks during the driest part of our construction season.

Finally the barrels' contents were identified as being radioactive phosphoric acid. When the acid made contact with the soil, which was a base, the acidity was neutralized, and since Energy Solutions was cleaning up radioactive-contaminated soil anyway, they agreed to continue their excavation of the site.

Energy Solutions had expected to remove about 2,000 cubic yards of waste, but by November they had packed 3,424 cubic yards into supersacks (and by the end of the project, had removed 4,107 cubic yards). The digging had gone as deep as 12 feet in some places until solid clay was found.

Two additional burial trenches had been discovered, and then a third. When the lifts began in those areas, the excavator unearthed bottles full of lab chemicals.

Again, excavation ceased as the bottles were removed.

The count reached 700 jars, bottles and other containers and about 5 cubic yards of broken bottles mixed in with the filter cake. The substances in each bottle would have to be tested and identified.

To enable the excavation to continue, large special containers were brought in to safely house the bottles of chemicals on one corner of the site, until a decision could be reached as to how to deal with them.

After some months, EPA agreed to an Emergency Removal Action and eventually the chemical waste was hauled away to labs.

Without EPA's agreement to deal with this unexpected non-radiation problem at the site, it would have been necessary for the government to reopen the entire 2002 Fruit of the Loom bankruptcy agreement to squeeze out more money for this part of the cleanup. That could have taken months or even longer to accomplish. We were grateful that the State was willing to apply for the Emergency Removal Action, and that EPA had agreed to undertake it.

Meanwhile, the snow came in December, and the site shut down until the following spring. We still couldn't cross the Breckenridge Site off our list.

As for the Smith Farm Site, the law firm in Traverse City wrote to say they could not "marshal sufficient resources" to go to litigation on a contingency basis. They closed out our file and returned our documents.

Well, it was a good try. When history looks back at the work of our volunteer group, I'm convinced they'll say we exerted every effort to get some of Velsicol's pollution insurance money back to Gratiot County for cleanups. And the legal action we'd taken to "perfect" the claim of Bethany Township and the CAG would remain in effect until 2015. There was still time to pursue another law firm to carry things forward.

Following my talk to the county commissioners in December of 2009, they sought more information about the landfill. They invited Matt Williams, the MDEQ project manager for the site, to come and give a power point presentation that was open to the public. I attended.

During his talk with the county commissioners, Matt said something that I'd never heard before.

He told the commissioners that a Landfill Maintenance Trust Fund had been set up with a $500,000 contribution from Velsicol to the Michigan Treasury Department (later he backtracked on his assertion that the money came from Velsicol). Instead of being a fund for all the landfills in the state, Matt said the wording on the Fund's document made it specific to the Gratiot County Landfill. For instance, the qualifying landfill had to contain PBB, and had to be part of a "response action," and had to have a judicially approved settlement.

The purpose of the fund was to generate interest from the principal which would be spent for upkeep at the site. I suggested that since the state was now requiring the county to take over the upkeep at the site, including monitoring the methane vents and taking samples from the groundwater wells on the site, the $500,000 should be transferred to them. He explained that another qualifier was that only the Michigan Treasury Department could hold the Fund and disburse from it.

When I told our local newspaper reporters about this rather mysterious Landfill Maintenance Trust Fund, it piqued their interest. One of them, Linda Gittleman, made arrangements to go through some old file cabinets at the courthouse looking for documents that might shed light on what had taken place back in the 1980s. Nothing was found.

Later Ed Lorenz went to the Bentley Library in Ann Arbor to search through documents from the administration of Governor William Milliken. We knew there must have been a law to establish the Landfill Maintenance Trust Fund, and since a governor signs a bill to make it a law, we thought Milliken's documents might have information about the Fund, but no luck. It was yet another document from the era of the PBB Disaster that seemed to have disappeared. And one more site on our list that had made no progress.

Despite our lack of accomplishments, our vision remained the same. In regards to the persistence necessary for a group of volunteers to work at such a large, long-term task, Ed Lorenz wrote an inspiring email about the necessity for us to stick to our primary goal for the land and river and not succumb to distractions emanating from EPA, MDEQ, or from ourselves. Then he exhorted us metaphorically to keep our simple demands "engraved in stone."

In reading his words, I thought of the tombstone erected at the chemical plant site with the warning words engraved in it.

Gary Smith also thought of the tombstone, but took the idea further and suggested that we place our *own* monument on the site with our simple demands etched in stone. His idea caught on within our group, and we decided to ask the City to join us in the plan. They did not hesitate, and voted to split the cost of a monument with us.

We discussed locations. Should it be on M-46 where the various churches had planted flowers to try to hide the ugly fenced site? Should we get approval from Jay Steinberg and EPA to place our monument inside the fence? Or should we stay outside the fence, but near the governmental tombstone to symbolically cancel it out? Joe Scholtz and I liked that idea.

One day he and I drove to the gates of the former chemical plant on North Street to view the government's tombstone with its words that declared the property a dead zone. Joe paced off 33 feet from the center of North Street toward the tombstone, and arrived at a spot on city-owned property, outside the gates, and just to one side of the tombstone. It was the perfect place for our monument.

I had already visited Bouchey's Monument Company in downtown St. Louis, and rather than a tombstone, I had been attracted to a bench that people could sit on -- instead of a symbol of death, a symbol of life. City Manager Bob McConkie and I went to the store together and agreed that the granite bench was our choice. The back of the bench had space for the words that we wanted engraved in stone:

<u>WE DECLARE OUR MUTUAL AIM:</u>
THAT OUR RIVER AND LAND BE RESTORED
TO THEIR NATURAL CONDITION
SAFE FOR ANY USE
City of Saint Louis and Pine River Superfund Citizen Task Force

The words fit nicely on the back of the granite bench, and Boucheys added engraved artwork of pine trees, deer, running water, and a jumping fish. City workers poured a concrete foundation for the bench, and soon Boucheys set the bench in place.

Our monumental task now had its own monument, with our simple demands etched in stone.

Chapter 18
(2011, part 1)
A Slingshot Victory

One of our CAG members said, "It's too good to be true." Prompting this remark was the comment by our MDEQ Project Manager Scott Cornelius that his retired boss desired to join our CAG. This man had helped convince EPA that the Velsicol plant site required more than a repaired wall and a new cap, and that the groundwater must be addressed, with extensive source removal needed from the depths of the plant site itself. And now this champion of our cause wished to join our CAG? It did seem almost too good to be true.

The next day Jim Heinzman e-mailed me explaining that in order to serve as a stakeholder in the Interstate Technology and Regulatory Council, he needed to affiliate himself with an environmental advocacy group. He hoped to be accepted into our CAG because of his past work on our site, and because he had a personal desire to see our project through to completion.

Murray voiced his concern to the Executive Committee about having Jim join us, fearing it would drive a wedge between us and EPA. The others thought having Jim in the CAG would strengthen us. As it was now, EPA easily sloughed off our "opinions," even when they were offered by well-educated people within our group. Because Jim's expertise at Superfund sites was known by EPA from their past dealings with him, they would have to meet head-on what he said, rather than dismissing it out of hand.

Jim paid his dues for a year ($5), and joined the CAG.

We still had not finalized our letter to the National Remedy Review Board. The date of the Board meeting had been moved ahead to March at this point in time. I sent the often-revised draft of our letter to Jim Heinzman to get his views, and he immediately responded with several suggestions for improvements of a scientific nature. I was very glad to get those.

Soon after Jim's contributions were added into the draft, along with some paragraphs from our paid Technical Advisor, Dr. Peter deFur, Murray wrote an e-mail response saying that the letter was "annoyingly negative" and contained nothing positive.

I don't know what motivated Murray to fail to contribute from his expertise to the letter, and yet to find fault with the contributions of others' additions and I had to hang on tight to my good nature in replying to his criticisms. In his zeal, Murray edited out one of the scientific paragraphs that Peter deFur had put in. Then Dianne, Murray's wife, did an edit and without knowing that some of the paragraphs had been put in by Murray, she edited those out!

I managed to write a halfway humorous response to everyone about these edits, and Peter wrote me a personal e-mail saying that I should win the national award of the century for my patience shown to my fellow CAG members.

Finally I sent around the 8th full revision of the letter, and received positive feedback from all the contributors, except Murray, who thought the letter was too wordy and too long, yet wanting things to be described more fully. Good grief.

By then the deadline for the RRB had been moved to May, yet our letter was finished in March, thank goodness.

Meanwhile, Klay Watson and I put in many hours on the video. I essentially "told" the story, using the various video clips and stills that we had accumulated, and he wove them into the voiceover that had already been laid down from work Ed had done at the college.

My background in making videos went back to the 1980s, prior to computer editing. Klay, however, had kept current, and now and then would suggest a new, modern way to do something. Some I thought we should use, and some I didn't. We wanted the video to be well made, but not slick.

We had members of the Executive Committee preview the video, and the response was gratifying. They thought the story was well told, and they were impressed with how much we had fit into 10 minutes. [The video is available on Youtube, and is entitled *From Mineral Springs to Toxic Town.*]

Finally, copies of the letter, printed on 70# paper, and copies of the DVD were mailed to Tom Alcamo at EPA in Chicago for him to include in the packages of information he was assembling for the members of the Remedy Review Board.

In addition, we had asked our members of Congress to write letters to the Remedy Review Board on our behalf, and they did, encouraging the Board to select a remedy that, in Senator Carl Levin's words, "upholds St. Louis residents' health and safety and provides a permanent solution to the threats that have plagued the well-being of the community for the past thirty years."

In the midst of all this, I received an award, and one that was deeply meaningful to me. The city of St. Louis gave me their citizen of the year award, called the Spirit of St. Louis. I wasn't the first member of our CAG to receive the award. Bill Shrum had been the recipient in 1997, Jerry Church in 2002, Joe Scholtz in 2007, and Norris Bay in 2010. I think the fact that so many of us were singled out for the award helps illustrate the character and integrity of the members of our CAG.

Later in 2011, the Alma College award for Community Service was bestowed on me. That was another unexpected honor, and deeply felt. Also, Klay submitted our video for a Philo Media award, and it won in the Non-Professional Documentary category. Amazing.

In February we lost another valuable elder from our CAG. For some time Arnie Bransdorfer hadn't attended meetings due to poor health, but prior to that he'd been an outspoken, opinionated and warm-hearted fixture in our group, and an important person in the history leading up to the CAG.

In 1979, while serving on the Gratiot County Board of Commissioners, Arnie had written a letter to Michigan's governor encouraging the involvement of local citizens in the decision-making process of how to deal with the demolished Velsicol site. The reply he received from the governor's office said state and federal officials did not want, and intended to actively discourage, any participation by citizens, because the facts of the matter would only serve to cause fear among them.

Arnie had shared that letter with us soon after our CAG formed in 1998.

And long before any of us saw our group as having historical significance, Arnie always asked for two copies of our minutes – one for himself, and one to place in the files of the St. Louis Area Historical Society. Even after he was unable to attend our meetings, I continued to mail two copies of our minutes to him.

Arnie had been in the thick of things during the closing and burying of the Gratiot County Landfill, and he had collected newspaper clippings from that time period of 1980 onward. He had given the file to Ed when Arnie knew his days were numbered.

After Arnie's passing, I borrowed the file from Ed, read through it, and summarized the articles. I could see that the county was, in fact, a potentially responsible party (PRP) for the illegal dumping of chemical and industrial waste at the Landfill, and the fact was acknowledged by county officials at the time. The news articles said that at least 20 various chemical compounds had been dumped at the landfill, including 269,000 pounds of PBB.

Ever since my talks with the Gratiot County Board of Commissioners in 2009, I'd kept in touch with Nicole Frost, the County Administrator, and Brian Denman, the Drain Commissioner. From Brian I learned that the county's Board of Public Works was the body that had actual jurisdiction over the Gratiot County Landfill property. He invited me to attend their next meeting when the Landfill would be discussed.

At that meeting, we talked about ways to possibly work together, despite the fact that their plans centered on maintaining the Landfill safely, while the goal of the CAG was to see the site cleaned up. They worried that any cleanup plans would involve money from the county, which they didn't have. Later, the CAG decided to apply for a TASC expert through EPA and share the results with the county prior to the upcoming 5-year review for the Landfill to help keep the county informed at no cost to them. The TASC expert (Technical Assistance Services for Communities) was an outside contractor paid for by EPA who would complete a task for us. Naturally, some of our CAG members were concerned that the TASC expert could skew the results in EPA's favor, but we decided to give it a try.

We asked the TASC expert to do three things:
- Oversee the current 5-year review for the Landfill that was being conducted by MDEQ's Matt Williams, and funded with $20,000 from EPA.
- Provide the CAG with suggestions for writing our comments on the 5-year review
- Read and interpret past data concerning the Landfill and write a report for the CAG

231

Our goal was to become better informed about the site, and perhaps to discover something that had been left undone that should have been done, which could re-open the project. In our view, the site was a potential threat to soil and groundwater contamination.

At the 5-year-review public meeting at the courthouse, Matt Williams gave a power point presentation, and answered questions. In the view of MDEQ and EPA, the site was protective of human health and the environment.

From the independent information gathered by our TASC expert, however, we questioned if the site *was* protective of human health and the environment, and we had many suggestions and comments, some of which we raised at the public meeting, and all of which we included in a letter of response to the 5-year review.

1) Even though the Landfill was known to contain a vast quantity of PBB, no testing for PBB had been conducted in either the groundwater or the drinking wells near the site for at least a decade.

2) Even though the clay cap had been graded in recent years, the permeability of the restored cap had not been tested.

3) It was known that several gaps existed in the clay wall surrounding the site, and an assessment made in 2001 by MDEQ found that the clay wall was not serving as a hydraulic barrier.

We questioned the accuracy of the 5-year-review from the agencies that stated "the remedy is operating and functioning as designed," because our TASC expert found that with the flaws in the wall and possible flaws in the cap, that the containment system was *not* functioning as designed.

Also, when the clay cap had been built, a lagoon was formed on top for the cap area to drain into, which went against current landfill design wisdom. Further, the Landfill lacked both a liner and a drainage layer.

We recommended that upgrades be made in all these areas. At the time of this writing, nothing has been done.

One observation that struck us at the public meeting on the Landfill was the seeming disconnect in the minds of the project managers in regards to the location of the Smith Farm Site, which also had been used as a dumping ground for PBB, as well as for DDT, mercury and vinyl chloride.

Both Matt Williams from MDEQ and Tom Alcamo from EPA didn't seem to think it was important that the two sites were adjacent to each other. Were there invisible and impenetrable borders around each site that we couldn't see, we wondered sarcastically? Not only were the sites next to each other on the soil surface, but surely they shared the same groundwater. But we couldn't get the project managers to view the proximity of the sites to one another as any cause for concern.

Ever since the law firm in Traverse City had told us they would not be able to move forward on the legal action against Velsicol over the Smith Farm Site, we had been trying to find another environmental law firm to take the case.

Vic Sher, the attorney for the city of St. Louis in their suit against AIG and Velsicol, recommended that we contact Richard Drury and Mike Lozeau in San Francisco, but they also turned us down. They then recommended we contact someone closer to Michigan, such as Howard Learner in Chicago, which we did, again with no luck. We learned that Steven Chester, the former MDEQ director, was now working as an environmental lawyer in Detroit. In response to our inquiry, he told us that his firm could not handle the case because it would be a conflict of interest due to their representation of some other parties. He suggested that we ask for legal help through an independently funded environmental organization. Contacts with the national Environmental Defense Fund and Wayne State Law School came up empty, and the Sierra Club never responded.

Legal success came, however, to the City of St. Louis.

One afternoon Joe called to share some momentous news. The city had reached a settlement in its lawsuit against AIG, Velsicol et. al. for $26.5 million. The papers had been signed. The city's lawyer, Vic Sher, had written a press release. The St. Louis City Council had met in a special meeting that afternoon and had approved the settlement. This was great news! In the press release, Mayor Joe Scholtz was quoted as saying,

"We are delighted to have achieved this settlement, which will help the City replace its water supply with a system that is safe and reliable. We have accomplished our goal of holding Velsicol accountable in court, and are pleased to end the lawsuit on these terms."

Yes. Good, clean water and holding Velsicol accountable for their mess were both long-term goals achieved with this settlement. Victory at last!

When EPA and DOJ had piled on to the versus side of the legal battle, along with Velsicol, AIG and the Trust, the case had become a true David and Goliath story, with powerful federal agencies and corporations fighting against small town America. Yet St. Louis had prevailed, aided by outstanding legal support from the Sher-Leff attorneys. It was a slingshot victory for our town!

Soon Judge Thomas Ludington signed the settlement, and City Manager Bob McConkie supplied me with a copy of the document.

I was especially curious to see how the major worry of EPA and DOJ had been addressed. In the court sessions I had attended, the agencies had carried on about how if the city tapped into Trust money allocated from the Fruit of the Loom bankruptcy settlement, it would set a bad precedent for any other negotiated deals the government might want to make with corporations. And yet, in this settlement, $6 million of the money coming to St. Louis would be drawn from that very Trust account.

Paragraph 3.4 of the legal document simply stated that nothing in this agreement would change anything about the Fruit agreement, and that was that. Now, honestly, why did the government have to pile on the heap and make such a fuss if all it took to fix the problem was one little clause?

The city had to give up some things to reach the settlement. For instance, they had to agree to a mutual denial that the water wells were contaminated or threatened with contamination, or that the "purported" contamination posed a health threat. Along with that, they had to agree that a replacement of the city's water supply was based on the fact that it would be more cost effective, rather than being done to mitigate an imminent and dangerous threat. We knew EPA had argued for the inclusion of that statement.

As I read through the document, I found a worrisome sentence on page 6. It said: "Nothing herein imposes any obligation on USEPA to secure funding for completion of construction of the City water supply."

Knowing that the city had estimated that it would require at least $35 million for a new water system, and that after the lawyers were paid, the remainder would be about $17 million, I had assumed EPA would pick up the rest of the costs as part of the remediation of the chemical plant site. The document seemed to exempt EPA from securing more money to complete the project. Worst case scenario, the city would spend their settlement money in designing and starting the project, and then EPA would not step forward to finish it, and it would sit half done.

I called the Trust president, Jay Steinberg, to talk about a number of things, including this worrisome scenario. He agreed that I'd interpreted the sentence correctly, and that it was put in there *intentionally* so that no one reading the document would think that this document actually *required* EPA to complete construction of a new water system for St. Louis.

He went on to say that it was made clear in the closed-door hearings that EPA wanted that sentence in there because they were unhappy about having to replace the city's water supply, and they didn't want other cities with contaminated water supplies to read this agreement and use it to force EPA to replace their water systems.

Also, EPA wanted to be bound *only* to the ROD (Record of Decision) for the plant site, and not to any other legal document. This sentence, which released them from any obligation to complete construction of the city's water supply, really did release them from that obligation. Supposedly, once the ROD was published, which would state that the chosen remedy would include replacement of the city's water supply system, then the worries about the project sitting half done would be alleviated.

The settlement agreement left the city responsible for coming up with a design plan for the new water system, and Jay cautioned that the city had to be very particular to not make any mistakes, since EPA, whose approval for the design plan was needed, would be looking for reasons *not* to reimburse the city for the expense of designing a plan.

He said "It is very important for the city to be nice to EPA." There were bruised egos at EPA, he explained, and all of us had to be careful to not fight them.

I asked if he had met Tom Alcamo, our new EPA project manager, and he hadn't. I told him it was very hard to not fight with Tom, because he seemed to want to fight. Jay said it was probably on purpose that EPA had given us a project manager like that. Despite that, we and the city had to "suck it up and be nice" in order to get the full $6 million from the Trust Fund, and the subsequent funding from EPA.

And even though Jay had used anti-St. Louis verbiage in the courtroom, he told me he was highly satisfied to have $6 million of the Velsicol Trust Account money go to help the city acquire a new water source. He added that our two Michigan senators "drove AIG crazy with letters and phone calls," and he believed that was why the insurance corporation agreed to a settlement that was larger than Jay had anticipated. He had thought that the city might get $10-11 million out of the insurance policy. Seeing them get double that delighted him.

To celebrate the city's David versus Goliath win, a large group of city officials and CAG members met at the River Rock bar in St. Louis to eat, and raise our glasses in toasts to each other for a job well done.

Chapter 19
(2011, part 2)
One Less Site

With the knowledge that a new water system was on its way to replace the city's contaminated drinking water wells, urgency diminished for the rat study on the effects of pCBSA.

We'd done everything we could to get the study by applying through EPA's IRIS (Integrated Risk Information System) as Tom Alcamo had instructed us, by having our senators write letters to EPA Administrator Lisa Jackson, by conversing on the phone with the EPA Office of Congressional and Intergovernmental Relations, and by applying for a study with NIH.

After all that, and with the knowledge that residents soon would no longer be drinking and bathing in pCBSA-contaminated water, we decided it was time to let our quest for a 90-day rat study die.

Having been told by IRIS that our lack of a comprehensive health study meant we most likely would not get a rat study frustrated us. How *can* a community get a health study done? Over the years our applications and requests to CDC, ATSDR, NIEHS and NIH for a comprehensive health study had come up empty, and we'd been told many times it was our lack of a health study that kept us from qualifying for the health study we were asking for, even a 90-day rat study.

In another area of our cleanup oversight, we had also asked for a study. Over the years CAG members had received phone calls about contaminated sites perhaps unknown to us. The latest phone call had come to me from a man who had witnessed slaughtered animals being buried at a nearby location. He saw a large truckload from a company located in Battle Creek, which is over 100 miles from St. Louis, placed in a hole and bulldozed over. This had occurred in the mid-1970s at the time of the PBB Disaster.

237

When I spoke about this anonymous call at our next CAG meeting, EPA Project Manager Tom Alcamo suggested we make a citizen request for a preliminary assessment.

I obtained the proper petition form, filled it out, attached a plat map with the location of the property marked, and mailed it in. Before long I received a phone call from EPA Region 5 telling me that an MDEQ person would be sent to walk over the property with us, and write a preliminary assessment report.

One afternoon, Phil Ramsey, Doug Brecht, Gary Smith and I hiked with Joe Walczak from MDEQ off Jackson Road onto one of the cattle burial sites. Gary knew where it was, because years ago while hunting in that area, he had seen cattle hooves protruding from the ground. We didn't see anything on the day we were there, nor did we see anything at the second site. Joe Walczak said he would gather information on the sites, using 1970s aerial photos, soil maps and other historical data. Then he would score the sites by using an EPA score sheet to see if they should be investigated further. If they scored high enough to warrant further investigation, soil samples would be taken and ground-penetrating radar would be used. If they didn't score high enough, there would still be a file created about them for use if further information was obtained.

About a year later we received the report on the preliminary assessment that said historical data showed cattle *had* been buried at the sites, but during the process of excavating clay from those areas to cover the Gratiot County Landfill, the burial pits were discovered. All the PBB-contaminated livestock remains then were relocated to the landfill, where they were re-buried under the clay cap.

The Breckenridge Site continued to run into difficulties as Energy Solutions pressed forward with their cleanup of radioactive filter cake. Rains in the spring and early summer had waterlogged the clay soils of the site, with over 500,000 gallons needing to be pumped out of the trenches, contained, and held until a permit was issued from the State of Michigan for disposal. Work came to a standstill.

I drove out to the site in mid-July, and there was no activity. No people, no equipment, nothing. Finally, the State determined the water was not radioactive, and they allowed Energy Solutions to pump it into Bush Creek, which ran adjacent to the Breckenridge Site. Work resumed.

Later in the year, the Nuclear Regulatory Commission tested the excavated trenches at the site and found them to be cleaned to a standard considered "safe for any use, including residential and agricultural." The trenches then were filled with clean soil, smoothed, and hydroseeded. For the last time, the workmen's trailer and equipment were removed from the site.

When Bill Snell of the NRC announced the end of the cleanup of the Breckenridge Site during a CAG meeting, the room burst into applause. Finally, after all these years, one of sites was finished, and with a full removal and cleanup.

David Heidlauf of Environ, the contractor for LePetomane Trust that held the deed to the property, was in attendance at the meeting. He said that once the land was sold, the money would go into the St. Louis Trust Account to help pay for the plant site cleanup.

The last official act for the Breckenridge Site came when the NRC's final report was published in the Federal Register early in 2012. The end. We celebrated with a toast of sparkling grape juice, because the city doesn't allow alcohol in the council chambers. Finally, one less site on our list of cleanup projects!

This was why we had formed ourselves into a task force and not a permanent organization. Our goal as a task force was to accomplish projects that had a beginning, middle and end, and eventually put ourselves out of a job. Our CAG had a few more projects to accomplish before we were out of a job, but at least this one had been seen through to the best end of all: land restored and clean enough for any use, including residential and agricultural.

I wish Mayor Joe Scholtz could have celebrated this victory with us. Sadly, he had passed away in August suddenly and unexpectedly at age 55. We were shocked and bereft to have him leave us. City Manager Bob McConkie called me to give me the news, and it was hard to handle. The city council members also were in shock, as was the whole town.

A number of us attended the funeral, including Theo von Wallmenich of CH2MHILL and Scott Cornelius of MDEQ. To have worked hard on the same goal for so long with Joe, it was like an earthquake under our feet, making us feel shaky, to know we had to go on without him.

Joe had been speaking out about pollution in the town of St. Louis since his teenage years. He'd poured his heart and soul into seeing the Pine River cleaned up, and the stigma removed from St. Louis of being known as the "toxic town."

I knew he would continue to pray for us, along with other CAG members who had left us, yet it wasn't the same as to be working side-by-side with him, to hear his voice and to see his smile.

A memory I clung to during this sad time was the boat trip that Joe, Gary and I had taken on our beloved Pine River the previous autumn, seeing a sand hill crane fly by, spotting bass in the water, and talking about our many years of working together to get the river cleaned up. That was a good day, and a precious memory.

Meanwhile, our sites expanded. We all knew that the river downstream from the dam in St. Louis was contaminated.

Following the 1982 remediation at the Velsicol Site, the DDT levels in wildlife living downstream had been expected to fall, but continuous sampling by MDEQ through the 1990s showed that instead of falling, the DDT levels in fish, birds, reptiles, amphibians and mammals continued to rise.

Back in 2003, we had been pleased when MDEQ began to gather samples downstream, but then we heard nothing more. It was while listening to our MDEQ Project Manager Scott Cornelius give a talk at Alma College that I learned the downstream portion of the river would now become part of the official Velsicol Site.

He told the audience that the Velsicol site had three (not two) operable units, and that OU-3 consisted of the riverbed and floodplains downstream from the St. Louis dam. That was great news, and I passed it on to the other members of the CAG.

Even as all these activities and changes happened at the various sites, our ongoing focus remained on the struggle for a thorough cleanup of the chemical plant site, which was a continuing source of contamination for both the river and groundwater. While DDT levels had ranged from 32,000 to 46,000 ppm in the riverbed, those in the soils of the plant site were as high as a million parts per million in some areas. Pure product.

Along with sending our 10-page letter and our 10-minute DVD to the Remedy Review Board, we also asked Senator Carl Levin, Senator Debbie Stabenow and Congressman Dave Camp to write letters to encourage the board to fund the plant site remediation. A reply to their letters from Mathy Stanislaus, Assistant Administrator for EPA, like most bureaucratic responses to Congress, explained the process, this time the process of the Remedy Review Board.

The letter, however, contained one short sentence of interest: Stanislaus wrote "We acknowledge the unfortunate history of the site, including the inadequacy of the containment remedy undertaken by the Velsicol Chemical Corporation." It was good for our CAG to see EPA state in this letter, as it had in a previous 5-year-review, that the 1982 cleanup hadn't been adequate.

A few days later, Scott from MDEQ and Tom from EPA traveled to Washington, D.C. to make their presentation to the Remedy Review Board.

When it was over, Scott sent us an e-mail to say he thought the board members had received the information well, and had asked many questions. Scott praised Tom's handling of the quizzing, and his ability to keep the members on topic. That was an aspect of Tom we hadn't seen. In our meetings he tended to deliver his reports in a disjointed fashion, and we were the ones working to keep him on topic.

Finally, the long-awaited comments from the Remedy Review Board were sent to Richard Karl, the director of the Superfund Division for Region 5, and Tom forwarded the document to us.

There were many surprises. First of all, only FPS-3 (former plant site alternative # 3) had been presented to the board, when we had thought alternatives 2, 3, 5, & 7 would all be presented.

Next, the Board expressed concern about both *in situ* thermal and chemical treatments because no treatability studies had been performed, because the source areas extended to 30 feet below the ground surface, and because the site contained a significant amount of construction debris.

They were also concerned about the high cost of thermal destruction.

We agreed about the construction debris as a potential problem, and later statements by both EPA and MDEQ indicated that they expected to have to dig up and remove much debris in the areas chosen for thermal or chemical treatment.

The more excavation the better, in our view.

Then the Remedy Review Board made some suggestions that really troubled us, such as recommending that the contaminated soils dug up from neighborhood yards be put on the plant site and buried under the new cap (an ugly reminder of Appendix F), and instead of replacing the slurry wall around the site with a steel wall, to simply repair the worst areas of the clay wall. The Board was also unhappy that the remedy plans included the replacement of the city's water supply.

To a community that had diligently worked during the past 14 years to get the best cleanup possible, these suggestions seemed a step backward.

The board's 1980s-like comments, however, did engender in us a greater appreciation for the work Scott had done, and Tom more recently, to persuade Region 5 of the necessity of new water for St. Louis, and a new wall, rather than a repair, and no more burying of contaminated wastes on plant site property!

Tom and Scott wrote a long and detailed response to the board, upholding their viewpoints, and they assured us that although the Remedy Review Board comments would carry weight in the decision process, it was the Region 5 leadership that would ultimately decide how to accomplish remediation at the plant site.

Now that the Remedy Review Board process was behind us, we again asked to see the draft Feasibility Study, but EPA still would not let us see it.

Instead Tom and Scott offered to give a presentation on the process of weighing the various plans under consideration. Because even though only FPS-3 had been presented to the Remedy Review Board, EPA supposedly had not yet chosen a remedy from the four under consideration. EPA and MDEQ kept up this fiction all the way through the time of the Public Meeting in order to fulfill the guidelines of not making a final decision until they had reached #9 of the CERCLA Nine Criteria, which is "community acceptance."

We were told that after considering eight alternative scenarios to accomplish the complicated cleanup of this site, EPA and MDEQ had settled on the four previously mentioned options (FPS-2, 3, 5, & 7) which ranged in upfront costs of $94 million to $186 million.

When 50 years of O & M (operation and maintenance) were factored in, the costs for the four alternatives ranged from $325 million to $481 million. Since all of the options required skilled operation of a complicated water treatment system, upkeep of a cap over the 52-acre site, and, in three of the options, maintenance of a steel wall around the site, factoring in O & M costs was necessary.

At this time, the most expensive EPA cleanup going on in Region 5 was costing $120 million, and it was dealing with one contaminant, lead. The Velsicol site contained multiple contaminants in the soil, plus the extensive groundwater contamination.

All four of the options included a replacement of the St. Louis water system, excavation and removal of polluted soils from residential yards, a groundwater extraction and treatment system at the plant site, NAPL recovery using collection trenches and sump pumps, ongoing groundwater monitoring, and the institution of laws and regulations regarding use of the site. FPS-2 included only these remedies and would cost a total of $325 million.

The next alternative (FPS-3) included all of the above and added in thermal destruction of NAPL and DBCP on about 12 acres of land in two areas of the site, prior to excavation of those areas. In the thermal destruction process, the contaminants are heated in the ground by the conduction of electricity through metal rods. When the contaminants reach the boiling point, they volatilize, and the gases are then captured in filters, which are disposed of in hazardous waste landfills. The process also causes liquid contaminants, such as DNAPL, to become less viscous, which makes the pumping of them possible. In FPS-3, chemical oxidation would also be used in two areas of the site to break down dangerous semi-volatile chemicals to non-dangerous forms. FPS-3 would cost a total of $374 million.

Alternative FPS-5 included all of the above-mentioned methods, but expanded the use of chemical oxidation to address both semi-volatile and volatile chemicals. It would cost $416 million.

Alternative FPS-7 utilized most of what was mentioned in the previous methods, but added a final step of excavating the entire top of the plant site down to the water table. In some areas this would be to a depth of 4-5 feet, and in other places up to 20 feet. In total, about 550,000 cubic yards of contaminated soil would be removed. The site would then be backfilled with sand and capped with clay and soil to more than 4 feet deep. FPS-7 also would not require a wall around the site, but would use extraction wells at the perimeter to keep the contaminants from moving into the river. It would cost $481 million.

Scott Cornelius said that alternatives 3, 5, and 7 all .targeted the source. And by controlling, eliminating and destroying the sources of contamination, the groundwater outside the perimeter of the plant site would be returned to drinking water standards in not less than 50 years, and probably many more. As for the groundwater beneath the site, it likely would remain contaminated forever.

In all the plans, a water treatment plant would be built on the plant site, and it would require many complicated processes in order to remove the wide range of pollutants contained in the contaminated water.

A total of twelve extraction wells would pump polluted groundwater up and then through the treatment plant. The groundwater, once cleaned, would be discharged into the Pine River. In part, the water treatment plant would separate out DNAPL from water, remove metals, use an air stripper for VOC's and treat the off-gases with thermal oxidation, and would use an advanced oxidation process, with a final filter of granular activated carbon.

DNAPL (dense non-aqueous phase liquid), a highly toxic substance, was present in three forms at the plant site, with most of it consisting of 82% DDT. Also dangerously toxic was DBCP (1,2-dibromo-3 chloropropane).

That is why the plans called for these chemicals to be thermally destroyed in the ground, to prevent danger to workers at the site, and to people in the neighborhood. In the location where DDT had been produced, some of the DNAPL was located 99 feet below ground.

As for future use of the site, there would be restrictions, such as no trees planted in the ground, because the roots could compromise the cap to be built over the site. A city law would have to be passed disallowing anyone to put in a private well, because the groundwater would not be cleaned to drinking water standards for many years to come, and perhaps not for centuries.

This was the presentation at one month's meeting. The next month we heard the second half which was described by Scott Cornelius of MDEQ as a "detailed, comparative analysis" of the four alternatives for cleaning up the plant site.

The alternatives were compared in terms of long-term effectiveness, short-term effectiveness, implementability, compliancy with established laws, reduction of toxicity, mobility and volume through treatment, overall protectiveness of human health and the environment, and cost. The acceptability to the community was not part of the comparative analysis.

To briefly define the terms, *long-term effectiveness* takes into account the amount of residual risk left at the site; *short-term effectiveness* deals with the protectiveness during construction to workers, the environment and the community; *implementability* covers technical feasibility; *compliancy* means meeting both federal and state standards for hazardous waste clean-up and disposal; reduction of toxicity, mobility and volume *through treatment* refers to the EPA's preference for treating pollution on site rather than hauling it elsewhere; and *overall protection* of human health and the environment considers how risks are controlled at the site.

After hearing this presentation, St. Louis City Manager Bob McConkie said that the City Council preferred FPS-5 in which almost the whole surface of the plant site above the water table, and in some places below it, would be treated with either thermal destruction or chemical oxidation. They felt that the FPS-5 alternative would be much more protective of the community and environment than FPS-3.

The CAG agreed with the city, and many CAG members continued to push for FPS-7 as being even more protective of the community, because it removed source contaminants down to the water table. Even in EPA's written evaluations, both FPS-5 and FPS-7 rated higher in long-term protectiveness that FPS-3, although Tom Alcamo said those remedies were off-set by the greater dangers in short-term effectiveness. In EPA's view, the FPS-7 excavation would expose the community to dust and volatiles over a long span of time.

In the view of many in the CAG, not only would FPS-7 rid the site of much more source material than FPS-3, but would also clean out the demolition debris that had the potential to disrupt other treatment processes planned for use at the site. As stated in the comments from the National EPA Remedy Review Board, the debris in place could be problematic because the gases and steam from the thermal process would likely follow "preferential flow paths caused by the demolition debris."

If excavation was to take place, about 550,000 cubic yards would be removed, requiring about 31,000 truck loads leaving the city. EPA and MDEQ presented these numbers to us with the intent, it seemed, to frighten us with their size, but we countered by pointing out that the residents of St. Louis had already experienced 750,000 cubic yards of river sediment being trucked away, with up to 70 truckloads a day leaving the city. The numbers didn't daunt us.

Despite good arguments put forth by the CAG membership for more widespread excavation of the plant site surface, EPA and MDEQ flatly said they would not choose FPS-7, even though they kept up the bureaucratic fiction that they had not yet decided on a plan.

Jim Heinzman, our newest CAG member, and retired from MDEQ, agreed to meet with the CAG Executive Committee and the St. Louis city manager to give us some behind-the-scenes details. In our talk with him, he spelled out in words what we had often sensed in the tension between our project managers.

Essentially, the State agency preferred to test until it could see as much of the problem as possible prior to remediation, and then to clean up as much as possible.

The EPA, on the other hand, preferred to avoid testing which might show a greater extent of the problem, in order to limit the outlay of money for the initial clean up.

These differing approaches had to do with the fact that the State pays 10% of the initial cleanup costs for a Superfund site, while EPA pays 90%, and, after 10 years, the State is left with the entire operation and maintenance costs. For instance, in the DNAPL discussion, the State's position was to remove as much source material as possible to reduce long term pump-and-treat maintenance, while EPA's position was the opposite--they wouldn't be paying for centuries of pumping and treating, so it was more cost-effective for them to clean up less source material.

As an example, Jim spoke about the 99-foot well on the plant site property that contained DNAPL. During the investigative phase, the State's sampling had shown DNAPL present at that depth, and they insisted it needed to be removed and not left for operation and maintenance. EPA took the view that the presence of DNAPL at that depth was a fluke, and the State would have no O & M to worry about.

To prove their point, they bailed out enough to fill a 55-gallon drum, thinking that would be the end of their DNAPL recovery. The well, however, filled up again.

After that experiment, EPA agreed to address DNAPL recovery as part of the initial cleanup plan, although it very well could remain part of the operation and maintenance of the site, too, depending on the quantity underground.

In the course of this discussion, I once again objected to the criterion of "community acceptance" being situated in last place on the list of the Nine Criteria EPA was required to meet. With the community acceptance portion of the process taking place only after the Proposed Plan and Feasibility Study were published, this effectively excluded the community from the decision-making process.

I suggested we send a letter prior to the publication of the Proposed Plan/FS, asking for certain concerns of ours to be addressed within the document.

Murray said the letter was not worth the time and effort to write, because it would be rejected, and I agreed that he was probably right.

And, in fact, at the last Technical Committee meeting when I'd told Tom that we had some statements we'd like to have written into the Proposed Plan, he replied, "*That* will never happen."

Even so, I wrote the letter to Region 5 Director Richard Karl asking that four provisions be included in the EPA's Proposed Plan document, one of them asking for bench studies to be performed prior to settling on a cleanup plan, and the other three asking for the involvement of the city and the CAG in any decision-making that might be necessary if the planned remediation ran into complications. I ended the letter by saying that these stipulations would need to be written into the Proposed Plan if the community was to give its acceptance.

The draft letter, when sent around, caused City Manager Bob McConkie some concern because of the delay it might cause in getting the cleanup underway. We shared his desire for the project to finally start, but we also remembered how the 1982 settlement had taken place with no community input. As I said to Bob, even if EPA refused to include our statements, we still needed to make the request. It was important for the record to show that we had asked and they had said "no."

The letter was sent, and, amazingly, Richard Karl agreed to include three of our four statements in a special paragraph called "Community Involvement" to be tacked onto the end of the Proposed Plan. As for the bench studies, those would be conducted during the design phase of the remediation, we were told, and not prior to choosing a remediation plan.

As a successful close to the year 2011, we were finally given a copy of the Feasibility Study. From the time it had first been promised until actually receiving it, nine years had passed! Even though many of us wanted more extensive excavation than was planned with FPS-3, we held out hope that once the shovels were in the ground, EPA would find it necessary to dig up far more debris and contaminated waste than planned.

With the Feasibility Study in hand and work at the plant site imminent, and with the city's lawsuit settlement, and the successful closing out of the Breckenridge Radioactive Site, it was a victorious year for the St. Louis community.

Chapter 20
(2012, Part 1)
Altered Circumstances

Having agreed to help us craft our comments on the proposed remedy for the plant site, University of Michigan Law School professor, Dr. Nina Mendelson, and her graduate students asked us which alternative the CAG wanted to advocate (FPS-3, 5 or 7), and that was the crux of our problem. Some members maintained that more excavation should take place on the plant site than what the Plan proposed, and some agreed with EPA that only the hotspots should be addressed, with a containment system constructed for the remainder of the polluted soil and groundwater. Furthermore, it was clear that EPA and MDEQ had settled on #3, yet the City of St. Louis preferred alternative #5, and many members in the CAG urgently felt that #7 was the only viable option for long-term permanence.

The Proposed Plan stated that all the alternatives met the EPA criteria of protecting human health and the environment. It also said that #7 scored higher in terms of long-term effectiveness and permanence, but less well in short-term effectiveness, because of the threat of airborne contamination to workers and the community. Those in our group who advocated for #7 argued that protective measures to contain airborne contamination were available and could be used at the site. Those that advocated for #3 said the use of those measures was not a perfect solution and contamination could still spread to the neighborhood, plus their use them would add to the cost. The city's position was that #5, in addressing the volatiles and semi-volatiles, would provide better long-term protection for its citizens, without digging up the entire site.

During several conference calls with Nina and her students, and with our paid Technical Advisor, Dr. Peter deFur, the majority opinion of the CAG settled on #7. Even if we ultimately did not get it, we felt we needed to be on record as having asked for this more complete cleanup, which would deal with all the source material that #'s 3 and 5 partially dealt with.

Peter said we should write a letter to the director of Region 5 prior to the Public Meeting, expressing our concerns about the proposed remedy and stating our preferences, and Jim Heinzman, the retired MDEQ employee who had become a CAG member, agreed.

Since I was flying out early the next day to visit family in British Columbia, I put together a letter that evening and e-mailed it to Richard Karl, the EPA Director of Region 5. Ordinarily I would have sent a draft of the letter around to members of the Executive Committee for their input, but this time I didn't. The consensus at the last Executive Committee meeting had been that the CAG believed #7 would more permanently protect our community, and that's what I explained in the letter.

While on vacation, I received an e-mail from Dianne Borrello, saying that the letter I'd sent expressed my personal opinion as if it were the opinion of the CAG, and that the CAG hadn't yet reached consensus. She was mistaken, due to the fact that neither she nor Murray had participated in the prior meetings, or the conference calls with Dr. Mendelson and Peter deFur, when the decision was reached. As dispassionately as I could, I wrote an explanation to her.

When I got home, Murray called an Executive Committee meeting, listing several agenda items, such as how to handle the writing of comments on the Proposed Plan, how we would use Peter deFur's expertise, and how to handle a response to the letter I had written to Region 5.

Predictably, none of the other topics were addressed at the meeting, but the letter I'd sent to Richard Karl came under great scrutiny. It was a three-hour session in which Dianne took the lead in angrily accusing me of having stepped out of bounds by not sending the draft letter around, and by stating facts in the letter which were incorrect. Despite my sense of ill treatment, I kept calm and continually asked how the letter was factually incorrect. Finally, she pointed out two things: first, I had stated the wrong purpose for the vertical barrier, or wall, and second, that ISCO (*in situ* chemical oxidation) was not part of the Proposed Plan. When I got home, I re-read the Proposed Plan document to see if I'd been mistaken, and found I wasn't. Rather, she was.

None of this, however, was the real cause of the discord, as far as I could see. If it had been about facts, why get so angry? I believed that Dianne and Murray had made up their minds that #3 was the best we could get and that we should accept it and not disagree with EPA. In fact, each of them had voiced at different times the concern that if we asked for #7 it would make us look ignorant in the eyes of EPA.

Of concern to me was the lack cohesiveness in our group as we entered this important phase of the remediation process. Pointing out where Dianne was factually wrong wasn't going to heal us, although it had to be done. What else could I do to help ease the tension?

I decided to withdraw the letter. Since Murray and Dianne had chosen to focus on the letter as the cause of their discontent, I hoped that by withdrawing it, their feathers might be smoothed. I wrote an e-mail to Richard Karl and Tom Alcamo at Region 5 asking them to withdraw the letter from the Administrative Record.

Then I wrote an e-mail of apology to the members of the Executive Committee for having sent the letter without their input. Gary Smith replied, saying no apology was necessary and that probably the others would have sent the letter as I had under the same circumstances. I wish he had said that during the three-hour meeting.

Also, Tom Alcamo called me, saying the letter was fine, and I shouldn't withdraw it. I explained that it had more to do with internal politics in our group than the content of the letter.

Next I wrote to Dianne and pointed out her inaccuracies, citing page numbers and quoting text from the Proposed Plan, and copying the e-mail to the Executive Committee members.

At the end of it I brought up another thing that had bothered me during the three-hour meeting. Gary had raised the idea of hiring our own employee to be on site during the plant site remediation work as a kind of overseer for the community. Recently, Jim Hall had rejoined our group after being gone for several years. As an Environmental Trainer for Consumers Energy, he had the qualifications to be on site in a hard hat while the rest of us didn't. He was the person Gary had in mind.

Both Dianne and Murray had criticized Gary's idea, saying that a CAG overseer would develop a buddy-buddy relationship with EPA and therefore would be ineffective. In my e-mail, I cautioned all of us about forming buddy-buddy relationships with EPA, because we might begin to push the agency's agenda rather than the agenda of the CAG and the wider community. Apparently this hit a sore spot with Murray. He fired off a response, asking if I was accusing him of this kind of relationship. I wrote back asking him to notice that the word "we" had been used in my statement.

This latest upset took place on the day of our CAG meetings. That afternoon, after our EPA, MDEQ and CH2MHILL project managers had arrived for the Technical Committee meeting, and our CAG members who regularly attended were there, including Dianne, we sat conversing, waiting for Murray to come and chair the meeting, but he didn't come through the doorway. Finally, I got up and went to where Dianne sat to asked her if Murray was on his way. She said he wasn't coming. After a pause, I asked if she planned to lead the meeting, as she sometimes did in Murray's absence. She said "no." So I got things underway.

That was how Murray quit the CAG. He hadn't been the person accused and grilled for three hours, but instead took offense at a cautionary sentence written to the entire Executive Committee. Writing cautionary statements was nothing new. Over the years, Ed, Gary and I, and even Murray, had written cautionary statements to the other members of the Executive Committee. And the topic wasn't new, either. Ed had warned us about being "captured" by the agency people time and again.

Over the next few days, I encouraged Murray to come back, as did Ed and Gary. Murray's only response was a short e-mail asking to be taken off the mailing list, and that any future messages from the group would be deleted without being read.

I thought back to his first resignation letter in 2002, and how I had convinced him he was needed, and he had stayed on. And to his second near-resignation in 2008, when counsel from Ed and Joe had helped him decide to continue in the CAG. I guess this time was different from either of those. Even Ed's email which admonished all of us to be mindful that we needed "to live together, forgive, and respect differences" didn't do the trick.

Dr. Peter deFur flew in the next day for the big Proposed Plan Public Meeting to be held that night. In the afternoon, the Executive Committee met to discuss our concerns about the proposed remediation. Dianne attended, but not Murray.

During the meeting, Gary said we needed a new chairperson for the Technical Committee, since it appeared Murray wasn't willing to continue in that capacity, and would Dianne be willing to take on the responsibility? She declined, saying she and Murray had always worked together in the CAG, and since he was through, she was also through.

She stayed on with us, though, until our comments were written for the Proposed Plan. Then she sent us a letter of resignation. With Gary's help, I composed letters to both Murray and Dianne thanking them for their many years of contributions to the CAG and letting them know they were welcome to return should they decide to do so in the future.

Following the afternoon Executive Committee meeting, several of us went to dinner with Peter deFur, Jim Heinzman, and David Heidlauf from Environ. Then we all went to the St. Louis Middle School cafetorium to attend the formal EPA Public Meeting on the Proposed Plan.

I was pleased to see the seats fill up with many citizens that I knew, and many I did not know. Scott from MDEQ and Tom from EPA alternated as speakers as they went through their power point slides. Despite the formality of going to the podium and the trickiness in negotiating the steps in the cafetorium, many individuals got out of their seats to speak into the microphone and ask their questions. We had arranged for the local public access television station to film the event and show it on their channel. All of that went well, and the program aired for several weeks following the meeting so that those who hadn't attended that night could watch the presentation on TV and perhaps get their questions answered.

During the Proposed Plan meeting, Peter deFur sat by me and passed me notes. In one of them, he suggested that the CAG hold its own community meeting to give people a chance to speak up in a less formal setting, and without the nervousness of standing at a podium.

It was a good idea, and we moved forward with it, planning to use our upcoming regular meeting date for that purpose. We got the word out through the city's newsletter, and by putting up fliers.

I couldn't attend on the night of the CAG's Community Meeting, and Gary Smith conducted it. We had a good turnout, with Jim Hall and Gary making a trip down to the basement to bring up more chairs. Again, public access TV recorded the event..

I think it was good for Gary to lead the event, considering what he was facing in his personal life. He had told me that the tumor growing in his chest was much worse than expected, and was environmentally caused. Later, he would have surgery to remove it, along with part of his sternum and the ends of two ribs. .

As for our own formal comments on the 60-plus page Proposed Plan, we were asked by Dr. Nina Mendelson and her U of M Law School students to lay out the CAG's greatest concerns about the proposed remedy.

Our number one concern had to do with permanence. I explained that the 1980s remedy of the chemical plant site had failed, and therefore, we worried that this new proposed remedy might also fail. We wanted language in place that would compel EPA to fix it immediately, should that happen.

Another concern involving permanence was the proposed pumping system. With the groundwater and upper aquifer underneath the site extensively contaminated, the plan called for a hydraulic pumping system to keep the pollution "contained" beneath the plant site. Since the pumping system would likely be a necessity through the course of many generations of citizens, we needed language that would mandate the establishment of institutional vigilance.

Recently, EPA had obtained a Technical Impracticability waiver for the area under the river, which allowed them to leave in place known and unknown deposits of DNAPL. The TI waiver made the claim that today's technology was not capable of addressing the DNAPL under the river.

This was our first acquaintance with a TI waiver, and we worried how it might be used again.

For instance, if EPA began work at the plant site and found the contamination to be more extensive or more expensive to easily clean up, would they seek another TI Waiver and leave the source material in place? We desired language that would circumvent future decisions to take the easy way out.

Also on that issue, we had been reminded by Jim Heinzman that it was *not* technically impractical for EPA to remove NAPL from under the river. The river could be sectioned with sheet piling, dewatered and excavated cell by cell. That was the method EPA had used from 1998-2006 in a 36-acre area of the river impoundment to remove DDT-contaminated sediment, and they could repeat that process in this other area if they chose to spend the money to do it. We wanted this stated in our comments.

As for the surface soil, we knew EPA had the technology to deal with it. They could excavate; they could apply electricity to thermally destruct the chemicals throughout the plant site; they could use chemical oxidation over the entire site to deal with volatile and semi-volatiles as well as chemical contamination. They could clean both the surface soil and the saturated soil beneath. We wanted the record to show that we were against having contaminants left in place that could be eliminated with today's technology.

We wanted our comments to express the specific ways in which we desired the quality of life for the residents of the community to be maintained throughout the cleanup process. The short paragraph that we had managed to have included in the Proposed Plan about community involvement needed elaboration. For one thing, even though the title of the section was Community Involvement, the verb used throughout the paragraph was "informed" -- that EPA would inform us of this and that. In our view, being informed was not the same as being involved in the decision-making.

We took the writing of these formal comments very seriously because we knew they would be included in the Record of Decision (ROD), and were an historical record of our efforts to get the best cleanup possible. Also, because I knew our formal comments would not include some of the things that individual CAG members wished to say, I encouraged our members to write their own personal comments and submit them and many of us did.

The e-mails went back and forth from me to the U of M law group. It was quite an experience to work with a soil chemistry expert, a hydrogeologist who knew our site in ways that we didn't, and a law professor and her students, one of whom had worked for EPA and was now studying environmental law. They and several CAG members funneled comments to me, and I kept piecing and re-piecing the text, and sending it to Nina at the Law School. It was invigorating and exhausting at the same time. Energizing me was the thought that this was the one and only opportunity in my lifetime to advocate for the best cleanup possible at the plant site.

When the first completed draft of the comments arrived from U of M, the facts and arguments were there, but it didn't read well. I resigned myself to the task of re-writing the document to bring together the various writing styles so that it didn't sound as if a committee had patched something together. Finally, in early April, the letter was written and on its way. It would be a few more months before the ROD was signed.

Meanwhile, I was making phone calls to find a person willing to chair the Technical Committee. After Dianne Borrello declined, I asked Jim Heinzman. He thought about it for a couple of days, but said he believed our CAG would be better served if he remained a member who could freely question EPA about technical matters.

I also spoke with Tom Rohrer, another former MDEQ employee who had worked on the Gratiot County Landfill site decades ago, and was now a professor at Central Michigan University. He also declined.

Next I spoke with Dr. Stephen Boyd, who had grown up in St. Louis, and who had interned one summer at the chemical plant, and was now a professor of environmental chemistry and soil toxicology at Michigan State University. He was willing to become a CAG member and to help us with reading and interpreting scientific reports. Later, he agreed to chair the Technical Committee.

Soon after Steve became chairperson of the Technical Committee, he wrote an e-mail comment on Alternative #3, saying that given the uncertainties of both the thermal and oxidation technologies, a complete removal of the contaminated soil at the plant site would be the best choice in the long run.

He said if the major concern for complete excavation was vapor release, it could be dealt with, and that in the long run, excavation would be less expensive than using the thermal and oxidation techniques because it was technically straightforward. That was what the consensus of the CAG had been, too.

In the long bureaucratic process of Superfund, the Velsicol Plant Site had passed the milestones of the Remedial Investigation report (in 2006), the National Remedy Review Board (in 2011) and the release of the Feasibility Study (at the end of 2011). Still ahead was the signing of the Record of Decision.

What we didn't know is that beyond the ROD lay the national EPA Prioritization Panel which would determine when funding for the work would begin to flow, and how much. We didn't know about the Panel because it had not been a step in the process back in 1998 when we'd traversed CERCLA for the sediment removal from the riverbed.

In May, Tom Short, a program manager for EPA's Region 5, came to our meeting to explain how the Prioritization Panel worked. He told us that the EPA Regions have no discretion over which sites are given priority in terms of time and money. The decisions are made solely by the people who sit on the Prioritization Panel in Washington, D.C. Short was a member of that panel, but he would not be allowed to score sites from his region, or to vote on those sites. After the panel had made its decision, the yearly allocations would be authorized by Mathy Stanislaus, the federal EPA Assistant Administrator who oversaw, among other things, the national Superfund program.

Superfund sites that were deemed "ongoing remediations" would receive priority over "new starts." Since the Velsicol Superfund Site had a newly approved ROD, it was considered to be a new start. This was the very worry we had faced back in 2004 -- that if the plant site cleanup did not get underway while the river impoundment cleanup was going on, the plant site would lose its place in the queue. At that time Senator Carl Levin had admonished EPA upper management about separating the river from the chemical plant, since they were contiguous to one another and part of the same cleanup effort. Despite his admonitions, and ours, the plant site was now back in the NPL pool of "new starts."

There was another major difficulty that our site faced -- we had money in a Trust Fund. If life was fair, our community would have been rewarded for having fought for a claim in the Fruit of the Loom bankruptcy back in 2002, which put money into the Trust Fund for our cleanups, and for cleanups in other states. The opposite was true. Because we had about $16 million in the Trust Fund, the Prioritization Panel would likely decide to withhold Superfund money, and make Region 5 use Trust Fund money instead.

If Region 5 was required to use money from the Trust, Tom Alcamo said only the residential areas marked with orange fences would be cleaned during the present construction season. No sampling of the neighborhood DDT and PBB levels would take place, nor would design plans for the plant site commence. That is, in fact, what happened later in the year.

Once again the whole plant site project was delayed, this time due to bureaucracy. We were in the middle of our fifteenth year as a CAG, and we still hadn't seen a shovel in the ground at the plant site. Joe used to say, "Once they stick a shovel in the ground, they'll have to keep digging." Phil Ramsey, who was almost 80 years old by now, said EPA was waiting for us all to die off so they could get away without doing anything ever. Sometimes it felt that way.

The declaration by EPA that the plant site was a "new start" and not an "ongoing remedial investigation" rankled us.

We contacted Dr. Nina Mendelson at the University of Michigan Law School wondering if we could find a way to overturn this designation to help speed up the funding.

She and her students determined that a logical case could be made that it *was* an ongoing investigation, since EPA had stated in its five-year-review that the first remedy had never worked as it was meant to, and that we were still dealing with the same environmental and health risks as we had been in 1982. It was logical to see the new proposed remediation as a repair of the old one.

It made sense, yet in the end, we learned the law was on the side of EPA in classifying our site as they chose. Another dead end.

At the same CAG meeting when we had learned about the Prioritization Panel, we were also told about the sampling technique planned for use in at least 54 yards in the 9-block residential area south of the plant site (which later became 117 yards). Our EPA Project Manager Tom Alcamo brought several of his upper management people to the meeting, including Region 5 Director Richard Karl; Karl's second in command, Joan Tananka; Tom's immediate supervisor, Ajit Vaidya; and Tom Short, the program manager who also sat on the Prioritization Panel.

Tom Alcamo told us that the sampling method used by MDEQ to first find contaminated areas in the yards, now enclosed with orange snow fencing, was not the method EPA would use. MDEQ had used a sampling grid and when a hot spot was found, they "stepped out" from it until the concentrations in the soil samples dropped below levels of concern. EPA, on the other hand, planned to take five random samples from an area, such as a front yard, mix the samples together, and then test to see if one small sample drawn from the mix tested above or below the cleanup criteria.

Members of our CAG immediately began to question the composite method, worrying that hot spots would be left if the mixing of samples determined that the whole yard taken together as one composite sample showed low levels. EPA's answer for that was that no person or animal was going to stand in the hotspot area of a yard long enough to be in danger.

Joan Tananka added that it would not make sense for one area of a yard to be high in concentrations and the rest to be clean, because contaminants didn't spread that way. When the wind carried them, they settled fairly evenly. I asked her if she was aware of the local knowledge about how the State had required Velsicol to dredge the river on the west side of the plant site in 1970; how the dredged wastes were piled up on the plant site; and how Velsicol offered free fill dirt from the piles to residents who wished to level low spots in their yards. She didn't believe that could have occurred, and Tom Alcamo kept echoing the same sentiment over the months until, in 2013, he found a layer of fill during the orange-fence excavations, and the fill material measured very high in DDT. We had the satisfaction then to know our local knowledge had been correct.

At the meeting, the EPA people went into a discussion about statistics, algorithms and risk communication, insisting that their method was more effective than the one MDEQ had used. Jim Heinzman agreed that their method had merit, but encouraged them to be "a little flexible" in their approach, and to not slavishly follow their statistical model, now that they knew this bit of history concerning the use of contaminated fill dirt.

Later Jim explained to us that there are two concepts, or philosophies, in thinking about sampling. The first is risk assessment and the second characterization. EPA was describing sampling from the first philosophy, and the CAG was questioning from the second.

As we learned more about sampling techniques from Heinzman, Dr. Peter deFur, and our MDEQ Project Manager Scott Cornelius, we came to see that the EPA method should be effective. Also, the sampling plan had changed.

Instead of taking only 5 samples from a yard, they now would take 14, and the mixing of samples was done level by level. By that I mean in each yard 14 samples from the first six-inch layer made up one composite sample, the 14 from the six-to twelve inch layer made up the next composite sample and so on. Most yards were being sampled at the six-inch, twelve-inch, eighteen-inch and twenty-four inch levels, with some yards being sampled as deep as four feet (later excavation in some yards went down six feet).

As for the process, each of the plugs from the six-inch level was sieved to get stones out, then mixed, and then combined into a composite sample. Those samples were then tested for DDT, PBB and TRIS. This plan seemed more thorough than the way it had been described to us at first.

Scott Cornelius had not been attending our meetings regularly, and Gary had raised the concern that the interests of the State were not being adequately represented without the project manager in attendance.

Then Scott sent us an e-mail saying it was time to transition to Tom Alcamo being the main person we dealt with, since we had entered the stage of the remediation process at which EPA was the lead agency.

This was worrisome. Maybe if a PRP had been involved, it would make sense. But without a PRP for EPA to push, the EPA became the de facto PRP at our orphaned site, not wanting to spend money, and always hoping to find the cheaper way to do only what they could not get out of doing at all. During the years when the State had served as a staunch ally with us, they had pressured EPA to do more, and without them, we felt at a disadvantage. But there was nothing we could do about it. We had to accept this latest circumstance and move forward.

Our circumstances altered yet again, due to the persistence of a CAG member. Teri Kniffen, who lived with an orange fence in her front yard, had complained for years about finding dead birds in her yard, sometimes as many as ten. She described seeing them stagger around before dying. Scott had told her to collect the birds and freeze them, and he would pick them up to have them tested. For some reason, this transaction did not take place in a timely manner. When the birds were finally transported to the lab in Lansing, they had been frozen too long and were worthless for testing.

In the spring of 2012, after finding two dead robins, Teri took pictures of them in place on the ground, collected them and put them in her freezer. She called the Michigan Department of Natural Resources Wildlife Disease Lab at Michigan State University, and drove the birds there herself a couple of days later.

When she called me with the lab results, I couldn't believe what I was hearing. The diagnosis was organochlorine poisoning; specifically, DDD, DDE and DDT in the brain. The male had over 237 ppm DDE in its brain and the female over 250 ppm DDE. Since whole, or total, DDT (DDD, DDE and DDT combined -- also known as DDX) is lethal for robins at 100 ppm or less, these adult birds had apparently died of acute DDT poisoning. Were our neighborhood soils really killing robins?

I asked Teri if it would be possible for her to attend the afternoon Technical Committee meeting the following week to share the necropsy reports from the lab with EPA at that time. I knew that EPA would have their ecological risk assessor, Dr. Jim Chapman, at the meeting, and I wanted him to hear the news first hand. She said she would be there.

She brought copies of the reports, and the photographs she had taken. Her news silenced the room. She said she'd been told that the robins were probably poisoned at the plant site and happened to die in her yard, but Jim Chapman said during nesting season, robins don't range very far from the nest. They gather worms close by to feed themselves and their young. That meant they had accumulated the DDT nearer her house. Teri had seen the birds pulling worms in the moist area near her sump pump outflow, and they also drank water from that source.

Tom Alcamo's reaction to the dead birds was about money. He was scheduled to go before the Prioritization Panel in Washington, D. C. the following week to argue that Superfund money should be used for cleanup of the residential yards, and he believed the dead robins would help him get the money he needed. He said the lab report from the DNR would add weight to his argument that the contamination problem in St. Louis was acute and needed priority funding.

To add backup to Tom's verbal argument, our CAG wrote letters to our Congressmen and women again, telling them how the robins were dying of DDT poisoning in St. Louis, and urging them to contact the Prioritization Panel with support for the funding of the neighborhood in St. Louis. I also wrote directly to Mathy Stanislaus, the person who would authorize the funding for Superfund sites, and I told him about the dead robins to illustrate the gravity of our situation.

Despite the extra clout of the DDT-poisoned birds, the Panel did not allocate any funding for St. Louis in 2012.

Chapter 21
(2012, Part 2)
Changing Faces

The orange snow fences staked around portions of people's yards were a visible sign of the contaminated soil within, and also of the long battle that EPA and MDEQ had waged against each other. For almost five years, the people on Bankson, Watson and Saginaw streets had lived with the ugly fencing put up by MDEQ, yet without it, EPA probably would not have cleaned up the yards at all.

Now the time for excavation was near. All that was needed was money.

Of the approximately $16 million in the Trust Fund for the Velsicol Site in St. Louis, the city's lawsuit settlement had channeled $6 million toward the new water system for the municipality. Of the remaining $10 million in the Trust Fund, half would go to MDEQ to be spent on operation and maintenance of the plant site once the remedy was in place. Now EPA Project Manager Tom Alcamo had to dip into the remaining $5 million to deal with the orange-fenced areas.

When the digging began, it went fast, and by the end of the year, each of the fenced locations had been excavated and the DDT-laden soil replaced with clean dirt. The orange fences disappeared. Everyone in town, from realtors to city officials to CAG members breathed a sigh of relief. Having an improvement that was visible counted for a lot.

During the excavation of Teri Kniffen's property and that of her next door neighbor, evidence of old fill material turned up which tested much higher in DDT than the surrounding soils. Even though the CAG was not glad about the contamination being there, we felt vindicated, since earlier EPA officials had refused to believe information we had offered them about Velsicol having given away free fill dirt contaminated with DDT.

The dead robins found in Teri's yard were mentioned in a two-part feature story published in the Detroit Free Press commemorating the 40th anniversary of the PBB Disaster. And the present-day dead robins were also a topic of conversation at a Rachel Carson *Silent Spring* gathering at Michigan State University.

Dr. Stephen Boyd had alerted us about an exhibit at the MSU museum that celebrated the 50th year of the publication of *Silent Spring*. There was to be a reception and official opening of the exhibit called "Echoes of Silent Spring: 50 Years of Environmental Awareness." Gary Smith and I drove down to East Lansing, and Scott Cornelius, Steve Boyd, and Jim Heinzman also attended.

The exhibit consisted of large panels with drawings, photos and text on them, as well as preserved dead robins which had been collected on the MSU campus by Dr. George Wallace, one of the scientists whose research was relied upon by Rachel Carson in the writing of *Silent Spring*. Also displayed were typewritten letters that had passed between Wallace and Carson, from 1958 through 1964.

Since Dr. Wallace had been my dad's PhD professor, and since our families were close, the exhibit held a depth of meaning for me beyond its place in American history. It was almost as if I was viewing part of my own early life. As I walked through the exhibit, I felt quite emotional to remember having known about DDT's devastating effects on robins and other birds even before Rachel Carson's book was published, due to our family connection. And I felt deeply honored to have been involved in the attempts to clean up the DDT pollution in St. Louis during the past 16 years. And I felt almost ashamed of the fact that the robins were still dying in St. Louis, despite the early efforts of Dr. Wallace, Rachel Carson, my mom and dad, and the more recent efforts of our CAG.

While sitting on a bench after viewing the exhibit, a woman sat down beside me, and I told her that the robins were still dying in St. Louis, where the DDT had been manufactured. I said, "For most people, viewing the dead robins in this exhibit is a remembrance of the past, but for the people of St. Louis, it is a present day reality." She was shocked to hear that. Later, during the reception, I sat with a group of retired MSU professors, and they, too, were shocked when I repeated my observation.

I introduced myself to Gordon Guyer, the main speaker for the celebration, and told him about my connection through my dad with Dr. Wallace. And I told him that earlier in the summer dead robins collected from St. Louis had been tested in the DNR lab housed on the MSU campus and were found to have died from DDT poisoning. He was shocked, as well.

Guyer had been a professor of entomology at MSU during the time of Dr. Wallace's research, and in 1970 became the director of the Pesticide Research Center at Michigan State University. He went on to become president of the university in the early 1990s.

When Dr. Wallace began to publish his DDT research, he was treated poorly by other professors and the administration of the university. Because the use of DDT was considered by agriculture to be a cure-all for every insect-borne disease that attacked crops, no one connected with agriculture at the university, or in state or federal government, wanted to hear anything negative about the pesticide.

In 1986, soon after the death of Dr. Wallace, Guyer was able to bring some well-earned recognition to him. The university issued a Special Commendation to "a true pioneer." In part it read, "Defying accepted fact, Professor Wallace was one of the very first to link mass deaths of robins and other birds to the use of the pesticide DDT."

It did my heart good to see Dr. Wallace hailed as a "true pioneer," which he certainly was. He blazed a trail for the rest of us to follow, and at a great personal cost to himself.

At the reception, Steve Boyd introduced Dr. Matt Zwiernik to us. Matt held a PhD in environmental toxicology and he was the director of the Wildlife Toxicology Lab at MSU. At present, he was working on an ecological study of the environmental effects of Dow Chemical Corporation's dioxin pollution in the Tittabawassee River, which our river emptied into. Steve thought Matt might want to serve as a technical advisor for us on the downstream portion of the Pine River. Matt was enthusiastic about helping out, and soon joined as a member of the CAG.

Finally, the Record of Decision (ROD) for the plant site was signed and distributed. The text was essentially the same as the Feasibility Study, so I skimmed through it and went to the Public Comments section to see the responses EPA had written.

I was surprised to see that the comments from CAG members and other citizens appeared with no identification as to who had made them. And a statement said the comments had been "redacted."

Over the previous 15 years we had commented on a number of formal documents from EPA, ATSDR and DOJ, and always the person making the comment was identified, and at the end of the document, complete letters people had sent were attached. I wondered why the comments had been handled differently in this document. Perhaps the privacy laws? But that didn't make sense, since all the comments were made during the Public Comment period and were intended as public, and not private, comments.

From my files I took out the ROD for the remediation of OU-2 (the river impoundment). Sure enough, both the oral comments received at the public meeting and the written comments included the name of the person who had made them. And I recalled how Ed had tracked down one of the people who had commented on the 1982 document for some information we needed. If his name hadn't been in the public ROD, Ed wouldn't have known who to look for.

I e-mailed my observations to the others, and none of us were happy to have had our signed, public comments made anonymous. At the next CAG meeting, we voiced our reasons for wanting the comments section to be revised to show the names of those who had commented. Gary had found that his comments, and those from another person, were not included at all, even in redacted form. His comment had to do with the new wall that was to be built to keep the plant site soil and the river water separated. He had expressed this comment at the Public Meeting, and neither the oral comment nor the written were included in the ROD.

At first our EPA Project Manager Tom Alcamo told us that *objections* were not included in the ROD, and that Gary hadn't made a comment, but an objection. Gary said that was something we'd never been told before, and in his view, he had made a comment.

Tom got defensive and started saying that all the comments were in the ROD, every single comment was in there, even Gary's comment was in there. Gary asked if he could tell him where it was located. I had brought a printed-out copy of the ROD with me, and Gary picked it up from the table, and asked Tom to turn to where his comment was located in the thick document. Tom said he would not do that, and Gary walked over and plopped the document in front of Tom, asking him once again to show him his comment.

The document hitting the table in front of Tom made a very loud noise. From my position at the front of the room, I could see Tom's face get white, and he started to rise from his chair as if he was going to walk out. I saw Theo give him a look, and a quick shake of his head, and Tom stayed put.

Then Tom went on the offensive, shouting that Gary's comment had been so long and rambling that he had no idea what point he was trying to make, so it had been left out. Tom was talking very fast, and interspersed with what I've written, he seemed to be insinuating that Gary didn't like the remedy EPA had chosen. Gary put a little distance between himself and Tom and leaned against the wall.

Then Theo spoke up and said that Gary was being "disingenuous" and that Gary's real motive in this discussion about the comments was to find fault with the selected remedy. Tom interrupted Theo to shout that Melissa Strait had liked the remedy, and Murray Borrello had liked the remedy, and he didn't see why the rest of us couldn't like it.

As chairperson, that's where I stepped in. I told them the fact was the CAG liked everything proposed in Alternative #3, but would have liked to see it be expanded to address more of the contaminants that EPA wanted to leave buried on the site. But tonight's discussion was not about the remedy, but how the comments from the community had been handled. We wanted them to understand that by omitting some comments and failing to identify the authors of the others, it seemed to us, at the very least, that our comments were not valued by EPA.

Tom countered that our comments were valued, and that's why they were summarized in the ROD. And Theo said the complete letters were published in the Administrative Record, a different document, and grouped together as having come from "concerned citizens" (again, anonymously).

After that we moved on to other business.

Such a troublesome exchange. And there was blame on both sides.

Often Tom was instantly defensive even in a quiet discussion. His interruption of others before they had finished speaking was typical, and throwing in the kitchen sink was one of his trademark moves to derail discussions. Plus, he was a shouter.

In my view of the exchange between Gary and Tom, I felt Gary had been wrong to plop the document in front of Tom and to demand that he find the comment. But at the same time, I questioned my view. After all, Tom claimed Gary's comment was in there, and this would have given him an opportunity to prove it.

Before I tackled that problem, I wrote a letter to Mike Joyce, our current Community Involvement Coordinator, making suggestions as to how the comments could be returned to their public status, and asking him to make the changes. I had looked up the CERCLA law regarding comments, and found that EPA is required to respond to comments both negative and positive, to criticisms as well as suggestions.

In other words, EPA staff could not ignore and omit comments that they chose to view as objections. According to CERCLA, Gary's "objection" still must receive a response, as should another omitted suggestion from a citizen who stated that the entire town of St. Louis should be moved to clean ground.

I went back through the CD's of what EPA had sent to find the file Theo had said was not in the ROD itself, called the Administrative Record. Sure enough, there were the comments.

First of all, I looked up Melissa's and Murray's comments, and saw that even though they were generally in favor of FPS-3, they had also made distinctions and suggestions as to ways that #3 could be expanded into something more. So Tom's outburst that they "liked" #3, while the rest of the CAG supposedly didn't, was nothing more than a divisive tactic.

My next task was to draft a letter to Tom and Theo and very clearly lay out the CAG's position on #3. I quoted text from our formal Task Force comments that said #3 was a good start, but not enough, and that EPA should expand and upgrade #3.

What was laying heavy on me, though, was the necessary task of calling Tom Alcamo in Chicago to talk about the incident, and then to talk to Gary. I didn't know what to expect from Tom. I was pleasantly surprised to hear him speak calmly on the phone, and with a sincere desire to discuss the confrontation.

As expected, he found fault with Gary, but added that he himself tended to be defensive, and he wanted me to "call" him on it at the meetings. I just said, "Really?" But he said he meant it.

He also asked for suggestions of ways to handle his presentations better at the CAG meetings. I told him I'd write down my suggestions and email them to him, which I did.

I suggested that he make it clear to the group that EPA had every intention of following through with what had been written in the Proposed Plan/FS/ROD; that Tom acknowledge out loud to the group often that he knew the community was gun-shy about EPA's claims that their new containment system would really work, and to explain why he was sure it would work; and, when possible, that he should let the CAG know that he expected #3 to be expanded in its scope during the actual cleanup.

I talked with Gary, and he said if he had it to do over again, he wouldn't toss the ROD document down on the table in front of Tom. Even so, he maintained that he and the rest of us had legitimate gripes about the way our comments were handled, and I fully agreed with him.

As I read through the comments on the disk, I saw that pages were missing. Certainly, only the first page of my personal comment was there, and it seemed that many other people's comments stopped in mid-sentence. I drew this to Gary's attention, and he began a search.

Meanwhile, I hadn't heard back from Mike Joyce. After repeated e-mails to him, I decided to go over his head. A few years previously, I had met his boss at an EPA conference in Seattle, Jeff Kelley, so I e-mailed him, asking him to intervene. I told him we preferred to settle this issue without having to appeal to the EPA ombudsman or taking the matter to our members of Congress.

Jeff replied that he no longer worked in Superfund, but that he would pass the message to Mike's current boss. Apparently that worked, because soon we received a response from Mike saying he had placed a link to the Administrative Record on the EPA website where the ROD was located.

Gary reported that pages from people's public comments were missing both on the CD and on the new link. It appeared that whoever had scanned the comments into the Administrative Record had only scanned one page of each person's letter. Good grief.

This problem required another month's worth of e-mails until EPA agreed to re-scan the documents correctly. That was the best we could do. We still think the summarized and redacted comments should have been identified by name in the ROD itself, and that the complete comments should have been attached to the ROD. But this was the best we could do at the time, and if anyone in the future needs to find one of us who commented, I wish that person luck.

As for the Gary vs. Tom confrontation, it led to a better working relationship over all. From my vantage point, I could see Tom's efforts to be less defensive, and Gary working to be more patient. Gary began to refer to the "new Tom," and I'm sure Tom had names for Gary, too.

The next time we were in the same room with Tom was at the Availability Session for the 5-year-review for the Velsicol Site. It was the "new Tom" who greeted me with open arms and a hug. That was a nice surprise.

Since none of us had ever attended an EPA Availability Session before, or even had heard of one, the term had to be explained to us. Tom said it meant that the 5-year-review for the plant site would be available for us to *look* at, but this was not an official 5-Year Review Public Meeting. He had convened it this way because nothing was completed at the Velsicol Site, so a review of the remedy wasn't really possible. The containment system for OU-1 (plant site) hadn't yet been built; monitoring of OU-2 (the river impoundment area) wasn't in place because the leaking plant site hadn't yet been remedied; and OU-3 (downstream) was just getting underway.

The 2003-04 MDEQ downstream sampling of water, sediment, floodplain soils, and living creatures had demonstrated DDT levels high enough to convince EPA that further sampling needed to be done in that portion of the river. Other chemicals of concern found downstream were PBB, HBB, TRIS and also PAH (polycyclic aromatic hydrocarbon) from the refinery activity upstream from the chemical plant.

One day Tom called to say he wanted to get to know the river better downstream.

Gary and I took him on a tour, accompanied by Theo von Wallmenich and Tom Hutchinson from CH2MHILL, and Chris Douglas from Weston Solutions, MDEQ's contractor who had done the sampling work in 2003-2004, and again in 2011.

We followed the river downstream by road, stopping at the bridges. Because of limited funds, MDEQ had sampled each end of the 36-mile stretch of river, and many miles in between had not been investigated. EPA planned to fill in the data gaps of MDEQ's work before determining how best to address the contamination in the river sediments and floodplain soils.

I knew the downstream work by EPA would be of interest to the Chippewa tribe in Mt. Pleasant, and notified Sally Kniffen, an Environmental Specialist, that it was beginning. The Tribe had told us back in 1998 to give them a heads up when the agencies turned their attention to the river downstream from the chemical plant, because that was what the 1819 Treaty between the United States and the tribe covered.

Throughout the Proposed Plan/FS/ROD processes for the Velsicol Site, Dr. Peter deFur had been our paid Technical Advisor. Now our contract with him was nearing its end, and a conversation started among members of the Executive Committee as to how to proceed next.

When we had hired Peter, we were looking for a person with a risk assessment background, which he had. Now we were looking for someone with both engineering and hydrogeology in his background to aid us in comprehending the design phase of the plant site remediation.

Our own CAG member Jim Heinzman had these skills. Moreover, during his years of employment with MDEQ, Jim had become acquainted with data about the plant site. In fact, my files contained a strongly worded memo he had written to EPA in the mid-2000s, taking them to task for suggesting another wall and cap for the site without addressing the contaminated groundwater. This memo had been written long before we knew Jim.

Everyone agreed that he seemed a natural fit as our next paid technical advisor.

With our hiring of Jim instead of Peter, yet another face changed in our CAG.

There had been a lot of changing faces in recent months. Murray and Dianne had chosen to leave. Dr. Stephen Boyd had come on board, as had Dr. Matthew Zwiernik from Michigan State University. Tom Alcamo had stepped away from two of our sites (the Burn Pit and the Landfill) and two new project managers had taken over. Jim Chapman, the EPA's ecologist was retiring, with Mark Sprenger taking his place temporarily. And Region 5's attorney, Gaylene Vasaturo, was also retiring, with Gary Steinbauer as her replacement.

There was yet one more big change in personnel to come before the year was out.

Here we were in 2012, a year that had seemed very distant to us when the CAG first formed in 1998. Nevertheless, it was a year in our thoughts back then. The date December 2012 was written into the 1982 Consent Judgment as when the decree would expire or be re-opened for changes.

Early in 2012, I had written an e-mail to Gaylene Vasaturo, the EPA attorney for Region 5, reminding her of our desire to replace the tombstone marker on the plant site with more conventional signage when the Consent Judgment was re-opened during 2012. We wanted the wording changed in the document to allow us to move the tombstone from the plant site to the St. Louis Area Historical Society Museum. She replied that she would talk to DOJ about it later in the year.

Meanwhile, Ed had asked the University of Michigan law group to read the 1982 Consent Judgment to help us compose the best replacement wording regarding signage, should the decree be re-opened at the end of the year.

In early December, Gaylene contacted me to say that EPA and MDEQ were looking into filing a Joint Motion to Terminate the Decree. When we passed on this news to Dr. Nina Mendelson at U of M Law School, she said first we should make sure all the good clauses of the decree had been replicated in subsequent legal documents, such as in the 2002 Fruit of the Loom bankruptcy settlement and the current ROD for the plant site. She didn't want us to lose any rights by letting the decree expire. Nina and her students drafted possible concerns, and I included them in a letter to Gaylene.

In Gaylene's response, she named other documents that contained the clauses of concern. So we gave our go-ahead for the joint motion to be filed.

We hoped this would be a quick and easy solution, because even after 15 years, we hadn't learned that nothing is quick and easy when dealing with governmental bureaucracy and legal documents!

Our December meeting was preceded by our annual Christmas Potluck. A few days before, we had received a long e-mail from Scott Cornelius, our MDEQ project manager who had worked with us since 2000. He said he had decided to leave MDEQ and take a job with a private environmental company.

This was quite a shock to the City and the CAG, since Scott had been the community's champion during his 12-year tenure. We worried about consistency in moving from the testing and sampling phases to the design and implementation stages of the remediation project. How could a new project manager get up to speed fast enough for the complicated plant site?

At the Christmas potluck, Scott spoke about his years with us, and encouraged us to keep moving forward. We gave him a round of applause and a farewell card signed by our members.

So that was one more familiar face gone, and soon a new person would be taking over as the project manager for the State.

At the meeting following the potluck, I announced that 2013 would be my last year in the role of chairperson. I planned to stay active as a CAG member, but twelve years as the leader would be enough for me.

Chapter 22
(2013)
Forward Progress

When one of Ed's students saw a new documentary about the 1970s PBB Disaster on TV, no mention was made of the town where PBB had been manufactured. Ed told us about the documentary at our January meeting, and we authorized him to contact the film makers to remind them that PBB didn't materialize out of nothing; that workers had made it, and plenty of leftover PBB was still piled up in our local landfill.

Sometimes it seemed as if we were invisible.

Later in the year, I was asked to speak to a class at Michigan State University about our CAG. Beforehand, I glanced through their textbook which used examples of environmental disasters, and saw that no mention made of the PBB Disaster, the largest food contamination accident in the history of our nation.

The chemical company in St. Louis had manufactured several different flame retardants, including TRIS, which was used in children's pajamas. The type of PBB that entered the food chain was BP-6, a hexabrominated biphenal. After the large, semi-transparent sheets came off the conveyor belt at the plant, they dropped into drums and were crushed into crystals, and the product was called Firemaster FF-1. The chemical plant also made a cattle feed supplement, and it was marketed under the name Nutrimaster. Although there are many suppositions, it is not known how Firemaster came to be bagged and sold as Nutrimaster.

Farm Bureau in Battle Creek mixed what they thought was Nutrimaster (magnesium oxide) into animal feed which was sold by the ton to farmers, and that is how PBB entered the food chain. As the meat from the animals, and the milk, eggs, butter and cheese were sold to households, the contamination spread until all 9 million people living in Michigan at that time had the chemical compound in their bloodstreams.

In the 1970s, the immediate human health effects of PBB exposure consisted of hair loss, skin rashes, joint pain, and memory loss.

More recent studies have shown that PBB is an endocrine disrupter, meaning that it can mimic or block the body's natural hormones, leading to various glandular problems and impairment of the reproductive system.

Accounts from the 1970s and 1980s state that 500 to 2,000 pounds of PBB were shipped and mixed. It was a very small amount. After production of the compound ceased, tons of leftover PBB were dumped at the Gratiot County Landfill, located on the south edge of St. Louis, and according to MDEQ, the substance was not de-grading over time. In some ways this was good, since the contaminant was not leaching into the groundwater. In other ways, it was a bad situation. Enough PBB is buried in that landfill to contaminate every animal and person on the planet, if it were to be misused in that way.

Increasing the danger, at least in my opinion, was the decision by the State of Michigan in 2013 to abdicate their caretaking position at the landfill and turn the complete responsibility over to Gratiot County. The county commissioners, knowing they did not have the skill to conduct the necessary sampling and lab work to maintain the capped facility, hired a contractor to fulfill the caretaking duties.

For awhile, due to extra income from the construction of wind turbines throughout our county, the commissioners will be able to afford a contractor. Once the wind money has died out, will their finances allow them to hire experts to oversee the landfill?

Through e-mails to the makers of the PBB documentary, Ed was given contact information for Dr. Michele Marcus at the Rollins School of Public Health at Emory University in Atlanta. We had known that Emory had taken over the long-term PBB study begun by the State of Michigan in the 1970s. The original study had included farm families and chemical workers, but the workers had been dropped from the cohort in the 1990s, partly because their bodies contained other chemicals which threw off the PBB findings.

After an hour-long phone call with Michele Marcus, Ed felt encouraged, saying that she showed a genuine interest in our community. Ed expressed to her our firm desire to see the chemical workers studied, and Michele was interested, but cautioned that it depended on funding.

A meeting was arranged, and in March Michele and three colleagues traveled up from Georgia to visit us, and also to introduce us to a few members of the PBB Citizens Advisory Board which consisted of people from Michigan farm families. That Board had been organized to assist the Emory researchers by giving them a community perspective on their studies.

At the joint meeting, Michele said the researchers were investigating the idea of applying for a supplement to the grant that would enable them to re-include chemical workers and their families in the study.

To begin this process, the CAG wrote a letter to Emory requesting that chemical workers and their families become part of the study. Then we contacted a few former chemical workers, asking them to have their blood drawn for a pilot study to support the grant. Twenty participants were needed, and we had no trouble meeting that number. Our local health department agreed to draw their blood at no charge.

One of the ongoing and major difficulties of the PBB study was the transfer of records from the State of Michigan to Emory University. Due to privacy laws, the state health department could not directly hand over the PBB Cohort records to Emory. Several years earlier, the health department had reached an agreement with the non-profit Michigan Public Health Institute that allowed the institute to hold the records for five years.

Then those individuals in the original registry who contacted MPHI could authorize them to allow the State to release the records to Emory. The researchers at Emory could not directly contact those in the original registry because neither the health department nor the institute would share the names on the records with the university, citing privacy laws. This meant it took word of mouth to let people know. It seemed terrifically inefficient and, in my opinion, not conducive to good public health.

Our group had old, incomplete lists of former chemical workers. There was no reason *we* couldn't contact these people to let them know about the need for them to transfer their records.

Gary Smith, aided by former chemical worker, Jim Buchanan, began a systematic search for current addresses, phone numbers and information on family members. This updated list greatly helped us to contact some of the people from the original study.

In October we received news that the supplemental grant had been awarded to the Emory research team to expand the study to include former chemical workers and their families. Could it be true that our community would finally get a health study? Over the years CAG members had been contacted by residents and former workers who wondered if the ailments and abnormalities of their children and grandchildren might have come from their own exposure to PBB, DDT and the other chemical compounds manufactured at the Velsicol plant. Now it appeared that the study proposed by the Emory University researchers could begin to answer some of the community's questions.

Planning began right away to bring the research team to St. Louis for two days in December to offer informational meetings, blood draws, and sign-ups for a long-term reproductive health study. The Emory team told us they hoped to have 50 people from our area of the state join the PBB Registry. Despite a December snowstorm, we had 213 people attend the blood draw and meeting, and join the registry. When the team returned in March, another 284 people joined.

In one year's time, Dr. Michele Marcus and her team had managed to bring a health study to St. Louis, Michigan.

To top it off, I received an email from Dr. Dana Barr who, when she was at CDC, had helped us with our pilot study on the infant blood spot cards. She was now working at Emory University and wanted to revive the blood spot card study. She asked me to write a letter from the CAG in support of an NIH grant proposal to determine the viability of dried blood spots as a blood collection tool, and to examine the historic exposure in our community from the archived cards. This grant was also funded. Forward progress at last.

Along with human health, we were concerned about the health of wildlife in our community. After learning the year before that the robins collected by Teri Kniffen from her yard had died of acute DDT poisoning, we determined that we should organize a collection of dead birds during the nesting season of 2013.

Dr. Matt Zwiernik,, a recent CAG member, and the director of the Wildlife Toxicology Lab at Michigan State University, was willing to design a proper collection procedure. Later, he offered to conduct the study, using trained volunteers, and to provide necropsies and brain and liver analysis on the collected specimens at his own cost.

After Matt had set up a Standard Operating Procedure, and after Jim Hall had lined up volunteers, then we were told by our new MDEQ Project Manager, Dan Rockafellow, that the state Department of Natural Resources could conduct the study. While Matt was willing to do the collection at no cost to us for one year, MDEQ/DNR was willing to do it free for 5 years. While Matt was willing to study livers as well as brains for DDT and PBB levels, the MDEQ would only look at the brains to determine the levels of DDT.

I wrote an e-mail to Dan asking him if the study would easily transfer; that is, if we were to work with Matt for the first year, using his protocols and his lab, and then switch to the state lab and protocols for the next five years, would the first year's data transfer smoothly? He assured me it would. That made our decision easier, and we continued with Matt's generous donation of time and talent for the first year of the collection.

Matt also advocated a study of robin eggs, but required funding to proceed. We spoke to both our MDEQ and EPA project managers about paying for the study. MDEQ said they would not foot the bill for an egg study, being convinced that it was unnecessary, since we were already going to do a study on the dead robin brains. EPA said that they might find money for the study, but left us hanging.

Meanwhile, nesting season was fast approaching. After much discussion within the Executive Committee, we decided to use some of our Oxford settlement money to pay for the egg study in the neighborhood.

It would be good to have this baseline information so that if we later found that DDT levels were still high in the eggs following excavation of the neighborhood yards, we could pinpoint where in town the soils still needed excavation.

Jim Hall recruited volunteers from among St. Louis residents who lived near the collection area to be trained in proper techniques for salvaging the dead birds. He settled on Jim Vyskocil, a retired chemistry teacher, Terry Jelenek, a former Total Refinery employee, Jerry Church, a retired Dow Chemical employee, and Mike Allen, a retired biology teacher.

Basic procedures that the homeowner should follow were published in the local newspapers, in the city newsletter, and hand delivered to the houses in the neighborhood. If a dead bird was spotted in the yard, a bucket should be put over it with a brick on top to keep the carcass away from the many feral cats that roamed the streets. Then a volunteer should be called.

Before collecting the bird, the trained volunteer would take a photo of it, along with GPS coordinates. The city manager agreed to have a small refrigerator installed in a room at city hall for storing the birds, and which could be accessed by the collection crew even when city hall was not open for business.

When everything was in place, we waited to hear if any dead birds had been found. We had hoped to collect at least a dozen. Before long, almost 70 had been collected. Most were dead adult robins, but some juveniles had also been collected, and a few starlings and bluebirds. In addition to the birds themselves, some video recordings had been made of robins in convulsions.

By autumn, lab results on the analyzed birds started to come in. The cause of death was acute DDE poisoning. The DDX in the brains ranged from a low of 25 ppm to a high of 811 ppm, with a mean of 300 ppm.

From the 20 active nests being monitored in the neighborhood, 14 eggs were collected for the egg study. Preliminary results showed that all the robin nests on Watson Street and on two blocks of Bankson Street had total nest failure.

That meant the parents had built the nest, laid the eggs, and even hatched some nestlings, but then they had died of DDX poisoning, which meant the nestlings and eggs also did not survive.

It was a strange mix of feelings to have these studies be successful. We were glad for the proof, yet sickened to think that our community was still responsible for the wretched deaths of so many robins. It was dreadful to think that our soils had been killing birds for decades.

After having seen the Rachel Carson "Echoes of Silent Spring" exhibit at Michigan State University the previous fall, we had talked about bringing it to our community, but hadn't accomplished that yet. Jim Hall offered to take the lead, and he spoke with the head of the MSU museum, worked out the price, and he and Ed Lorenz solved the logistics to bring the exhibit to Alma College.

Although there were many people in the CAG who were good leaders, I had spoken with Jim about replacing me as chairperson. I favored him as my replacement because he had a personal passion to follow through with the cleanups that were underway. Not only had his daughter been born with birth defects (and died at age 2), but of his several brothers and sisters, three had experienced thyroid problems with subsequent removal of that gland, and his eldest brother had died from non-Hodgkins lymphoma when a teenager. The family had lived a few blocks from the plant site, and Jim's father had grown up across the street from the chemical plant.

When Jim asked me why I thought he could lead the CAG, I told him it was because I could see he had the heart for it. Also, he was fifteen years younger than I!

We were able to rent the Rachel Carson exhibit, and we set it up in the large lobby of the science building on the Alma College campus. The thirty 4x8 panels were erected on easels built by the college carpenter.

I contacted the St. Louis Area Historical Society and they loaned us many items from their collection of chemical plant memorabilia, including a calendar that the chemical company had distributed (ironically, featuring birds), and a can of DDT from the World War II era with directions written on it in many foreign languages.

Gary Smith and I also gathered up CAG items, such as T-shirts with our logo, buttons that said "EPA Haul It Away," and our big Carter Partnership Award trophy. I also sorted through my newspaper clippings and chose several with headlines that told our story. Dead robin carcasses were brought up from the basement of the science building, and I could recognize my dad's penmanship on the labels indicating when and where they had been collected. With all of this material, we arranged two display cases to go along with the panels of the exhibit.

For our opening night, we provided refreshments and a viewing of the PBS documentary *"Rachel Carson Silent Spring."* We had invited our legislators, and local elected officials, our EPA and MDEQ project managers and their bosses, our membership and the community at large. After the grand opening, we kept the exhibit up throughout the spring and summer and into fall so that individuals and groups could come and tour through it.

Even though the death of robins from DDT was still going on in St. Louis, we hoped the end was in sight. Thirty neighborhood yards had been sampled and results showed most of their soils contained DDT at levels above 5 ppm, the cleanup level, some in the first six inches of soil, many to a depth of 18 inches, and some as deep as two, three and four feet. Forty-four more yards were slated to be sampled in 2013, and later we learned that 54 more yards would be sampled in 2014. Thankfully, there was EPA money in place to fund the excavation, soil replacement, and landscaping of the yards. Tom, along with his superiors at Region 5, had been successful in convincing EPA to grant almost $4 million to clean up the neighborhood, even though it was technically a piece of the unfunded 52-acre plant site project (OU-1).

We were also seeing forward progress on the new water system for St. Louis. Two water mains were being built, with booster stations along the way, to bring water from Alma. If all went as planned, in 2015 St. Louis would shut down its current well field and begin sharing water with Alma through the Gratiot Area Water Authority.

Tom and his Region 5 superiors had been awarded money from Superfund for both the neighborhood and the water system partly because they were able to convince the Prioritization Panel to look upon both remedies as "ongoing remediations," when in reality they were "new starts."

The irony is that the plant site, which was in reality an "ongoing remediation" had been put back in the big pool of unfunded "new starts." In the spring of 2013, however, we learned that the plant site was now out of the pool and on a list scheduled for funding in 2014, depending on the amount of money available.

Progress was being made downstream on the portion of the river below the dam in St. Louis, known as OU-3 of the Velsicol Superfund Site. Tom Alcamo had requested and received $400,000-500,000 from Region 5's "pipeline" budget to be used for sampling downstream. The data would supplement the data gathered in 2003-2004 and in 2011 by MDEQ.

The most hopeful downstream study had to do with fish. In 2010 MDEQ had conducted another fish study downstream, and the recently released data showed that the DDT levels in fish tissue had dropped dramatically following the 1998-2006 removal of polluted river sediment from the impoundment area behind the St. Louis dam. Most fish sampled were at or nearing a level at which some of them could be eaten, at least some of the time, by some people.

We continued to press forward with having the tombstone removed from the plant site and placed at the historical society. I called Jay Steinberg, the president of the Trust, and deed holder of the plant site property, asking if he objected to having the tombstone removed. He said, "More power to you."

Gaylene had retired as EPA Region 5's attorney, and her successor, Gary Steinbauer, drafted a motion to terminate the 1982 consent judgment. When we hadn't heard anything by the end of April, I wrote to Gary, telling him we would like to coordinate our tombstone removal celebration with the annual July 4th Blues Festival that took place in St. Louis, and needed confirmation by the middle of May that we could move the stone in order to have time to prepare for our ceremony and parade.

By the middle of May, things were still at a standstill. Gary had met resistance at the Department of Justice to the idea of terminating the judgment. He was now working on a motion to simply modify the wording of the Consent Judgment to allow removal of the granite marker, without doing away with the entire Consent Judgment. He asked for a formal letter of request from us. I wrote the letter and sent it.

I also met with the St. Louis Area Historical Society to ask if they would be willing to accept the donation of the tombstone, assuming they would agree. As I described our plans for short speeches by the CAG, EPA and MDEQ at the plant site gates, and then having the tombstone paraded through town to the museum, I sensed resistance in the room.

Later I learned that several members were not sure the museum should come into ownership of the tombstone that symbolized the toxic reputation of our beleaguered town. Was it history that should be remembered? Parading it through town instead of crushing it or burying it went against the grain with them.

The St. Louis City Council had voted to partner with us in staging the celebration. They offered to pour a slab of concrete on the museum grounds for the stone to stand on, and to have their workers lift the stone out of the ground for transportation in the parade.

The idea of displaying the tombstone at the historical society museum had come from CAG member Bill Shrum, who was also a long-time city council member and a member of the St. Louis Area Historical Society. Thirteen years earlier he had expressed his hope to live long enough to see the stone moved to the museum. Bill was now in his 80's. Norris Bay, also an elderly member of both the CAG and the historical society, had dedicated many years of his retirement to acquiring and displaying items from the chemical plant at the St. Louis museum, including some excellent infrastructure drawings that enabled both MDEQ and EPA to know where various chemical compounds had been manufactured on the 52-acre site. Both Bill and Norris would ride in the lead classic cars in the parade.

Things were in place in St. Louis. Not so at EPA and the Department of Justice. Apparently our request had put the DOJ into a tizzy. Tom Alcamo said DOJ did not want to terminate the Consent Judgment, no matter what, even if the document was not being implemented nor had any bearing on future work at the site.

This didn't make any sense to us. If a legal document had an expiration date, then it should expire on that date. In fact, we had seen it happen to benefit Velsicol. Their pollution insurance policy through the AIG subsidiary had an expiration date of midnight, December 21, 2009, and if we hadn't had an attorney file "Intent to Sue" documents to extend the date, the policy would have expired at that date and time

I wrote a letter to Alan Tenenbaum, the attorney at DOJ who had crafted the Fruit of the Loom bankruptcy settlement.

Using language from the University of Michigan Law School responses to our questions about the Consent Judgment, I made it plain that there was no legal reason for the tombstone to remain on the site. I wrote that the CAG and the City of St. Louis had worked tirelessly since 1998 to heal our community's reputation, environment, and economic well-being, which had all been severely damaged by the terms of the 1982 Consent Judgment, because it had allowed the perpetrator of the damages to leave the community without cleaning up after themselves. I said, "At the time... the placement by government agencies of a tombstone on the Velsicol Site seemed to mock this small town that was nearly ruined not only by Velsicol's bad actions, but also by the act of EPA, DOJ and other governmental agencies in signing off on the 1982 Consent Decree, which clearly benefited Velsicol and clearly disregarded the community of St. Louis."

Later Tom Alcamo told me that my letter to Tenenbaum helped spur things along at the federal level. After much behind the scenes bureaucratic discussion, the U. S. Department of Justice, instead of EPA, decided to file a motion to dissolve the 1982 Consent Judgment. I learned this from Jay Steinberg. He called me and said, "Well, you've done it again!"

By now it was June, and our plans to move the stone during the July 4th celebration had to be postponed.

At the end of July, Judge Thomas Ludington held a hearing and asked the DOJ attorney what impact the termination of the Consent Judgment would have on the Trust that had been set up during the Fruit of the Loom bankruptcy settlement, and what impact it would have on the cleanup of the plant site. The attorney said it would have no impact on either.

On July 31st, the judge signed the order granting the motion to terminate the consent judgment. We were especially pleased that he singled out the tombstone, saying that the termination included "the Consent Judgment's requirement in Section XI for a granite marker."

As for that granite marker, over the years we had come up with some theories that gave the crafters of the Consent Judgment the benefit of the doubt.

Perhaps they thought if they specified a "granite marker" and not a granite rock, they could bring a little business to the Brewer-Bouchey Monument Company in St. Louis, which provided gravestones for local residents. Or perhaps they preferred a flat granite gravestone, and not a big rock, so that the words of warning could be carved deep and last as protection for the community. A little later, we would learn the real reason the tombstone was chosen.

Meanwhile, we began to finalize our plans for the celebration. Jim Hall arranged for the classic cars for the parade. Ed Lorenz suggested that a tour of the Rachel Carson exhibit be on the agenda of events. Gary Smith said we should have something to give away, and settled on refrigerator magnets that showed a photo of the tombstone with the words, "Hauled Away, 2013." My duties were to finalize the parade route with the city manager and the police chief, and to write and send the invitations and an agenda of activities.

The tombstone removal excited a lot of interest, and I was interviewed by WNEM, a Saginaw television station, and by Michigan Radio that aired the interview throughout Michigan. Several friends from around the state contacted me to say that they had heard it on the radio in their areas. Our local newspapers in Mt. Pleasant, Ithaca and Midland gave us extensive coverage. The press release I'd written was run as a guest column in the Morning Sun newspaper.

In it I contrasted our planned parade with one that had taken place in 1946. Paul Van Note, a former St. Louis resident, described that earlier parade, which celebrated DDT. He remembered decorating his bicycle in red, white and blue crepe paper, and fastening a DDT garden sprayer to the handle bars to ride in the parade down the streets of St. Louis. At that time, DDT production was aiding the war effort. The pesticide had been used to delouse soldiers, and was still being used for that purpose on refugees to prevent them from contracting or spreading diseases carried by body lice.

In the press release, I wrote, "That was then. This is now," and that phrase became the theme of our celebration.

The day of the event, October 16th, was a rainy one. First I went to the Rachel Carson exhibit in the lobby of the science building at Alma College, where I was introduced to Anne Couture, a senior advisor to the current director of MDEQ, Dan Wyant. As we sat and visited, she told me about being a state employee working at the Gratiot County Landfill remediation back in the 1980s, and at the same time, the initial work was underway to bury and cap the chemical plant site. She told me about the choosing of the tombstone as a warning marker for the plant site, and none of our theories that gave the benefit of the doubt to those in charge was valid.

She told me that the man responsible for choosing to use a tombstone did it intentionally, and with amusement. He thought since the chemical facility was being buried in place, they should mark the spot with a gravestone. At the time, Anne and others objected, saying that the town had suffered enough without having a large tombstone in its midst. Their voices were ignored, and the decision was made, even to the extent of having the granite marker designated in the Consent Judgment, and with the words to be engraved on the marker spelled out in the document. The phrase I had used in my letter to DOJ was not too strong -- it was true, the town had been mocked by the intentional placement of the tombstone.

After hearing the true story, I was doubly glad to see the tombstone already lifted out and loaded in the back of a truck when I arrived at the gates of the plant site.

Woody Black of Woody's Music had set up a microphone for the speeches. Miraculously, the rain stopped as people gathered.

Mayor Jim Kelly led off, saying that when the CAG had formed, he hadn't expected it to accomplish much of anything, but that the group had surprised him with one accomplishment after another. And now, the tombstone was actually going to be removed.

When it was my turn, I said that it was time to move the tombstone, a symbol of death, because, due to the efforts of the CAG and the City, the town had been restored to life. This day was to celebrate our accomplishments so far, and once the plant site was cleaned up, we would celebrate again.

Both Anne Couture and Daria Devantier spoke as representatives of MDEQ. Anne said that when she learned we had planned a ceremony to remove the tombstone, she knew she had to be here, no matter what!

Our EPA people could not attend our event because a government sequester had shut down their travel budget. But Theo von Wallmenich of CH2MHILL, the contractor for EPA at the site, spoke about the cleanup plans for the neighborhood and the plant site.

The parade, led by a police car, traveled south on Bankson, where the yards had finally lost their "lawn decorations" of orange fences, then east on Saginaw to Main, and then south on Main to the St. Louis Area Historical Society's museum. A police officer held back traffic on M-46 as our parade crossed the highway.

A local barbershop quartet sang a few numbers as people gathered at the museum, and then I spoke, making the formal offer of our donated item to the historical society. City Manager Bob McConkie spoke next, and then Judy Root, president of the historical society, formally accepted the donation. Cookies and punch were served inside the old railway depot. Just as the ceremony ended, it started to rain again.

Seeing the tombstone moved to the museum was personally satisfying for me as I neared the end of my twelve years as chairperson of the CAG. Although symbolic, it was also a highly physical act, and represented for me a contribution to the improvement of the community.

Most of what the CAG had accomplished in 16 years was barely visible to the community at large. For instance the $97 million sediment removal from 36 acres of the river impoundment area was often thought by people to be still underway because of a long stretch of sheet pile wall having been left standing in the center of the river.

Or, some people thought that once the river impoundment area had been cleaned up in 2006, it meant that the entire plant site had been cleaned up, also. They were surprised to learn that the CAG was still trying to get EPA to put shovels in the ground.

When the granite tombstone was paraded through town, however, it could be seen and understood. People could look at the gates of the plant site and see that the stone was no longer there, or they could look at the museum and see that the stone was now there. To do something that could be seen and celebrated assured me that my years of volunteerism had accomplished at least one concrete task!

As the time for our biennial elections neared, I encouraged several members of the Executive Committee to run for the office of chairperson. I learned then that both of our secretaries, who had divided the duties for many years, planned to step down. Carol Layman had been battling illnesses and surgeries, and thought it was time to retire, and Melissa Strait planned to be on a year-long sabbatical from her teaching position at Alma College.

I also learned that Gary Smith was adamant about wanting to remain in the office of treasurer, and that both Ed Lorenz and Jim Hall felt worried that they could not give enough time to the position of chairperson. Following an Executive Committee meeting held at my house to plan the tombstone ceremony, Jim, Ed and I were alone, and I raised the issue with them. Jim said he wanted the opportunity to serve as chairperson, but was concerned that his job would not allow him to do all the tasks that I had carried out each month. Ed said he could help out, but didn't want the full responsibility. We decided that Jim could run for chair and Ed for vice chair. That way they could share the work load. To do that, we would need to change our bylaws, as our original bylaws had allowed only for a chairperson, treasurer and secretary.

I drafted a bylaw change to add the office of vice chair, and also re-drafted the position of secretary to allow that officer to take on several of the writing duties that the chair had until now handled, such as writing the quarterly performance report for our TAG grant from EPA, and doing much of the necessary correspondence of the CAG. The membership voted in favor of making these changes.

In December, Jim Hall was elected Chair, Ed Lorenz Vice-Chair, Gary Smith Treasurer, and Jane Keon Secretary.

Onward and upward!

Sites Mentioned in Chapters

Breckenridge Site 2,3,4,5,6,9,13,14,15,16,17,19

Burn Pit/Golf Course Site 8,13,14,17,22

City drinking water 7,11,12,13,14,15,16,17,18,19,22

Fruit of the Loom/NWI 4,5,6,7,11,12,13,15,17

Gratiot County Landfill 2,8,16,17,18,19,22

Horse Creek 3,4,5,8

Injection Well 2,5

Oxford Automotive 2,5,9,10,12

Plant Site 1,2,3,4,5,6,7,8,9,11,12,14,15,16,17,18,19,20,21,22

Residential Properties 1,3,5,7,14,17,20,21,22

River Impoundment 1,2,3,4,5,7,9,11,12,17

River Downstream 1,2,7,9,11,13,15,19,21,22

River Upstream 5,9,10,11,13,17

Smith Farm Site 2,5,6,7,8,9,10,11,16,18

Total Refinery 2,3,4,7

Glossary of Acronyms

A&I	Assumption and Indemnity
AEC	Atomic Energy Commission
AIG	American International Group
AISLIC	American International Specialty Lines Insurance Company
ATSDR	Agency of Toxic Substances and Disease Registry
CAFO	Concentrated Animal Feeding Operation
CAG	Community Advisory Group
CDC	Centers for Disease Control
CERCLA	Comprehensive and Environmental Response Compensation and Liability Act
CIC	Community Involvement Coordinator
DBCP	1,2-dibromo 3-chloropropane
DOJ	United States Department of Justice
DDT	dichlorodiphenyltrichloroethane
DNAPL	Dense Non-Aqueous Phase Liquid
DNR	Michigan Department of Natural Resources
DNRE	Michigan Department of Natural Resources and the Environment
ECCO	Environmentally Concerned Citizens Organization
EPA	United States Environmental Protection Agency
ERA	Emergency Removal Action
FOIA	Freedom of Information Act
FPS	Former Plant Site
FS	Feasibility Study
ITRC	Interstate Technology and Regulatory Council
JSAP	Joint Sampling and Analysis Plan
LNAPL	Light Non-Aqueous Phase Liquid
MDCH	Michigan Department of Community Health
MDEQ	Michigan Department of Environmental Quality
MOU	Memorandum of Understanding

MUCC	Michigan United Conservation Clubs
NAPL	Non-Aqueous Phase Liquid
NIEHS	National Institute of Environmental Health Sciences
NOAA	National Oceanic and Atmospheric Agency
NRC	Nuclear Regulatory Agency
NRD	Natural Resource Damages
NWI	Northwest Industries/NWI Land Mgt.
O&M	Operation and Maintenance
OSHA	Occupational Safety and Health Adm.
OU-1	Operable Unit 1 (the plant site)
OU-2	Operable Unit 2 (impoundment area)
OU-3	Operable Unit 3 (downstream)
PAH	Polycyclic Aromatic Hydrocarbon
PCB	Polychlorinated Biphenyl
PBB	Polybrominated Biphenyl
pCBSA	para-Chlorobenzene Sulfonic Acid
ppm	parts per million
PRP	Potentially Responsible Party
RCRA	Resource Conservation and Recovery Act
RI	Remedial Investigation
ROD	Record of Decision
RPM	Remedial Project Manager
SEP	Supplemental Environmental Project
TAG	Technical Assistance Grant
UDS	Ultramar Diamond Shamrock
VOC	Volatile Organic Compound

Minutes of the meetings of the Pine River Superfund Citizen Task Force are available at pinerivercag.org.

Documents generated by MDEQ and EPA for the Superfund sites are available at the T.L Cutler Memorial Library, 312 Michigan Avenue, St. Louis, Michigan 48880 and at this website address: www.epa.gov/region5/clanup/velsicolmichigan/documents.html

Letters, e-mails, and newspaper articles are archived at the Alma College Library, 614 W. Superior St., Alma, Michigan 48801

Bibliography

Bay, Norris (compiler). *Michigan Chemical 1935-1984*. Saint Louis, Michigan: Michigan Chemical Corporation.

Carson, Rachel. *Silent Spring*. Boston: Houghton Mifflin Company, 1962.

Chen, Edwin. *PBB: An American Tragedy*. Prentice Hall Int'l, 1979.

Christensen, Laird Evan. *Recovering Pine River*. Alma, Michigan: Gratiot CountyCommunity Foundation and Alma College Service Learning Office, 2000.

Cronin, John and Robert F. Kennedy, Jr. *The Riverkeepers: Two Activists Fight to Reclaim Our Environment as a Basic Human Right*. New York: Scribner, 1999.

Dave Dempsey. *Ruin and Recovery: Michigan's Rise as a Conservation Leader*. Ann Arbor: University of Michigan Press, 2001.

Dunlap, Thomas. *DDT: Scientists, Citizens and Public Policy*. Princeton, New Jersey: Princeton University Press, 1981.

East Michigan Environmental Action Council. *Groundwater Contamination Sites: A Citizen's Guide to Fact-Finding and Follow-up*. Birmingham, Michigan: East Michigan Environmental Action Council, 1984.

Egginton, Joyce. *The Poisoning of Michigan*. East Lansing: Michigan State University Press, 2009.

Fischer, Frank. *Citizens, Experts and the Environment: The Politics of Local Knowledge*. Durham, North Carolina: Duke University Press, 2000.

Gibbs, Lois Marie. *Love Canal: My Story*. Albany: State University of New York Press, 1982.

Halbert, Frederic and Sandra. *Bitter Harvest: The Investigation of the PBB Contamination: A Personal Story*. Grand Rapids: Wm. B. Eerdmans Publishing Co., 1978.

Lear, Linda. *Rachel Carson Witness for Nature*. New York: Houghton Mifflin Harcourt, 2009.

Lorenz, Edward C. *Civic Empowerment in an Age of Corporate Greed*. East Lansing: Michigan State University Press, 2012.

Quarles, John. *Cleaning Up America: An Insider's View of the Environmental Protection Agency*. New York: Houghton Mifflin, 1976.

Roberts, Donald and Richard Tren. *Excellent Powder: DDT's Political and Scientific History*. Indianapolis: Dog Ear Publishing, 2010.

Steingraber, Sandra. *Living Downstream: An Ecologist's Personal Investigation of Cancer and the Environment*. Cambridge, Massachusetts: Da Capo Press: 2010.

Touzeau, Lois. *Our Side of the Story: Other Victims of PBB Contamination in Michigan*. New York: Vantage Press, 1985.

Wallace, George J. *My World of Birds: Memoirs of an Ornithologist*. Philadelphia: Dorrance & Company, 1979

About the Author

In addition to serving on the Pine River Superfund Citizen Task Force, Jane Keon sits on two other boards with goals to improve the Pine River for the benefit of the people and wildlife of mid-Michigan. Her great-grandchildren represent the eighth generation of family members to live on or near the Pine River in the middle of Michigan.

53196776R00165

Made in the USA
Lexington, KY
25 June 2016